Anonymous

The Empire of Brazil

at the Vienna Universal exhibition of 1873

Anonymous

The Empire of Brazil
at the Vienna Universal exhibition of 1873

ISBN/EAN: 9783337271374

Printed in Europe, USA, Canada, Australia, Japan

Cover: Foto ©Andreas Hilbeck / pixelio.de

More available books at **www.hansebooks.com**

THE EMPIRE OF BRAZIL

AT THE

VIENNA

UNIVERSAL EXHIBITION

OF

1873

Rio de Janeiro

PRINTED BY E. & H. LAEMMERT
61 B, Rua dos Invalidos, 61 B

—

1873

INTRODUCTION

A perfect knowledge of the American continent is at present a necessity for all the European nations, where population is superabundant.

The luxuriance of the Brazilian soil, and its manifold treasures of natural riches offer a vast field to all kinds of industrial energy.

With the intention of proving it, and in order to promote immigration into this Empire, the opportunity offered by the Vienna Universal Exhibition was availed of, in order to revise and improve the «SHORT-SKETCH» published in 1867, on the occasion of the Paris Universal Exhibition.

A work of this description cannot be accomplished with immediate perfection.

However, with the encouragement given to the zeal of official contributors, and with the increase of private information, which, on this occasion, have already been elements of great importance, it is to be hoped that for future Universal Exhibitions, more perfect results will be obtained.

It must be observed, however, that the leading purpose, in the publishing of the «SOHRT-SKETCH» of 1867, as well as in the present work, was not that of a false patriotism, which, exaggerating the advantages of a country, hides its defects.

The principal object in view, being to make the Empire of Brazil well known abroad, as also to afford the necessary information to immigrants, a particular care was taken in order to say the truth, only the truth.

THE EMPIRE OF BRAZIL.

Geographical position and extent of Brazil.

The Empire of Brazil is situated in the most eastern part of South America.

'It comprehends 1/15 of the terrestrial surface of the globe, 1/5 of the New World, and more than 3/7 of South America.

It has a sea-coast of 1,200 leagues or 7,920 kilometers.

Area.

According to the estimate of Baron Humboldt its area is valued at 2,311,974 square miles of 60 to a degree, or 7,952,344 square kilometers.

According to the estimate of senator Pompeu, which is almost equal to that made in the Statistical Board, the surface of the country is divided as follows:

Provinces.	SQUARE LEAGUES.	THEIR AREA IN SQUARE KILOMETERS.
Amazonas	66.000	2.874.960
Pará.	40.000	1.742.400
Maranhão	16.000	696.960
Piauhy	10.500	457.380
Ceará.	3.627	157.992
Rio Grande do Norte	2.000	87.120
Parahyba.	2.600	113.256
Pernambuco.	4.467	194.582
Alagôas	2.035	88.644
Sergipe	1.360	59.242
Bahia.	14.836	646.256
Espirito-Santo	1.560	67.954
Rio de Janeiro.	2.400	104.544
Municipality of the capital	32	1.394
S. Paulo	10.120	440.827
Paraná	7.700	335.412
Sta. Catharina	2.580	112.385
Rio Grande do Sul.	8.230	358.499
Minas–Geraes	20.000	871.200
Goyaz	26.000	1.132.560
Mato–Grosso	48.000	2.090.880
	290.047	12.634.447

Topography.

The soil of Brazil is, in the most, mountainous, though it contains vast plains, both in the north and south, and is traversed by extensive valleys. In the interior, the ground gradually rises into extensive and high plateaux and numerous mountain ranges, that stretch in several directions.

The most extensive and the highest mountain ranges in Brazil are three: the Central chain called Serra do Espinhaço or Mantiqueira; the Eastern or sea-coast chain called Serra do Mar; and the Western chain called Serra das Vertentes (Watersheds).

All the other ranges generally derive from the above, and constitute with them the so called Brazilian system; since the Parima system slightly penetrates into various points of the northern boundary line.

Of the three mountain ranges, the most important, both geographically and geologically, is the central one.

Its culminating point lies in the province of Minas Geraes, where it is more developed; and without transposing the 10th., and 28th. parallels of South Latitude, from the banks of the river S. Francisco to those of the Uruguay, it traverses the provinces of Bahia, S. Paulo, and Paraná, slightly touching that of S. Pedro do Rio Grande do Sul on its northern extremity, and that of Rio de Janeiro at the point where the boundary lines of the provinces of S. Paulo and Minas Geraes intersect each other.

It is the highest of all, the Serra d' Itatiaia being actually acknowledged as its loftiest altitude, as well as of all Brazil: the average elevation above the level of the sea is 2,714 meters, according to some, or 3,140 meters, according to others.

The second or eastern chain begins on the banks of the river S. Francisco in 10° S. Lat., and terminates on the banks of the Uruguay in latitude 28° S.

The third, the most extensive and yet the lowest, runs from Ceará to the confines of the province of Mato-Grosso. This long range separates the waters of the affluents of the Amazonas from those of the River Plate, and at the same time supplies the rivers Tocantins, Parnahyba, S. Francisco and Paraná.

The above mountain ranges bear various local denominations in the different provinces through which they run.

Capes.

The principal capes in Brazil are five in number: — Orange, Norte, S. Agostinho, S. Roque, S. Thomé, Cape Frio, and Santa Martha.

Ports.

With the exception of the provinces of Amazonas, Minas-Geraes, Goyaz and Mato-Grosso, all the others are maritime. The former, however, though they lie in the interior, yet have got the advantage of navigation along their rivers, which flow into others that, in their turn, empty into the sea. In the coast of Brazil there are not less than 42 ports, holding the first rank, by its capacity and safety, that of the capital of the Empire, which is above 30 leagues or 198 kil, in circuit. Next to it, from North to South, there are those of Pará, Maranhão, Pernambuco, Bahia, Ilhéos, Victoria, Santos, Paranaguá, Santa-Catharina, and others.

Lakes.

They are numerous, though, in the most, they be not of considerable extent. The chief ones are: those of *dos*

Patos and *Mirim*, in the province of Rio Grande do Sul, the former being 46 leagues or 303,6 kil. long, by 10 leagues or 66 kil. wide; and the latter 26 leagues, 171,6 kil. long by 7 leagues, 46,2 kil. wide; those of *Maricá*, *Araruama* and *Feia* in the province of Rio de Janeiro; and those of *Jiquiá* and *Manguaba* in Alagôas.

In the island of *Bananal* or *Santa Anna*, in the province of Goyaz, there is a lake of 24 leagues, 158,4 kil. from North to South, and 6 leagues, 39,6 kil. from East to West.

In the Brazilian Guyana is worthy of notice the lake *Saracá*, that lies between the rivers *Urubú* and *Anibá*, which communicate through it. Besides the above mentioned, there are others in the valley of the Amazonas which, like the lake *Xaraes*, the *Periodical Sea* of the province of Mato-Grosso, become dry during some time every year, on account of the going down of the waters.

Islands.

Not far from the sea-coast there is a great number of islands, the most remarkable of them being that of *Marajó*, 37 leagues or 244,2 kil. in length, and 27 leagues or 178,2 kil. in breadth; that of *Maranhão*, the seat of the capital of the same province; that of *Itamaracá* in Pernambuco; of *Itaparica* in Bahia; the *Ilha Grande* in Rio de Janeiro; those of *São Sebastião* and *Santos* in the province of São Paulo; that of *Santa-Catharina*, the seat of the capital of the province of the same name.

Far from the sea-coast there are: the island of—*Fernando de Noronha*—in the province of Pernambuco, lying North-East, 195 miles, 360,7 kil. off the cape of São Roque; and that of *Trindade*, 600 miles or 1.112,8 kil. distant from the eastern coast of the province of Espirito-Santo.

There are likewise some remarkable islands in several first-class rivers, chiefly that of—*Santa Anna* or *do Banal*—in the interior of Brazil, between the provinces of Goyaz and Mato-Grosso, formed by two branches of the Araguaya; it is not less than 60 leagues, 396 kil. in length.

Rivers.

Brazil possesses three large fluvial basins, besides many others of a lower order. In the first rank we must place that of the Amazonas; afterwards that of the Paraná, and finally, that of the São Francisco.

The majestic Amazonas spreading its waters along 580 leagues or 3,828 kilometers in the territory of the Empire, receives within its limits, 19 first-class tributary streams viz: the *Tocantins*, the *Xingú*, the *Tapajós*, the *Madeira*, the *Purús*, the *Coary*, the *Teffé*, the *Jurud*, the *Jutay*, the *Javary*, on the right margin; the *Jary*, the *Parú*, the *Trombetas*, the *Nhamundá*, the *Uataman*, the *Urubú*, the *Negro*, the *Japurá* and the *Içd* on the left margin. Some of them have a course of above 500 leagues, or 3,300 kilometers.

Beyond the frontier of Brazil, the Amazonas pursues its course free to steam navigation for above 300 leagues or 1,980 kilometers, in the territory of Perú, receiving the important tributary streams, the *Napó*, the *Morona* and the *Pastaza* on the left bank; the *Ucayaly* and the *Uallaga* on the right. Those rivers afford free navigation as far as the first mountains of the chain of the Andes, allowing an easy communication to the most important part of the two Republics of Perú and Equador, lying eastwards of the said chain.

The extent freely navigable to steamers, through thé Amazonas and its affluents, in the territory of Brazil, is 7,351 leagues or 48,517 kilometers, according to the following table.

	Leagues.	Kilometers.
Amazonas	580	3,828
Basins of its principal affluents.	5,771	38,089
' Lesser affluents and lakes . .	1,000	6,600
	7,351	48,516

Through the Amazonas and its tributaries, the republics of Bolivia, Perú, Equador, New-Grenade and Venezuela have their intercourse with the port of Pará, as well as the central brazilian provinces of Mato-Grosso and Upper Amazonas.

It is more than 18 years since steam-navigation, with the aid of the government, is established along the 580 leagues or 3,828 kilometers of the Brazilian Amazonas, and 200 leagues or 1,320 kilometers along the Tocantins and other rivers, in the neighbourhood of Pará.

In 1867 the government granted a subsidy to 2 companies more, which now carry on the steam navigation on the rivers Purús (240 leagues, 1,584 kilom.); Negro (120 leagues, 792 kilom.); Madeira (186 leagues 1,228 kilom.); Tapajós (50 leagues, 330 kilom.) and Upper Tocantins (230 leagues, 1,518 kilom). The whole extent of steam navigation in the basin of the Amazonas, therefore, being now 1,606 leagues or 10,600 kilometers.

On the upper part of the falls, the Madeira and its

affluents are freely navigable along 1,000 leagues or 6,600 kilom, and they afford easy conveyance to almost all the republic of Bolivia as well as to the western side of the province of Mato-Grosso.

In order to join the upper navigation to the lower one, in this river, and to foment the intercourse of the interior of South America with the port of Pará, the government subsidised a company that undertook the construction of an important rail-road along the margin of the river, these being the only means of profitably avoiding the falls. The works have already begun and must be over within 4 years.

In order to join, in the like manner, the navigation of the 230 leagues or 1,518 kilometers of the Araguaya to the lower navigation of the Tocantins, which is 100 leagues or 660 kilometers, the government is constructing, at its own expense, a road of 70 leagues or 462 kilometers, by means of which, the falls of the above rivers are to be avoided. The said road will afford communication to the provinces of Goyaz, Maranhão and Pará, to the extent of 400 leagues or 2,640 kilometers, and in after times shall be joined to the capital of the Empire by the D. Pedro II rail-road; and to the navigable portion of the river Paraguay by another road long of 40 leagues or 264 kilometers.

The Paraná is formed by the junction of the rivers Grande and Parnahyba, in the latitude 20° S. On the East, it waters the provinces of S. Paulo, Paraná, and that of Corrientes, belonging to the Argentine Confederation; and on the West, the province of Mato-Grosso in Brazil, the republic of Paraguay, and the

Argentine territory. Besides the rivers Grande and Parnahyba, the Paraná possesses a great number of affluents, some of them remarkable for their navigability, others for their extent, and all for the fertility of their valleys.

Of all those affluents the most considerable is, unquestionably, the Paraguay, which rising in the province of Mato-Grosso about 13° 30" S. latitude, pursues its course through the territory of Brazil and that of the republic, that borrowed its name. Is is navigable from 16°, and as its tributaries it has several rivers, likewise navigable, and among them, in the Brazilian territory, the S. Lourenço, along which and the Cuyabá small steamboats go up to the capital of Mato-Grosso.

On the side of the latter province, the Paraná takes in the rivers Pardo, Ivinheima, Nhanduhy, Iguatemy and Igurey. On that of the provinces of S. Paulo and Paraná, flow into it the Tieté, the Paranapanema, the Ivahy, the Pequiry and the Iguassú, which are more or less serviceable to navigation.

The navigation of the Paraná, quite free from the mouth of the Iguassú to the River Plate, is interrupted through the space of 30 leagues or 198 kilom, on the side belonging to the Empire, in consequence of the rapids of Urupungá, and of the Sete Quedas, 80 leagues or 528 kilometers below the former.

Those obstacles being overcome by the construction of marginal roads, either they be of the common or iron rail systems, the Paraná will become very serviceable to the future commercial intercourse of Goyaz, Mato-Grosso, Minas-Geraes, S. Paulo and Paraná, with the cities of Buenos-Ayres and Montevidéo.

The river S. Francisco flows through the central part of Brazil, watering the provinces of Minas-Geraes, Bahia, Pernambuco, Alagôas, and Sergipe.

Amongst its affluents, the rivers das Velhas, Paracatú, Verde and Grande are worthy of notice.

Its course is interrupted by the great and majestic falls of Paulo Affonso, up which it affords free navigation in a space of 230 leagues or 1,518 kilom. Downwards of the falls, in an extent of about 40 leagues, 264 kilom, it is navigable to steamers as far as its mouth, below the town of Penedo, in the province of Alagôas, and gives entrance to ships of 15 palms, 3,3 meters draught.

Besides those three first-class rivers, there are likewise others, which importance is well known, and that run into the sea, viz: the Gurupy, the Tury-assù, the Mearim, the Itapicurú, the Parnahyba, the Paraguassù, the Rio das Contas, the Jequitinhonha or Belmonte, the Pardo, the Mucury, the Doce, the Parahyba do Sul and the Rio-Grande do Sul.

Some of the latter are navigable to steamers for about 100 leagues, 660 kilom.

The government being convinced of the great advantages resulting from the exploration of the most important rivers in Brazil, in order to get a thorough knowledge of their navigable streams, of the obstacles that prevent their being navigated, and the means of removing them, continues to apply its serious attention to that subject.

The explorations performed in the last years before 1867, were the following ones:

By Dr. José Vieira Couto de Magalhães and the engineer Ernest Vállée, those of the river Tocantins and the Araguaya, which should served to establish a regular river navigation between the provinces of Goyaz and Pará. The result of those studies are to be found in a report and plan that were presented to the government.

By the engineer Dr. João Martins da Silva Coutinho, those of the rivers Purús and Ituxi, tributaries to the Amazonas; the result of these is also contained in a long and detailed report on that subject.

By the aforesaid engineer those of the rivers Japurá and Madeira.

By Mr. Chandler, the engineer, that of the river Agary, an affluent of the Purús.

By the same engineer that of the river Purús, from its mouth to the distance of 1,618 miles, 3,001 kil. southwards, and 1,602 miles, 2,971 kil. northwards.

By the engineer Gustave Dodt that of the river Ceará-mirim.

By the engineer Newton Burlamaque that of the river Parnahyba, in the province of Piauhy.

By the engineer Ferdinand Halfeld that of the river S. Francisco, from the falls of Pirapora down to the ocean.

By the engineer Mr. Em. Liais, with the assistance of Drs. Ladisláo Netto and Edward Moraes, that of the aforesaid river, from the falls of Pirapora up to its source.

Those explorers have also examined the river das Velhas, in the province of Minas, an important tributary to the S. Francisco.

The studies concerning those two rivers were published in Paris.

The engineers José and Francisco Keller explored the

river Parahyba do Sul, from the town of Pirahy, in the province of Rio de Janeiro, to that of Cachoeira, in the province of S. Paulo ; and the river Pomba, in the province of Minas, one of the tributaries of the above mentioned Parahyba.

The river Ivahy, in the province of Paraná, was explored by the engineers Gustave Rumbelsperger, José and Francisco Keller.

The two last mentioned engineers explored a part of the river Paraná, from the mouth of the Ivahy to the Paranapanema, and the rivers Ivinheima, Paranapanema, and Tybagy.

The engineer Eusebio Stevaux made some explorations for the canalisation of the rivers Pomonga and Japaratuha, in the province of Sergipe.

The engineer Vignolles made studies for the canalisations of the rivers Poxim and Stª Maria, in the said province, the works being already in execution ; and the engineer Charles Demoly for the canalisation between the lake of Patos and the river Mampituba, in the province of Rio Grande do Sul, and the north of Laguna, in the province of Stª Catharina.

Besides that, commander José da Costa Azevedo has drawn up a chart of the river Amazonas.

Professor Agassiz explored the amazonian region, and delivered a series of lectures on that subject, which were published in the papers of the capital of the Empire.

Both the Upper Uruguay and the Upper Paraná have been explored by several engineers and officers of the Imperial Navy.

All those explorations are highly important both for

the special advantage of Brazil and the navigation and trade of the whole world.

Since the year 1867, the following explorations have been carried on :

That of the river Madeira, in that part where lie the falls, from the place called Santo Antonio to the mouth of the Mamoré, by the engineers José and Francisco Keller, who by order of the government drew the plans the most suited for the improvement of that important mean of communication between the provinces of Pará and Mato Grosso and the republic of Bolivia, both by river and the land.

With the view of opening a communication between Mato-Grosso and Pará, through the river Tapajós, and a road along the margin of that river, which is calculated at about 33 miles, or 61,2 kil. in length, the president of the last of said provinces ordered the convenient explorations, being charged of them the engineers Julião Honorato Corrêa de Miranda and Antonio Manoel Gonçalves Tocantins.

In order to recognise the practicability of steam-navigation through the river das Velhas, from the place called Jaguará, as well as that of the river S. Francisco, the government has, not long since, commissioned the lieutenant of the Navy Francisco Manoel Alvares d'Araujo, upon a voyage of experience which was successfully effected, the waters of the Upper S. Francisco being for the first time furrowed by a steam-boat.

A committee of engineers is now exploring and studying those parts of the rivers Araguaya and Tocantins, where the navigation becomes difficult on account of the falls and rapids, in order to propose such means as may improve their navigable conditions, or in case of impossibility to study the direction of a marginal road to avoid those natural obstacles.

The river Iguassú, in the province of Paraná, was explored by the engineer Dr. Eduardo José de Moraes.

The government has likewise treated upon the exploration of the rivers *Carinhanha, Paraná, Grande, Preto,* and *do Sonho,* so that such sections of them, that may be liable of steam-navigation, should be rendered serviceable to the rail-road, which is about to be constructed between the basins of the river S. Francisco and that of the Tocantins.

A contract has also been drawn for recognising the navigability of the rivers Ivahy, Paraná, Ivinheima, Brilhante and Mondego in order to make them serviceable to the road projected between Coritiba, in the province of Paraná, and Miranda, in that of Mato-Grosso. Those studies have already begun and are being carried on very rapidly.

The river Parnahyba, though it had been already examined, was again explored by the engineer Gustave Dodt, from its mouth up to the sources, according to the report given by him.

In order to promote the agrandisement of the Empire, by constantly drawing closer international intercourse, and by encouraging the navigation and trade of the river Amazonas and its affluents, as well as that of the Tocantins and S. Francisco, those rivers from the 7th of September 1867 were declared open to the merchant vessels of all nations; I the Amazonas up the frontiers of Brazil; the Tocantins as far as Cametá; the Tapajós as far as Santarém ; the Madeira as far as Borba; the Rio Negro as far as Manáos, and the S. Francisco as far as the town of Penedo.

The navigation of the tributaries of the Amazonas, in places where only one bank belongs to Brazil, will depend on treaties to be made with the other bordering states, as to the respective limits and police and fiscal regulations.

The present dispositions in no manner altered or interfered with the existing treaties of navigation and commerce, with the republics of Perú and Venezuela, in accordance with the regulations already issued out for that purpose.

Climate and temperature.

The Empire of Brazil enjoys two quite distinct climates ; in the torrid zone it is hot and damp during the wet season; temperate and dry beyond those limits.

In the interior of the provinces of Ceará, Pernambuco, Parahyba, and Rio Grande do Norte, the want of rain, in some years, causes extraordinary droughts, so as to present a psychrometrical difference of 10° cent. Nevertheless, in many localities of the torrid zone, the climate is very mild and modified by the woods, the prevailing winds, and the elevation of the soil.

In places where the greatest heat prevails, the thermometer as a general rule, does not rise above 36° cent. ; and in those where the greatest cold is felt, it is an exception to the general rule, when it goes below 3°. 2, as for instance in the mountain range of Itatiaia, where in the

months of June 1858 and 1859 the thermometer marked
6° cent. below 0°; the daily maximum not exceeding
13°. There it often snows, and the small lakes are covered
with a coat of ice 0ᵐ,055 thick. In the plains of the
province of S. Pedro do Rio Grande do Sul, likewise, it
sometimes happens that the thermometer falls to 0° cent,
and as an exception to 2°. 5, below 0°.

In the valley of the Amazonas the mean temperature
is 27°; the effects of the heat, however, are not much
felt on account of the east-winds that sweep across the
whole country.

The difference of temperature between day and night sometimes attains to 12°, but the mean does no exceed 9°, and
from summer to winter there is only a variation of 3°.

The nights are always cool.

These circumstances become gradually and slightly modified towards the province of Ceará and Rio-Grande do
Norte, where the mean annual temperature is 26°,7 ; the
maximum of the averages during 24 hours being 30°,4,
and the minimum 23°,1.

Temperatures of 36° are of frequent occurrence during
a few hours of the day in summer, and the heat is not
much felt on account of the extreme dryness of the air.
During the rainy season, and at the same hours, the thermometer marks 26°, and the heat is then much felt.

The mean summer temperature exceeds that of winter
by 3°, as in the province of Amazonas ; and between day and
night there is only a difference of 7°.

A series of observations made with the aid of Dollond's
meteorograph during 5 years, gives the average of the daily
maxima as 27°, 13 ; the average of the daily minima as
19°,63 ; and the mean of the averages as 23°,42.

The cases have been very rare in which the thermometer has risen above 32°, or fallen below 16° The
minimum almost always occurs in July, and the maximum
in February.

From Rio de Janeiro to the Amazonas, under the torrid
zone, the mean temperature is 26°,0.

From Rio de Janeiro to the extreme south of the Empire the heat sensibly decreases, the climate becoming
very cool.

This occurs in the province of S. Paulo, Paraná, Santa-
Catharina, S. Pedro do Rio-Grande do Sul and in a part
of the province of Minas-Geraes. In the latter, which is
wholly situated on the central plateau of the Empire, and
on the mountainous portion of the others, the difference
of temperature is much felt, comparatively to that part of
the sea-coast lying between the corresponding parallels.

Mr. Em. Liais ascertained, by a series of comparative
observations, that each degree of low temperature is correspondent to 203 meters, 666 feet, of altitude.

The climate of Brazil is, in general, very healthy.

With the exception of the banks of some rivers and
the low and marshy lands, where in some seasons of
the year intermittent fevers prevail, there are not, in
a remarkable proportion, those dangerous diseases that
commonly waste the population of large cities. Such
was the opinion of the well known work — *Du climat
et des maladies du Brésil* — the author of which considered
Brazil as one of the best regions in the globe, even
reputing it, in regard to the two Americas, just in the
same case as Italy with regard to Europe.

Such was also the opinion of Lind, testified by his
experience. He used to say that the air is generally

pure on the torrid zone; and indeed salubrity is, amongst other numerous precious gifts, the best one that this american region is indebted of to the Creator of the universe.

On the sea-coasts and the neighbourhood of the maritime provinces, some epidemies such as the yellow fever in 1850, and the cholera-morbus after 1855, have some times wasted away the population, but it is worthy of notice that both those diseases have been imported, and that the asiatic plague has not renewed, to this day, its dreadful eruption.

The mortality in the most populous cities, as well as in the capital, of the Empire is a proof of its salubrity, which is comparatively superior to that of many of the healthiest cities in Europe. Cases of longevity are numerous in Brazil.

The climate, according to the latitudes and peculiar circumstances of the localities, offers all desiderable advantages to the european emigration which, besides such favorable conditions, meets with many other elements for the acquisition of wealth and independence offered them by a most feracious soil.

Rains.

The rains in Brazil usually commence in November and continue until June; but these periods vary according to the localities.

It rains considerably from the Amazonas to the Parnahyba, but little from thence to the S. Francisco, and more from the S. Francisco towards the South.

The immense zone of the S. Francisco, that comprises

those districts which the inhabitants designate by the name of *Sertão*, is subject to two seasons, which differ in a remarkable manner : the rainy season and the dry season ; the former lasts from January to May, and the latter from May to December.

In June, all vegetation ceases, the seeds are all then ripe or nearly so ; in July, the leaves begin to turn yellow and fall off ; in August, an extent of many thousands of leagues presents the aspect of an european winter, without snow ; the trees are completely stripped of their leaves, except the rare *joazeiros* (Zisyphus) ; and the *oiticicas* (Moquilea).

The gramineous, and other creeping plants, that grow in prodigious abundance in the wilderness and amidst the bushes, dry up and serve as a natural hay for the sustenance of numerous herds of cattle.

This is the period more favorable for the preparation of the coffee that grows on the mountains. Being picked up and laid on the ground, which gives forth no moisture but, on the contrary, absorbes it ; surrounded by an atmosphere possessing the same properties, the coffee dries rapidly without fermenting.

From December to January the rains begin to fall, and the rivers, up to that time nearly dry and only preserving in one place or another a few pools, which serve as watering places and as a refuge for fishes, swell to enormous volumes of water. The vegetation becomes once more verdant, within a few days, and the vast country is covered, as by enchantment, with all varieties of flowers ; all kinds of vegetables grow vigorously up and produce in abundance.

On the brazilian coasts the mean annual rain-fall is 2.^m,

0.9 fathom and above, as it occurs in Pernambuco, where according to the observations of Dr. Sarmento, referred to by M.' Em. Liais, it reaches to $2^m,62$ or $1^m,19$ fathom.

Thunderstorms are not of frequent occurrence. At Río de Janeiro the average number of days in which this phenomenon is observed, is 26 per annum.

Winds.

Along the extensive coast of Brazil, the winds generally prevalent are those from the S. E. and N. E. ; the former from September to March ; and the latter from April to August.

The sea-coast currents vary in the same manner.

In the vicinity of the coast, the land-breeze blows from 4 to 9 o'clock in the morning ; and the sea-breeze in the opposite direction from 10 o'clock in the morning to 6 in the evening ; the latter wind extends more or less towards the interior according to the physical nature of the locality, reaching to a considerable distance over the plains, as it happens in the north of the Empire ; and suffering an immediate modification in the mountainous regions.

In the basin of the Amazonas, completely deprived of mountains, the east winds penetrate to more than 500 leagues, 3,300 kil, in the interior of the country, chiefly from July to November. During this period, sailing vessels easily ascend this mighty river in 25 to 30 days from Pará up to Manáos, a distance of 300 leagues, 1,980 kil.

In the interior of the country, the south winds generally prevail during winter, and the north winds during summer.

The Animal Kingdom.

Brazil is extremely rich in the animal kingdom. Its immense territory, comprehending, as it were, all the climates, covered either with forests, virgins in the most. or extending through prairies, is peopled by numerous quadrupeds and birds, many of which are fit for food, as for instance: the tapir ; deer ; *paca*, agouti (Cœlogemys) ; *cutia* (Chloromys) ; wild boars ; armadillo, among the quadrupeds ; and the partridge, quail, *jóó* (Tinamus) ; *jacús* of several kinds (Penelope) ; *macuco* (Tinamus) ; *mutum,* curassow, (Crax galeata Sp.) ; and many species of pigeons, among the birds.

The sea, the line of coast, and the rivers of the interior are abundantly supplied with excellent fish, as the *mero* (Perca guttata); *bijupird; garoupa* (Perca atra) ; *badejo* (Perca cœrulescens) ; mackerel ; whiting ; mullet ; besides some cetacea as the whale and the porpoise, suited for the extraction of óil, and many other sinhabiting sea-water : the *suruby ;* dourado (Chetodon aureus) ; *pirarucú,* (Sudis gigas); sturgeon, *tambaqui, tucunaré, pacú* (Tetraodon lineatus), and many others living in the rivers.

The ordinary consumption of the population, both of fresh and salt or preserved fish, supports considerable fisheries, and there can be no doubt that as soon as this branch of trade is better regulated, the supply of fish, for the requirements of the population, will become a very important business.

There exist already some fishing-companies and, in a short time, that one recently organized in the capital of the Empire, under the name of Guanabara, will begin its operations; the fund being Rs. 600:000⚡000, nearly £60,000.

The law grants to fishing-companies the following concessions : A guarantee of interest till 5°/₀ within a period not exceeding 5 years, for the capital effectively employed in the purchase of boats and all the necessary fishing apparatus, as well as in the construction of factories for the salting and preserving of fish, and to shelter the workmen and the whole material of the companies. 2. A grant of marine grounds of national property, on the islands and coasts on the dry land for the establishment of factories. 3. The landing free of importation duties of all the materials indispensable for the companies,own use, whilst there be no alteration in the laws concerning those ones which are applied to the consumption of the national manufactories. 4. Also the landing free of import and of consumption duties of the salted or preserved fish, caught up and prepared by the company. 5. The exemption of military service for such as have been lately employed in the companies; as well as the exemption of the service of the navy for the masters of boats, boys and apprentices under 18 years old, and for the masters or superintendents of the business of the factories.

These exemptions, however, are only granted for a period of 10 to 20 years.

There is a great plenty of shrimps, lobsters, crawfish, and other species of crustacea, as also of oysters and several species of shell-fish which, in some of the sea-coast localities, constitute almost exclusively the food of the poor inhabitants.

Game, although it has not yet risen up to a special

trade, is, however, exported already from one province to another, either salted or preserved.

Notwithstanding the numerous attempt to improve the breeds of the domestic animals of Brasil, these have not shown any melioration, as it was to be desired. Nevertheless they are still carried on, and in the National Exhibition of 1866, as also in that of the Agricultural School, in Juiz de Fora, some breeders were rewarded who exhibited some horses brought forth by the crossing of foreign stallions with native mares.

The raising of sheep of improved breeds, imported from abroad, is like to prosper in the provinces of Paraná, S. Pedro do Rio-Grande do Sul, and the Municipality of New Friburgo, in the province of Rio de Janeiro. Some very fine wool has already been prepared and exported, besides a great quantity of it, which is consumed in the Minas-Geraes manufactories.

From the latter province numerous flocks of sheep come down to the capital of the Empire, to supply the butcheries.

The Brazilian Fauna, extremely rich, chiefly as regards insects, fishes, and birds, is not yet well known in its various, numerous, specific types. In order, however, to give a general idea, we shall mention the most remarkable species belonging to the classes and orders, already known, and existing in the zoological collections of the Brazilian Museum.

Class of the Mammalia.

Order of the Quadrumana.

In this group Brazil possesses several species of the genera Mycetes, Ateles, Lagothrix, Cebus, Pithecia, Jacchus, Midas, and Callithrix.

To the genus Stentor belong the *Guaribas* or Howling monkeys, the biggest and the most perfect animals of this order, that inhabit the Brazilian woods. The following species are already described: Stentor fuscus; S. seniculus; S. ursinus ; S. niger; S. flavimanus ; S. palliatus ; S. flavicaudatus ; S. discolor ; S. stremineus ; S. chrysurus.

The *Coatds*, Prehensiles or spider monkeys, pertain to the genus Ateles ; the principal species are the Ateles marginatus, and the A. paniscus.

The *Barrigudos* belong to the genus Lagothrix, found out by Baron Humboldt, who described the following species: Lagothrix Humboldtii, L. Castelnavii, and L. canus.

Many species of the genus Cebus live in Brazil ; we shall mention the following ones : Cebus robustus ; C. cirrifer ; C. xanthocephalus; C. gracilis ; C. cucullatus; C. libidinosus.

The *Saguis* (wistit), the most delicate type of this order belong to the genera Jacchus, Midas, and Callitbrix.

In the genus Jacchus we shall mention : the common *sagui* (Jaccbus vulgaris), a handsome animal $0,^m 20, 0,9$ palm, long, not including the tail, which is skirted all over with black, gray rings: the Pará *sagui* (J. humeralifer silver coloured on the back : the long eared *sagui* (J. auritus), of a dark, gray colour : the Bahia *sagui* (J. penicillatus), bearing a brush of long black hair over the ears : the Rio de Janeiro *sagui* (J. leucocephalus), whose hair is reddish and the head and breast white.

Of the genus Midas, are known the following species : the Maranhão *sagui*, Silky Tamarin, (Midas rosalia) of a fine golden colour ; the furry *sagui* of Pará (Midas ursulus), the body of which is covered all over with long black hair and the back is of a reddish hue ; the Midas labiatus, with black head and white nose ; the Midas chrysomelas, quite black except the forehead and the upper part of the tail, that are of a golden colour : the Midas bicolor, whose breast, fore legs, and neck are covered over with long, white hair.

To the genus Callithrix belong the following species the black *sagui* (Callithrix amictus) : the masked *sagui* (Callithrix personatus), and the red *sagui* (Callithrix moloch), discovered by Hoffmansegg in the forests of Pará.

Of the genus Pithecia there are several species, such as : the black *Parauassú*, saki cuxio (Pithecia nigra), that inhabits the forests of Pará and the banks of the Orenoque : the Pithecia Saturnina, a pretty monkey quite black, described by Dr. Emilio Maia : and the Pithecia hirsuta, a monkey much like the Sloth.

Order of the Cheiroptera.

In this order Brazil possesses a great deal of species of bats, principally pertaining to the genera Vampirus, Vespertilio, Plecotus and Phyllostoma.

Amongst others, the most remarkable are : Phyllostoma lineatum ; P. perspicillatum ; P. rotundum ; P. lilium ; Verpertilio naso ; V. polithrix ; V. brasiliensis ; V. lœvis ; V. Hilarii ; Plecotus velatus.

Order of the Carnivora.

Of this group there exist several individuals of the genus Felis, such as : the Ounce or Jaguar (Felis onça), which is as big and fierce as the royal tiger of Asia, and is found through all South America, chiefly in the south forests and central mountains of Brazil : the black Ounce (Felis nigra), considered by some naturalists as a mere variety of the Felis onça : the *Suçuarana*, cougar, (Felis concolor); the *Maracajá* (Felis pardalis), not big ; and the wild cat (Felis tigrina), a species still less big than the preceding ones.

Of the genus Canis, almost through the whole country there are to be found : the Guará or red wolf (Canis jubatus), which is as big as the european wolf but not so fierce ; the Brazilian fox or Wild dog (Canis brasiliensis), not so big as the european kind, but as sly and mischievous as the latter ; and the *Guaxinim* (Procyon cancrivorus), a native of South America and very common on the coasts of Brazil, feeding almost exclusively on crabs.

Order of the Rodentia.

Many species of this order are peculiar to Brazil, such as : the *Capivara*, Water-hog, (Hydrochœrus Capibara) the biggest rodent known ; the *Pacas* (agouti), that form two different species : the Cœlogenis fulvus and the Cœlogenis sub-niger, the flesh of which is very relishing; the *Cutia* (Chloromys aguti); the *Mocó* (Kerodon Mocó) ; the *Caxinguelê* (Macroxus variabilis); the *cuandú* (Hystrix insidiosus) ; the *Preá* (Cavia cobaya).

Order of the Pachydermata.

This order is represented by the *Anta* Tapir, (Tapirus americanus), the largest mammifer, native of the country ;

and by the *Caetetús* or Wild boars (Dicotyles labiatus, and
D. torquatus), which is the best game of the brazilian forests.

Order of the Ruminantia.

To this group belong divers species of deer (Cervus), that
inhabit the forests and prairies from the N. to the S. of
the Empire. We shall mention : the *Cervus campestris ;
C. palustris ;* C. nemori-vagus ; C. rufus, etc.

Order of the Edentata.

To this group belong the Armadillos, that constitute various species of the genus Dasypus, many of which are
esteemed as excellent game ; the Ant-eaters, of the genus
Myrmecophaga, of which there are several species, and
that feed on ants ; and the Sloths (Bradypus), remarkable
for the slowness of their movements.

Order of the Marsupialia.

In this remarkable order of the mammalia are found
the *gambás*, opossums, (Didelphis) that comprise several
species, almost all native of Brazil, and more or less re-
sembling one another.

Order of the Cetacea.

In this order we must mention the sea-cow or manatee
(Manatus americanus), a cetaceous, herbivorous mammal
that grows up to a great size, and lives in the waters of
the Amazonas or in the adjoining lakes.

Besides the Whales which, in certain periods of the
year, haunt the coasts of Brazil, on their migration from

the Southern seas, there are to be found in large troops, in the inlets and bays of the seacoast, the dolphins or *botos* (Delphinus rostratus), a cetaceum that attains more than 2 meters, 9,1 palms, in length.

Class of Birds.

Order of the Accipitres or Rapaces.

FAMILY OF THE DIURNAL—In this group Brazil possesses divers species of the genera Cathartes, Nysus, Falco, and others. To the first of them belong the common *Urubú*, vulture (Cathartes jota), and the *Urubúgereba* (Cathartes aura).

FAMILY OF THE NOCTURNAL—Many species of Owls, belonging to the genera Strix, Noctua and Scops, inhabit Brazil.

Order of the Passeres.

In this group there are numerous species, some remarkable for their song, some for their handsome plumage, and others for their singular habits. As songsters, are worthy of mention the sundry species of the genus Turdus, vulgarly known by the name of *Sabids,* Mocking-birds ; the *Currupião* of the genus Xanthornus ; the *Caraúna* (Icterus) ; the *Japús* and *Xexéos* (Cassicus), and many others that can hardly be mentioned in this brief survey.

Order of the Scansores.

Brazil possesses several species of Toucans (Ramphastus); *Araçaris* (Pteroglossus); Macaws (Ara); Maracans (Conurus);

Parrots (Psittacus); Paroquets (Psittaculus); and others pertaining to the genera Coccysus, Crotophaga, Picus, etc.

Order of the Gallinæ.

There are various species of *Jacús* (Penelope); *Mutuns*, curassows (Crax); *Inhambús*, Partridges and Quails (Tinamus); Pigeons (Columba) and other birds of the same family, that are likewise much esteemed.

Order of the Grallæ.

FAMILY OF THE BREVIPENNES. — In this small family, Brazil numbers the Brazilian Ema (Rhea americana), the only species that represents in America the ostrich of the old continent.

FAMILY OF THE BREVIROSTRAL. — There are a few species of the genera Charadrius, Vanellus, Hematopus, Dicolophus,

FAMILY OF THE CULTIROSTRAL. — To this family belong the various species of Herons (Ardea), the *Arapapá* (Cancroma); the Spoonbill (Platalea); the *Jaburú* (Mycteria), all of which live in flocks on the margins both of lakes and rivers.

FAMILY OF THE LONGIROSTRAL. — In this family are found different species of Snipes (Scolapax); Curlews (Numenius); and many others belonging to the genera Tringa, Rynchœa, Limosa, Totanus, Himantopus, Ibis, etc. In the latter genus is worthy of notice the *Guará*, Ibis (Ibis rubra), that inhabits the sea-shores both in the North and South of the Empire.

FAMILY OF THE MACRODACTYLS. — This Family is represented by various species of Jaçanas or Surgeons (Parra); *Anhumas* (Palamedea); Water Fowls (Gallinula), and many

others, among which mention can be made of a species of
the genus Phœnicopterus.

Order of the Palmipedes.

FAMILY OF THE LONGIPENNES.. — Of this family, to which
belong the birds of highest flight over the seas, as for
instance the *Procellariæ*, are found some species both of
the genus Larus, and the genus Sterna.

FAMILY OF THE TOTIPALMATÆ. — This small family is represented by few species of the genus Plotus, by some
of the genus Carbo, and by one species of the genus Pelecanus, the Pelecanus brasiliensis.

FAMILY OF THE LAMELLIROSTRAL. — There are in this family
many species of ducks and widgeons (Anas), that could be
easily domesticated, and a species of drake, native of the
valley of the Amazonas (Anser jubatus).

Of the genus Mergus there is one species, the Smew,
Mergus brasiliensis, and one species of Swan, the Cygnus
nigricollis.

Class of the Reptilia.

Order of the Chelonia.

It comprehends the Tortoises, both of land and water,
turtles, and the *Jabotis*, Greek tortoises, which are represented by numerous species, many of which are not
yet perfectly known.

Amongst those that are most known we shall mention
the species of the genera: Emys, Testudo, Chelonia, Ca-
retta, and particularly the curions turtle *mata-mata* (Tes-
udo fimbriata.

Along both the margins of the Amazonas and its tributaries, the turtle affords a precious food to the population.

With the eggs of the several species of the chelonia, inhabiting that region, they prepare the so called *turtle butter*, that makes an important branch of trade, in the province of the said name.

Order of the Sauria.

There are many species of which we shall mention : the common Alligator (Alligator cynocephalus) that grows up to 2 or 3 meters, 9,1 to 13,6 palms, in length, and inhabits almost all the rivers of Brazil : the Alligator palpebrosus, a smaller species, but not less mischievous; the *Teju-assú* (Tupinambis nigropunctatus) ; the Iguana delicatissima ; the Lacerta marmorata (Polychrus marmoratus) ; the Lacerta scincus; the Lacerta striata ; the Tubinambis viridis ; the Chameleons (Agama picta and Agama marmorata), and several others.

Order of the Ophidia.

The forests of Brazil are inhabited by numerous species of Ophidia of all sizes and colours, some of them being extremely venomous, chiefly those of the genera Trigonocephalus, to which are belonging the *Surucucús, Jararacas, Jararacussús* , etc. ; and Crotalus, represented by the Rattle Snake.

Of the genus Coluber there exists a great number of harmless species, such as the *coral* (Coluber formosus; C. venustissimus, and others) ; the *caninanas* (Coluber pœcillostoma) ; besides other species belonging to the genera Elaps, Scytale, Cophias, and others.

In the genus Boa, that comprends snakes of the largest size, we shall mention the *Giboia* (Boa conchria) ; and the *Sucurиú* or *Sucuriuba* (Boa Anaconda).

Class of the Batrachians.

There are in Brazil several species of the genera Bufo, Ceratrophys, Crossodactylus, Brachycephalus, Trachycephalus, Hyla, Rana, and others.

Class of the Fishes.

It is hardly possible to enumerate all the species of fishes that are to be met with, in the seas and rivers of Brazil, so immense is their quantity. Moreover, many of them have not yet been studied.

Professor Agassiz, on his recent voyage through Brazil, collected, only in the valley of the Amazonas, thousands of species, many of which quite new.

Amongst the most remarkable and best known species of that region there are: the *Pirarucú* (Vastres Cuvierii), a fish that grows up to a great size, and is the principal article of food for the greater number of the inhabitants of Pará and Amazonas; besides three other species of the same genus Vastres: the Phractocephalus hemiliopterus ; the Doras niger ; the *Poraqué*, electric eel (Gymnotus electricus); the Asteoglossum Vandellii, the only species known of the genus Osteoglossum, and divers species of the genus Lepisosteus.

The genus Salmo is represented by one species, the *pirapitanga* (Salmo pirapitanga, that lives in the waters of the Cuyabá.

Molusca.

CLASS OF THE CEPHALOPODS.—In the seas of Brazil there is to be found one species of this class belonging to the genus Argonauta.

CLASS OF THE GASTEROPODS. —There are various species, pertaining to the genera : Patella, Dentalium, Siphonaria, Fissurella, Crepidula, Helicinæa, Bulla, Helix, Clausilia, Bulimus, Panorbis, Paladina, Ampullaria, Natica, Janthina, Scutaria, Trochus, Murex, Triton, Cassis, Cassidaria, Purpura, and many others.

CLASS OF THE ACEPHALA. — Of this class there exist sundry species of the following genera : Ostrea, Serpula, Pecten, Limax, Pinna , Mytilus, Solen, Lustraria, Crassatella, Petricola, Sanguinolaria, Donax, Capsa, Cardium, Venus, Arca, Unio, Anodonta and many others.

Crustacea.

In the section of the Decapoda Macrura there are several species of shrimps and crawfish (Palemon), as also some of the genera Scyllarus, Penœus, Squilla, besides others not yet well ascertained.

In the section of the Decapoda Brachyura, that comprehends all kind of crabs, there are found numerous species of the genera : Xanthus, Maia, Pericera, Lupa, Eriphia, Trichodactylus, Guaia, Gelasimus, Grapsus, Sesarma, and Uca.

Class of the Insecta.

This class is extremely rich in species of all the genera, many of which are quite harmless, some mischievous, and some remarkably useful. We shall mention only the latter.

In the order of the Hymenoptera, are worthy of notice many species of *melliponæ* that afford not only a delicious honey, but also a soft wax from which trade derives much advantage. Of those *melliponæ* which are known in Brazil by the general denomination of *abelhas*, bees, some are cultivated, and other live in a wild state, having not been domesticated to this day.

The european bee (apis mellifera) is likewise brought up in Brazil and it is already so accustomed to the climate, that it swarms spontaneously in the woods. In some localities of the provinces of S. Paulo and Rio de Janeiro, the production of bees constitutes an important and very profitable industry.

In the order of the Lepidoptera there exist various species of silk worm worthy of cultivation, amongst them the *saturnia*, that furnishes excellent cocoons, of which some remarkable specimens were exhibited at the last national exhibition. These species, however, have not been regularly educated, what should undoubtedly prove of the greatest advantage to the national industry.

The exotic species (Bombix mori) is still brought up and yields perfectly in the south provinces. At Rio Grande do Sul, the cocoons have just become an article of exportation. The Imperial Agricultural Institute of Rio de Janeiro, with the assistance of the government, is endeavouring to give an impulse to the silk trade, as it is related in another place of this book.

In the order of the Coleoptera, there are some insects which, on account of their bright, metallic, reflex, and variegated hues, are used as ornamental, to make flowers, garlands, necklaces and for many other fashionable purposes.

The province of Santa Catharina is the most advanced in this branch of trade, its products being sent down to the capital of the Empire.

The Vegetable Kingdom.

The vegetation of Brazil is one of the most wonderful in the world. In the plains, on the mountains, on the highest tops, on the coast itself and in the midst of the sands, through steepy rocks and precipices ; in short, every where the most vigorous vegetation is continually exhibited in an everlasting spring.

The Brazilian Flora is perhaps the most luxuriant in the world because of the abundance and variety of its most important species, of which more than 17 thousand are already known.

In the forests of Brazil are found some of the best kinds of timber for naval or civil constructions ; and for cabinet-work, the richest and finest known in this industrial department.

Amongst the former are worthy of notice : the *peroba* (Aspidosperma peroba) ; *tapinhoã* (Sylvia navalium) ; *cabiuna* or black *jacarandá* (Dalbergia nigra), also known by the name of rose-wood ; *páo-brazil*, Brazil-wood (Cæsalpinia echinata) ; *bacuri* (Platonia insignis) ; *sucupira* (Bowdichia major) ; *aroeira* (Astronium) ; *páo d'arco* or *ipé* (Tecoma speciosa) ; *pequiá* yellow (Aspidosperma sessiliflorum); *massaranduba* (Mimusops elata) ; *páo-ferro*, iron-wood (Cæsalpinia ferrea) ; *cedro*, cedar (Cedrella brasiliensis); *louro*, laurel or bay-tree (Cordia frondosa) ; *itauba* (Acrodiclidium Itauba) ; *sapucaia* (Lecythis Pisonis) ; *baraúna* (Melanoxylon Brauna) ; *paracaúba* (Andirá) ; *grapiapunha* (Apuleia polygamea) ; *pequiá-marfim* (Aspidosperma eburnea) ; *guarabú* (Peltogyne-guarabú) ; *angelim amargoso* and *pedra* (Machœrium andira) ; several species of cinnamon, *canella* (Nectandria and Cordia) ; *mirindiba* (Terminalia *Mirindiba*) ; *gruçahy de azeite* (Moldenhauria) ; *ipé tobacco* (Tecoma) ; and many others.

For cabinet-work, the most remarkable are : the *oleo* (Mirocarpus frondosus) ; the *muirápinima* (Centrolobium paraense) ; *cajarana* (Cæsalpinia monosperma) ; *páo-cruz* (Leguminosa?) ; *vinhatico* (Echyrospermum Balthasari, ;*páo-setim*, satin-wood (Aspidosperma) ; *jacarandá* red, rose-wood (Machœrium firmum) ; *gonçalo alves* (Astronium fraxonifolium) ; *sebastião d'arruda* (Phylocalymma floribundum) ; *páo-marfim*, ivory-wood (Aspidosperma eburnea) ; *muira-piranga* (Cæsalpinia) ; and so many others that it is hardly possible to enumerate them all.

For dyeing purposes the best woods are : *páo-brazil*, Brazil-wood (Cæsalpinia echinata) ; *talagiba* (Maclura affinis) ; *mangue vermelho*, red mangrove, (Rhizophora mangle) ; several species of *anil*, indigo (Indigofera) ; and *urucú*, annatto (Bicho Orellana).

Besides the above mentioned, there also spring up abundantly and spontaneously in the forests, the *grum-marim* (gen. ignotum), which is an excellent substitute for box (Boxus sempervirens) in engraving ; the *seringueira*, gum-elastic tree (Syphonia elastica), from which caoutchouc is extracted, as also from the *mangabeira* (Hancornia speciosa), and from other plants ; *myristicas* which produce a vegetable tallow ; the *cacao* (Theobroma cacau) and many other plants of vast and acknowledged utility, which constitute an extensive and important matter of trade.

There is a great variety of aromatic plants such as : the *vanilla* (Vanilla aromatica) ; the *cumarú* (Dipterix) ; the *cuyumari* (Ocotea), the seeds of which are used to impart their flavour to chocolate ; the *Brazilian nutmeg* (Criptocaria) ; the *pichurin* (Nectandra) ; and the aboriginals'peper, *pimenta de gentio* (Xylopia).

Amongst many wild plants abounding with tannin, we must mention the *barbatimão* (Stryphnodendron), which yields 80 % of that substance ; the mangue, mangrove (Rhizophora), which yields five times more tannin than the european oak (Quercus) ; the *jurema* (Acacia), and the *aroeira*, lestisk-tree (Schinus).

Among the plants fit for food (and they abound in Brazil), the most remarkable are the manioc (Manihot), of which a particular mention shall be made; the *pinhão* (Araucaria), which fruits are excellent ; *jacatupé* (Pachyrrhizus) and several kinds of dioscorea.

There are also to be found, in great abundance, in the different provinces, numerous plants of which the fruits, shells, seeds or stones are used for medicinal purposes, as for instance *sarsaparrilla* (Smilax sp) ; *ipecacuanha* (Cephœlis Ipecacuanha) ; *caferana* (Tachia Guianensis); *urari* or *curary* (Strychnos); *guarand* (Paullinia sorbilis) ; *mururé* (Bichetea officinalis) ; *jalap* (Ipomœa) ; *caroba* (Jacarandá procera) ; and various plants which for their febrifugal qualities are known under the name of *quina*, quinine, but which belong to the genera *Exostemma, Coutarea*, and *Hortia* ; as also in some places are found a species of *strychnos*; the *pdo-pereira* (Geissospermum sp.) ; *pareira brava* (Cocculus platiphylla) ; *maiden hair* (Adianthus sp.); *cahinca* (Chiococca anguifuga); *tamaquaré* (Laurineæ), and many others ; the most precious balsams and valuable oils ; and finally a large variety of resinous, oleous, and lacteous plants, as the *jatahy* (Hymenœa sp.) ; *angico* (Pithecolobium gummiferum and Acacia

angico) ; *andiroba* (Carapa guianensis) ; *copahiva* (Co-
paifera sp.) ; *oiticica* (Moquilea) ; and others.

In grounds once occupied by virgin forests, as well as
in the prairies and along the coast, there grow up spontaneously numerous plants, which produce varied and
excellent fruits.

Among the trees the most useful of Brazil, is worthy
of a special mention the carnauba-palm (Copernicia-ce-
rifera), which grows uncultivated in the provinces of
Ceará, Rio Grande do Norte, and some others in the
North of the Empire.

Perhaps there is no region of the globe, where can be
found a tree of such varied uses and so serviceable as
the carnauba-palm.

It resists the most severe and longest droughts, keeping always green and flourishing.

The roots possess the same medicinal properties as
the sarsaparilla. From the trunk they extract strong,
light fibres, that are susceptible of a nice lustre; and
the wood is used for props, joists, and other building
purposes, as also for stakes and fences.

The inner rind or cabbage, when fresh, is used as a
highly esteemed and most nutritive food; it also affords
wine, vinegar, saccharine substance, and a great quantity
of gum like sago, possessing the same properties and taste.
It has often been the only food of the inhabitants of Ceará
and Rio Grande do Norte, in times of severe drought.

From the wood they make musical instruments, tubes,
and pumps.

The soft, fibrous substance in the interior of the stalk,
and that of the leaves, is a perfect substitute for cork.
The pulp of the fruit is agreable to taste, and the kernel,

which is very oily and emulsive, after being roasted and poundedl, is used, as coffee, by some people in the inte-rior of the country.

From the trunk, a species of flour, like maizena, is ex-tracted, as also a whitish liquor like that produced by the fruit known by the name of Bahia cocoa-nut.

Of the dried leaves they make mats, hats, baskets and brooms; and the straw is already sent to Europe in great quantity, to be made into fine hats, some of which are sent back to Brazil. The value both of the quantity exported and of that employed in the national industry, is estimated at about Rs. 1,000:000$000, nearly £ 100,000.

From the leaves is extracted a kind of wax, much used for making candles, which are extensively consumed in the northern provinces, especialy at Ceará, where this article is already an important branch of trade.

The annual exportation of this wax is calculated at above 60,000 arrobas, 871,400 kilog; — the internal con-sumption at above 50,000 arrobas, 734,500 kilog. ; — the value of the annual production amounting to above Rs. 1,500:000$000, (£ 150,000).

The Mineral Kingdom.

Brazil abounds in

Precious stones.

Diamonds are found in the province of Minas-Geraes, along the Serra do Espinhaço; on the north of the said Serra as far as the northern boundaries of the province; as well as in the mountains that lie S. W. of the sources of the river S. Francisco. They are also found in the plains and in the southern mountains that lie nearer to the valley of the S. Francisco, in the province of Bahia.

In the provinces of Goyaz, Mato-Grosso, Paraná, S. Pedro do Rio Grande do Sul, and S. Paulo, diamonds are also to be found, but these are of small value, and occasionally met with in the ïtacolumitie rocks. It is probable that in aftertimes, with the increase of the inland population and the progress of the minereal industry, many other and more abundant mines shall be found out.

The diamond mines belong, at present, exclusively to private parties, in accordance with the terms and conditions of the laws, that regulate the special administration of the diamond mines and their workings.

Emeralds, euclases, sapphires, rubies, topazes, beryls and tourmalins, either black, blue or green, also called brazilian emeralds, are all met with in the Empire, especially in the province of Minas-Geraes, where together with the ordinary zarconites are found other gems of less value.

Garnets, though not of the first quality, are found in great quantity throughout the whole country.

Quartz and its varieties.

Perfectly pure rock crystals and of enormous sizes are already exported, chiefly from the provinces of Minas-Geraes, Goyaz, S. Paulo and Paraná, whence beautiful, large amethysts are likewise extracted, which are sold at a high price.

Opals, chalcedonies, agates and jaspers are also found nearly throughout the whole country, the province of S. Pedro do Rio Grande do Sul being the most remarkable for the exportation both of agates and chalcedonies, which already constitute there an important branch of trade.

Metals.

GOLD. —There is scarcely any point in the Empire where this precious metal does not appear among its natural produces.

As, however, we must refer only to those localities acknowledgedly auriferous and destined as such for mineralization, we should mention a great part of the province of Minas-Geraes, and especially the upper basin of the S. Francisco, along its eastern side, from whence a few english companies and many private persons extract gold.

Such is also the case with the municipalities of Caçapava, Rio Pardo, Santa Maria, and Cruz Alta, in the province of S. Pedro do Rio Grande do Sul. A brazilian company under the name of « South Brazil gold and copper mining company », with a fund of 800:000$000 (nearly £ 80,000) is already carrying on gold-mining in the municipality of Caçapava.

Next to those we must mention the district of Tury-Assú, in the province of Maranhão; and many other places in the provinces of Bahia, Pernambuco, Parahyba, Piauhy, Goyaz, Ceará, and S. Paulo, for the exploration of which the imperial government has granted privileges during those last years.

The gold that is met with in all those veins, is usually found mixed with compact quartz, and quartzite, within primitive rocks. ·

The system, used to this day, for the extraction of this metal, either by the national or the english companies that have been lately established, is the same as employed in Australia.

Private parties, however, make use of the old method of washing the sands proceeding from gold-mine rocks, and deposited in the bed of the nearest rivers. In those above mentioned sands, the gold is found mixed together with platina, iridium, and more seldom with palladium.

In some mines the gold also is found mixed with tellurium and a great quantity of arsenious pyrites.

From the assays made at the Rio de Janeiro Mint, the gold mixed with palladium has been found to give the following results:

	I	II	III
Gold. . . .	88,9	90,25	92,3
Palladium . . .	11,1	9,75	7,7

SILVER.— This metal accompanies many of the galenic formations, that are to be met with in all the provinces; but its proportion is always inferior to 1 % of lead.

It is known, however, that amongst the minerals of copper in the municipality of Caçapava, in the province of S. Pedro do Rio Grande do Sul, silver was met with, in a proportion of 2, 5 %.; it being probable that, upon a closer exploration of the former, by the brazilian company that undertook the gold workings, in the aforesaid municipality, silver may soon be looked upon as one of our richest and most important commercial produces.

It is nearly two centuries since this metal was extracted and cast at the mount Araçoiva, in the municipality of Sorocaba, in the province of S. Paulo, together with gold which, a few years ago, was still worked out there.

MERCURY.—In the province of Paraná, not far from the capital, there are some mines of mercury, that can bear competence with the richest either of Europe or Perú. We are also told that, in the beginning of this century, this metal was met with in the province of Santa-Catharina.

COPPER.— It is found in abundance in the provinces of Mato-Grosso, Goyaz, Minas-Geraes, Bahía (not far from the capital), Maranhão, Ceará, and chiefly in that of S. Pedro do Rio-Grande do Sul, in the municipality of Caçapava; and especially in the hamlet of Santo-Antonio das Lavras, one league, 6,6 kil., distant from the village of the same name ; whence it can easily be transported in a distance of 13 leagues, 85,8 kil. to the city of Cachoeira, a port in the river Jacuhy, navigable to steamboats.

The copper of the above said municipality, where lie the richest copper-mines of Brazil, yields 60 °/₀ of pure metal, according to the veins chosen out for exploration.

In those mines there are to be found malachites, azurites, scorodites and the so called klaprothine.

MANGANESE.— In Minas-Geraes and other provinces, this metal is met with; it exists in great abundance in the neighbourhood of Nazareth, a town in the province of Bahia, which has an easy communication, by water, with the capital of the same province.

TIN.—This metal has been found out in such a small quantity that it can hardly be considered as an industrial product of the country.

It is said that this metal has been discovered among the sands of the river Paraopeba, in the province of Minas-Geraes, and also in some of the granite rocks of that of Rio de Janeiro ; and that some traces of it have appeared in the province of Ceará and Santa-Catharina, but as yet there are no reliable proofs of its existence there.

LEAD. — There is a great abundance of it in the state of galena, the composition of which is 86, 5 % of lead, 12, 5 % of sulphur, and from 0,6 to 0,7 % of silver.

The mines of Iporanga, Sorocaba, Iguape, in the province of S. Paulo, of Rio Abaeté and of the neighbourhood of Sete Lagôas in Minas-Geraes, are well known ; as well as those of Rio de Janeiro, Parahyba do Norte, Bahia, Santa-Catharina, Ceará, Maranhão, Piauhy, and finally the seams or beds in the mountain chain of Ibiapaba, in the province of Ceará.

Chromate of lead is pretty abundant at Congonhas do Campo, in Minas-Geraes; being found in the extent of a few kilometers ; but no great profit is taken from it as yet. It is composed of 69 % of oxyde of lead, and 31 % of chromic acid.

Of all the lead-mines the most remarkable is the one at Rio Abaeté, whence has been extracted not only lead, but even silver, when it was worked in former times.

ANTIMONIUM. — There are in the national museum some specimens of sulphuret of antimonium from the province of Minas Geraes; they say it has also been found in S. Paulo and Paraná.

BISMUTH. — It has been found in the province of Minas-Geraes, as well as in other localities, in great quantity.

ARSENIC. — It generally accompanies the pyrites in the auriferous formations, being also found out in the state of carbonic acid combined with iron, forming scorodite, that is to be found in the parish of Antonio Pereira, in Minas-Geraes.

IRON. — It may be said, without fear of error, that there is not, through the whole Empire, a single hectare of land, 2.066 square fathoms, which does not contain iron under one or other of its varied forms; being in many a locality met in the most valuable conditions.

At the summit of Itabira, in the neighbourhood of the city of Ouro-Preto; on the mountain chain of Espinhaço, near Piedade Hill; and in many other points of the province of Minas-Geraes, it is incalculable the quantity of iron there existing, not only magnetic, but oligistic and micaceous too, which in a great measure enters in the composition of the mountains of that province. The oligistic iron undergoes a decomposition at the surface, owing to the action of atmospheric agents, forming beds of limonite that stretch over a considerable extent.

In the northern provinces, in the interior of Minas, in S. Pedro do Rio-Grande do Sul, and in Paraná, iron is found in a remarkable quantity, more or less decomposed, amidst the argilous beds, that cover up the plains and the skirts of hills.

The richest iron mines, which do not constitute an independent formation, are more or less abundant seams like those of S. João de Ipanema, and others in the provinces of Alagôas, Ceará, Rio-Grande do Norte and Parahyba.

There are in Brazil some iron-mines that possess the incontestable superiority of being free from pyrites, an advantage which not even the most famous mines of Denmark and Sweden enjoy.

The brazilian magnetite (loadstone) contains 72,5 %. of iron; the oligist, the martite, and the best micaceous iron 70 %., lowering down in the inferior qualities to 25 and 20 %.

Iron, by itself, is one of the greatest elements of wealth in the Empire, for its abundance and quality, as well as for the facility and economy with which it can be worked, being commonly found near extensive woods, that reproduce themselves in the space of 6 to 10 years, affording of course an excellent fuel for a long while. There are besides, at hand, abundant currents and water-falls that can be availed of as motive-power to machines.

Some people, in Minas-Geraes, encouraging with so promising conditions set to iron-mining with a great advantage. That province consumes a great deal of iron, extracted from its own soil and wrought even there.

Every thing leads to the belief that this useful industry shall spread within a few years, through many points of the Empire.

In S. Paulo there exists the most important iron-work in South America.

That establishment founded and supported by the State, actually possesses sure elements of prosperity.

These iron works can employ important and valuable resources, such as : first rate mineral, carbonate of lime for casting purposes, refractive material for the construction of ovens, sufficient water to set in movement the principal machinery, and capital woods at a short distance.

That important establishment will have besides, after the conclusion of the rail-way from S. Paulo to Ypanema, across Sorocaba, an easy and convenient means of conveyance for its products.

Its director is at present in Europe, charged by government to engage skilful workmen, who may concur for the thriving of the manufactory, forming there at, the same time an industrial school.

Such school may be considered as already in way of execution; for some orphans and many young slaves under the guardianship of the nation, having been sent thither, as soon as they got their freedom, are already learning to read, to write and accounts; the oldest ones being obliged, in the leisures hours, to attend the iron workings.

The Ypanema iron-works possess several workshops, for clay and sand moulding, for refinery, carpentry, and other purposes: it may soon rival with the best iron-works of Europe in the sale of its products, since the capital employed in wood-lands is but too small compared to that required there, for the same extent of woods.

Those woodlands occupy a surface of 6.651,5 hectares, 1,5 square league, that can furnish daily 15 metrical tons of charcoal, 18,9 tons, a sufficient quantity to keep in full activity all the various departments of the iron-workings.

Besides the high furnaces and work-houses, already existing, a flood-gate was now set up in the central part of the mines to retain the waters of the brook do Furo, producing thus a moving power of 6 horses.

There is also in way of construction an ustulation-muffle, like those of Sweden and Russia. Iron rails are being set too, for the transport between the ovens and the work-houses; as well as for the rapid communication with the calcareous mountains. Some other important works are likewise going on.

Very near the ironworks there spread rich and extensive quarries of excellent marble, the specimens of which were much valued at the last national exhibition. They are being availed of conveniently.

[handwritten marginalia]

Building-stones.

A vast tract on the southern coast of the Empire, comprehended between 12° and 30° Lat. is almost exclusively constituted by primitive rocks, such as granites of various kinds and colours, gneiss, more or less foliated, green and black diorites, clear, and dark quartzites, porphyry stones in large dikes, generally intercalated in ancient rocks; and in some sites there are beautiful varieties of syenite.

In the interior, where many or rather, we may say, all those rocks extend to a great distance, there is equally a great number of ferruginous rocks, of grit òr grit ferruginous rocks, and of calcareous, quite fit for sculpture and possessing the polish of true marble; there is, finally, plastic clay in thick layers.

Even within the bay of Rio de Janeiro, a large collection of dark granitic porphyry mixed with large crystals of rosy feldspar, can be obtained on the hills, that surround it, as for instance those of Armação in Nitheroy, of the island of Paquetá, which are grayish and slightly spotted with micaceous nidulations, those of serra do Matheus, near the railway station of Engenho Novo, as also whitish, slightly yellowish or rosy ones, such as those met with at Botafogo.

The gneiss is some times whitish, as those ones o Santa Thereza, and other times streaked of white and black, as those of S. Christovão, in the suburbs of the city of Rio de Janeiro.

Dykes of variegated porphyry, under the form and nature
of diorite, are found at the foot of Corcovado, at Santos
Rodrigues-Hill, at the fortress of Villegaignon and
other places near the Capital. The stones extracted from
such rocks, as also the compact diorite, that is equally
found nearly in all the mountains of Rio de Janeiro, are
now beginning to be employed in the construction of
rustic walls, where they produce the most beautiful appearance.

The granitoid-diorite is very fit for the pavings that
have to support great burthens, as it is a very hard
rock, on this account being scarcely made use of in
common paving.

CALCAREOUS. — Saccharoid calcareous are found in many
localities, being, in the most, eruptive from gneiss.

From the compact varieties of all colours met with
in the province of S. Pedro do Rio-Grande do Sul,
many works have been made. They are known in our
country by the name of marbles of Rio-Grande.

A company has been lately organized to work the
quarries at a place named Encruzilhada, in the above
mentioned province, from which are extracted marbles
of different colours ; the green being remarkable for its
hardness and variegated veins, and the black variety for
its exceptional lustre.

This is not, however, the only province holding such
riches ; Minas-Geraes, S. Paulo in many places and very
near the capital, Bahia, Alagôas and other provinces,
produce beautiful marbles too. The most remarkable are
extracted from the municipality of S. Roque, a few leagues
from the capital of S. Paulo, where there exists already
a manufactory for the purpose of splitting them over.

Besides being liable of polishing, these carbonates are to be seen under the most beautiful varieties; the black one especially rivals with the best marble of Europe.

The lime, generaly used for building purposes on the sea-coast towns, is almost exclusively made from the *Sambaquis*, or enormous mounds of shells, or also from shoals of shell-fish that grow in the inlets or beds of coral, that follow along the coast of Brazil, from the Abrolhos northwards.

Gypsum appears in Minas-Geraes and in many of the northern provinces.

Alabaster is rather scarce : some specimens have been sent from Bahia, and from the banks of the river S. Francisco.

At Maranhão, Parahyba do Norte and Pernambuco there are cretaceous marbles, characterized by the fossils that occur in them.

CLAY. — It is found throughout the Empire, proceeding from the decomposition of rocks standing still and forming, therefore, large beds correspondent to the volumes of the decomposed rocks. It is in a great part, however, produced by alluvion.

Clay is much employed in pottery. The white varieties, fit for the manufacturing of earthen-ware, are abundant.

That clay, more or less white, and known by the name of *tabatinga*, has been much employed by the primitive inhabitants, and so it is even now-a-days, in the interior, for the making of rough earthen-ware, and other purposes.

Kaolin is abundant in Rio de Janeiro, but in most cases is accompanied with numerous grains of quartz, which it was united to before its decomposition.

There are many varieties of refractive clay, from which

excellent crucibles are made ; as for instance those exposed
at the French Exhibition of 1867, and analyzed by Mr. Dess
cloiseaux and by other competent persons, who acknowledged and testified their fine quality.

Combustible Minerals.

Coal. — Recent analyses of our combustible mineral-
have proved that some provinces possess the true fossil
coal.

Not only the proportion of carbon and other deductions ₍
confirme this assertion, but it is furthermore powerfully ₍
demonstrated by the union of our coal with fossil plants ₍
of the genera *Calamite*, *Lepidodendron* and *Sigillaria*,
that have hitherto served as characteristic of carboniferous ₍
lands.

The specimens of this combustible, extracted from the
mines existing in the provinces of Paraná and Sta Catharina, are well known.

In the province of S. Pedro do Rio Grande do Sul the
most important mines are those of Candiota, and of the
Arroio dos Ratos.

The former was granted to an english company, that
is about to construct a rail-way for the transportation of
the coal.

The latter wrought by another english company, has
already a tram-road through which is conveyed the coal,
that is employed for different purposes, especially for the
steam-boats that ply along the Lagôa dos Patos and some
rivers of the province.

The coal of Tubarão, of Araranguá, and ist neighbourhoods, in the province of Santa Catharina, are also of quality.

The mining of all those coal-beds has been allowed, and it is to be hoped that, in a few years, this great element of industry and civilisation will contribute to the progress and prosperity of Brazil.

Lignites.—They are abundant nearly through the whole Empire, especially in S. Paulo, in Santa-Catharina, at Rio-Grande do Sul, Marianna in the province of Minas-Geraes, and on the banks of the Parahyba do Sul, the exploration of which was granted not long since.

Like coal-beds are also to be found in Ceará and Maranhão, where they are already being wrought.

Bituminous Schists.—In most of the provinces, bituminous schists have been discovered. We may, however, point out as the best those in the southern coast of the province of Bahia, and of Camaragibe, in Alagôas.

The first mentioned are now explored by an important commercial house at Bahia. There are other grantees who are about to promote therein the extraction of petroleum.

The exploration and extraction in other provinces were not long ago granted to an undertaker, who is going to organize a company for such a purpose.

Graphite.—It is as yet known in more abundance in the province of Ceará, forming nidulations in gneiss ; or then under the shape of little spangles in the eruptive saccharoid limestone.

Sulphur. — The sulphur hitherto discovered exists in a native state in the province of Rio-Grande do Norte, in a small quantity in Rio-Grande do Sul, and at the parish of Furquim in Minas-Geraes. It is, however, very abundant in Corrego do Ouro (golden brook), a district

of Minas-Novas, where it has been tried with success
for the making of gun-powder.

Salts.

One of the most remarkable for its importance is salt-
peter, which is abundantly formed on the beds of the
calcareous caves in Minas-Geraes, Piauhy, Ceará, Mato-
Grosso, Goyaz, and other provinces, chiefly from the city
of Ouro Preto down to the banks of the river S. Francisco,
in the proximity of Bahia.

Alum has appeared in plenty about Paraná, Minas-Geraes,
Piauhy and Ceará, and in many other places of Brazil,
since in all its soil there is a great quantity of lignites
and bituminous schists, from the pyritic nidulations of
which a large portion of this salt is extracted.

In Mato-Grosso and Goyaz, in the interior of the province of Bahia, in Piauhy, and chiefly in Minas-Geraes
there is a great quantity of rock-salt. Sulphate of magnesia and of soda, though in less quantity and sometimes
in the form of efflorescences, are also to be found, as for instance, in the calcareous strata of the Serra d'Araripe, in
Ceará.

The most curious saline efflorescence is, no doubt, that
of the chlorid of sodium in the gneiss of Serra de Uru-
buretama as far as Serra da Meruoca, in the last mentioned province.

A like phenomenon is observed in Piauhy, and, as it is
said, on the mountains, that lie between Minas and Goyaz.

Salt is extracted, in Rio Negro, from stomapods, that
grow on the rocks in spite of the great current of the
water.

Mineral Waters.

Mineral waters of different kinds are to be found in plenty throuhgout Brazil.

Most of them, however, not being as yet analysed, brief is the mention now made of their properties.

Ferruginous Waters.

Such waters are to be found almost in the whole country. There are, in the capital of the Empire, nine springs already examined, two of which within the city.

The most important of them, for their abundance and for containing iron in greater quantity, are those of Andarahy Pequeno, Larangeiras, Riachuelo and Silva Manoel streets, Serra da Tijuca, and Lagôa de Rodrigo de Freitas. The two first ones are public fountains much frequented and well built, situated in two of the most agreeable and healthy suburbs.

In the capital and other spots of the province of Rio de Janeiro there exist eleven springs, already examined, as also seven of them in the province of Minas Geraes, in whose capital there is a public fountain; five in the province of Pernambuco, and several in Maranhão, Piauhy, Espirito-Santo, S. Paulo and other provinces too.

They all, in general, contain iron in the state of carbonate dissolved excess of in carbonic acid, but in very irregular proportions.

Aerated Waters.

The most resorted to are those called *Aguas Virtuosas,* in the parish of Lambary, about 3 leagues, 19,8 kilom.

from the town of Campanha, and nearly 60 leagues, or 216 kilom, from the capital of the Empire; and those, formerly called Aguas Santas, and actually de Caxambú, in the district of Baependy, at the distance of 1 league, 6,6 kilom, more or less, from the town of the same name; all of them in Minas-Geraes.

They generally contain a great quantity of carbonic acid and some salts in small proportion, such as bicarbonate of soda, chlorid of magnesium, of sodium, of calcium, and sulphate of soda.

In the waters of Campanha, according to well informed persons, the carbonic acid forms two thirds of their volume in dissolution.

The use of such waters has been lately spreading beyond the place of their springs, being exported to the Capital and some provinces.

There are springs of the same kind in a little hamlet of recent date, named Cambuquira, which, since three or four years, begin to be searched chiefly by the inhabitants of certain places of the province of Minas-Geraes.

They are also to be found at the farm das Contendas near the road that goes from Lambary to the hamlet of Caxambú.

All those fountains are in the province of Minas Geraes.

In the district of Pajeú de Flôres, in the province of Pernambuco, there are equally several springs, the waters of which in their composition and effects are like the above mentioned.

In order to avail the springs of Lambary and Caxambú, the provincial government and the municipal administrations, assisted by some inhabitants, have ordered several works, and still go on undertaking new ones, to keep the waters as pure as possible, and at the same time to render comfortable the stay of the numerous visitors going there every year.

Thus in the parish of Lambary, besides a bathing house with furnished rooms, spacious and aired, and marble bathing-tubs, they deviated, on a long extent, the stream, that ran close by the principal springs, in order that its overflowing might not endamage their water.

The efficacy of these waters in diseases of the digestive apparatus, and such like, is, long ago, out of question, so many are the instances that prove it.

Not far from the principal fountains, and within the village, there is an abundant spring of sulphurous aerated water, known by the name of «Paulina» which has been usefully applied in chronical diseases of the liver.

It is, however, not yet conveniently improved and, on that account, cannot be of any use during the rainy season.

The parish of Lambary, besides its water, possesses the advantage of an excellent and mild climate, being of course very wholesome.

The travel from the capital of the Empire to that place is now easier than it was a few months ago; and this is owing to the 4th section of the rail-way D. Pedro II having attained the extent of 32 leagues, or 211,2 kilom., reaching to the neighbourhood of the Serra of Picú.

This great improvement is also very much advantageous to the waters of Caxambú and other aerated springs in the province of Minas-Geraes, affording to people, that intend to go there from the capital of the Empire and from the province of Rio de Janeiro, easy means of conveyance.

In the hamlet of Caxambú, equally remarkable for its wholesomeness, several works were made, in 1868, to render it more comfortable to they who apply for its waters.

Some improvements were accomplished, concerning the opening and leveling of new streets and squares, in a great measure by the efforts of the inhabitants and other persons, that have stayed for some time in that place.

It may be also mentioned the channeling of the stream Bengo which, in former times, from November to May, muddled the pureness of the waters; in 1868 were built there bath-rooms.

There were also built 6 elegant *chalêts*, that shelter an equal number of springs, making them serviceable in any season.

The springs thus sheltered are the following :

1st. The one called of D. Pedro II containing too much aerated and somewhat alcaline water, which is thought powerful in curing dyspepsy and other chronic diseases: of the stomach and bowels it is made use of either in drinking or in bathing.

2nd. That of « D. Thereza, » a slightly ferruginous, aerated water, which is recommended in the obstructions of bowels, chlorosis and other complaints.

3rd. That of « Duke of Saxe » a very sulphurous and somewhat aerated water, advisable in the chronic uterine affections, as well as in nephritic complaints.

4th. That of magnezian aerated water, good for chronic complaints of the bowels, which is known by the name of « D. Leopoldina. »

5th. The one called « Comte d'Eu », which, being a very ferruginous water, not much aerated, has been successfully employed against chronic anemy and chlorosis.

6th. That called « D. Izabel » a slightly ferruginous, aerated and sulphurous water, chiefly prescribed for the liver and spleen chronic affections, as well as for all nervous complaints, the chlorosis, and other diseases.

All those springs are situated within a short perimeter.

A statistical account, published in 1867, shows that, from 160 patients who went thither at the time when there was in the place no comfort to be had, only one died, 54 recovered, and 94 grew better.

Since that time the visitors to the waters of Caxambú are becoming every day more and more numerous.

No doubt the concourse of visitors will encrease, as soon as the road be finished or the projected branch of the D. Pedro II rail-way is carried into execution.

Saline Waters.

The most remarkable are those of Itapicurú, in the province of Bahia; they spring from the mountains near the river of that name, and spread along its banks in the extent of about 11 leagues, 72,6 kilom.

The principal springs are: Mãi d'agua do cipó, near the village of Soure; that of the Mosquete; that of the village of Itapicurú; the Rio Quente and others.

They have all been examined by order both of the general and provincial governments.

The temperature of the different springs varies from 31° to 41° C.

They contain carbonic acid, sulphate of soda, bicarbonate of soda, chloruret of sodium, of calcium and of magnesium, silicic acid, carbonate of lime and of magnesia, and peroxyde of iron in small quantity.

They are aperient and have been employed internally

for jaundice, stones, and other infirmities, and in baths principally in cases of paralysis, chronic rheumatism, dartres, and cutaneous infirmities.

The president of Minas ordered the enlargement and improvement of the building now existing at the springs.

Sulphurous Waters.

They are found in great abundance in several springs of the town of S. Domingos do Araxá, on the confines of the provinces of Minas-Geraes and Goyaz, having been already noticed in the Corography of Ayres do Casal and in the works of Auguste de Saint-Hilaire.

They are applied in many diseases, and are also much sought for by wild beasts, and made use of for cattle, as a substitute for salt, which is sold very high there.

There are also some springs like the aforesaid, on the banks of Rio-Verde, in the province of Minas-Geraes.

Thermal Waters.

Considered as such, are those of Santa-Catharina, known by the name of Caldas de Bittencourt with a temperature of 35° 1/2 C ; Caldas do Norte do Cubatão, temperature 36°; Caldas do Sul do Cubatão, temperature 45°; and Caldas do Tubarão.

To avail some springs lying at a short distance from the capital of that province, further up the town of S. José, there is an establishment called Hospital das Caldas da Imperatriz, which is situated in a delightful and healthy place near a falling brook of excellent water and shaded by in a great virgin forests extent.

There is a road leading to it, which, with some repairs, would be a very good carriage road.

Those waters are not in the least sulphureous and, when cold, they are nice to taste.

Their use has been efficacious in many a case of paralysis, chronic rheumatism, pulmonary and vesical catarrahs and cutaneous infirmities, in their commencement.

There are thermal springs, that have not been well examined yet, such as those of Seridó in the interior of the province of Rio-Grande do Norte, about 6 leagues, 39,6 kilom. from the village of Principe. Their brackish and ever warm waters produce a copious perspiration.

In the same case is the water of Lagôa Santa, in the province of Minas-Geraes, which in the extent of nearly 0,5 league, 3,3 kil, and width of 0,25 league, 1,65 kil, keep always tepid. Medicinal virtues are also attributed to them.

Alcaline thermal Waters.

There is a great abundance of them in the neighbourhood of the very high mountain of Caldas, district of Santa Cruz, in the province of Goyaz, at the places called : Caldas Novas, Caldas Velhas, and Caldas do Parapitinga.

At the first place there are 13 springs used for bathing, besides other springs in the bed of the brook Lavras. At the second there are copious sources, springing out from an auriferous quartz rock, and forming a stream.

The springs of the third, turn into a lake, 150 palms (33 meters) long, and from 15 to 20 wide (3,3 to 4,4 meters); at the bottom of which spout up many springs. The temperature of the waters of this pool is in some places as high as nearly 48° C., and to be made use of they must be cooled first.

By order of the provincial government of Goyaz these springs were all examined in 1839 ; when the number of those who used the waters was estimated at 110 persons, only in the month of September.

They were again examined in 1842, by order of the government ; and though the accounts of their beneficial effects on the treatment of elephantiasis of the Greeks are at present considered as exaggerated, there is, however, not the least doubt about their efficacy in cases of tetter, in chronic rheumatisms, in old scrophulous sores, and such like complaints.

Chlorurets, carbonates, and silicates of potash, soda, lime, magnesia and alumina, in a small quantity, predominate in these waters.

Their temperature, in general, varies from 34° to 40° C, rising up, in one of the wells, to 43°.

Thermal Waters somewaht sulphureous.

The most frequented, and decidedly the best, hitherto known, are those in the province of Minas-Geraes.

The springs are six leagues, or 39,6 kilom., distant from the village of Caldas. There is one, having the temperature of 41° on the right bank of the Rio-Verde one league 6,6 kil. distant from that village.

There are three of these springs or larger wells, viz : *Pedro Botelho*, the most remarkable for the quantity of water and the temperature of 45° ; — *Mariquinhas*, having about the same temperature, the waters not being so much aerated ; and finally — *Macacos*, divided into two, the temperature of one of them being 41°, and of the other, which abounds more in bicarbonate of soda, 42°.

These waters have been very successfully employed in all chronic rheumatisms, and in rheumatic inveterate paralysis, in which they prove of a great efficaciousness.

They are actually frequented by 2 or 3 thousand persons, every year, in the less cold season.

The provincial government, in order to render easier the use of such fountains, is about to construct reservoirs, bath rooms and make other improvements.

The plan of the village, that is going to be built there, is already drawn up, being pointed out in it every brook, stream and spring of thermal waters.

Acquisition has, not long since, been made of the necessary ground for building houses and inns.

In the opinion of some native and foreign physicians these springs are perhaps the best in the world.

The thermal springs are situated at the height of 6 thousand feet, or 1.828,8 meters, above the level of the sea, in one of the most wholesome places of the Empire.

The climate is as mild and nice as may be wished. There are no bogs or marshy lands in the vicinity of the springs.

The air is pure, dry and transparent, not being known there either the morning fogs or the copious evening dews. The sun rises all of a sudden, in his splendour, and a constant wind sweeps and keeps clear the atmosphere.

In Monte-Sião, near the boundary of S. Paulo and Minas-Geraes, but on the soil of the first mentioned, there is an abundant thermal spring of about the same temperature, and as it is presumed, with the same qualities as those of the district of Caldas. It springs from the height of 5 thousand feet, 1.524 meters, above the level of the sea.

In the village of Apody, in the province of Rio-Grande do Norte, there is a hot spring, that is also said to be sulphureous, the water of which, though of not so high a temperature, has been proficuosly employed on the treatment of several cutaneous diseases.

Population.

The official proceedings, concerning the census of the Empire and committed to the charge of the Board of General Statistics, lately created, being not yet terminated, no reasonable alteration can be made to the reference contained in the book « A Glance at the Empire of Brazil » edited in 1867. The basis for those calculations was taken from the official census organized in 1817-1818 as well as from other true and respectable sources. The population of the Empire is there estimated at 11,780,000 souls, including 500,000 wild aborigenes and 1,400,000 slaves.

Under the head of catechising we shall treat about the wild aboriginals.

The slaves are very kindly treated and generally well housed and fed. In most of the plantations they are allowed to cultivate portions of land for their own account and to dispose freely of their produce.

Their labour is now-a-days moderate, and usually lasts only throughout the day time ; the evenings and nights are devoted to rest, to religious pratice or sundry amusements.

They can make up a stock by means of their savings, and apply it for their ransom.

Slavery, which was imposed on Brazil by the force

of circumstances, since her discovery, shall be extinguished within a few years.

By the law of the 28th September 1871 it was declared that, from that date, every new-born of a slave should be free. It also declared free all those slaves that belonged to the nation and were at the public service or at that of the imperial household.

For slaves belonging to private parties, the said law raised up an emancipation-fund, which is to be annually applied for their ransom, in accordance with the regulations that the government has issued out, and are already in execution.

From 1871 to 1873, the sums applied to this fund amounted to Rs. 1.776:717$176 or nearly £ 177.670.

It is owing to those proceedings, as also to the sums enacted in the provincial budgets, added to the proverbial philantropy of the Brazilians, that a considerable number of slaves annually obtain their freedom, some of them by the generosity of their own masters, some with the help of private contributions.

The above said law contains still other indirect measures which, joined to the former, assure a result wished for even by the slave-owners, that is, the total extinction of slavery without any danger to public safety nor any harm to private property, which is guaranteed both by the Constitution and the laws.

The following table contains an estimate of the population of the Empire distributed by its several provinces, comprising in that of Rio de Janeiro, the municipality of the Empire.

PROVINCES.	POPULATION.		
	TOTAL.	FREE PEOPLE.	SLAVES.
Amazonas.	100,000	95,000	5,000
Grão-Pará.	350,000	325,000	25,000
Maranhão.	500,000	450,000	50,000
Piauhy.	250,000	230,000	20,000
Ceará	550,000	520,000	30,000
Rio Grande do Norte	240,000	235,000	5,000
Parahyba	300,000	260,000	40,000
Pernambuco.	1,220,000	970,000	250,000
Alagôas	300,000	250,000	50,000
Sergipe	320,000	285,000	35,000
Bahia	1,450,000	1,170,000	280,000
Espirito-Santo	100,000	90,000	10,000
Rio de Janeiro and Municipality of the Capital	1,850,000	1,550,000	300,000
S. Paulo.	900,000	825,000	75,000
Paraná.	120,000	110,000	10,000
Santa-Catharina	200,000	190,000	10,000
Rio Grande do Sul.	580,000	550,000	30,000
Minas-Geraes.	1,600,000	1,440,000	160,000
Mato-Grosso	100,000	95,000	5,000
Goyaz	250,000	240,000	10,000
	11,280,000	9,880,000	1,400,000
Wandering tribes of aborigenes.	500,000	500,000	
Total. . . .	11,780,000	10,380,000	1,400,000

Political Constitution of Brazil.

Government. — Reigning dynasty.

Brazil was proclaimed a free and independent State on the 7th September 1822.

Its territory is divided into 20 large provinces, besides the Municipality of the city of S. Sebastião do Rio de Janeiro, the capital of the Empire, which is under a special administrative organization.

The government is a hereditary, constitutional and representative monarchy. The political constitution (the third in the world as regards antiquity) dates from the 25th of March 1824.

The reigning dynasty is that of His Majesty D. Pedro I. Emperor and Perpetual Defender of Brazil, the founder of the Empire, and father of the present Emperor D. Pedro II.

His Majesty D. Pedro II. Constitutional Emperor and Perpetual Defender of Brazil, was born on the 2d December 1825, and succeeded his august father on the 7th April 1831.

Having been declared of age, he took possession of the sovereign power on the 23d July 1840.

He was sacred and crowned on the 18th July 1841.

He was married, by proxy, on the 30th May 1843, and received the matrimonial benedictions on the 4th of September, in the same year.

Her Majesty the Empress, D. Thereza Christina Maria, his august consort, daughter of Francisco I, king of the Two-Sicilies, was born on March 14th 1822.

From this marriage the issue is : His Imperial Highness Prince D. Affonso, born on the 23d February 1845, dead on the 11th June 1847. His Imperial Highness Prince D. Pedro, born on the 19th July 1848, dead on the 10' January 1850. Her Imperial Highness the Princess D. Izabel, heiress presumptive to the crown, born on the 29th July 1846. Her Highness the Princess D. Leopoldina, born on the 13th July 1847, dead at Vienna on the 7th February 1871.

The Princess D. Izabel married, on the 15th October 1864, His Royal Highness D. Luiz Philippe Maria Fernando Gastão d'Orleans, Comte d'Eu, Marshal of the Brazilian Army and Counselor of State.

The Princess D. Leopoldina married His Royal Highness D. Luiz Augusto Maria Eudes de Coburg-Gotha, Duke of Saxe, Admiral of the Imperial Navy, on the 15ᵗʰ December 1864. Of this marriage the issue was: Prince D. Pedro, born on the 19ᵗʰ March 1866. Prince D. Augusto born on the 6ᵗʰ December 1867. Prince D. José born on the 21ˢᵗ May 1869; and Prince D. Luiz born on the 15ᵗʰ September 1870.

Established Religion.

The established religion of the Empire is the Roman Catholic. All other religions, however, are tolerated, with their domestic or private form of worship, in buildings destined for this purpose, but without any exterior form of temples.

No one can, in Brazil, be persecuted for religious motives. All that is required is a regard for the public moral and respect for the religion of the State; in the same manner as the State respects all other religions, and even punishes, by its penal code, with fine and imprisonment all persecutions for religious motives, or the abuses and insults directed against all forms of worship established in the Empire: those crimes being considered as public are charged and tried ex-officio.

Moreover, the powers of the State have, more than once, voted funds for building houses of prayer, and for the support of ministers of different religions, in the colonies of the State: the children of those who are not catholic not being obliged to receive the religious instruction given to those who profess the Roman Catholic Religion.

The marriages of Protestants are respected in all their legal effects. This matter is now regulated by a law which guarantees the civil condition of the children, who are considered legitimate, whether the said marriages be effected in the Empire or abroad.

Political Powers and National Representatives.

The Constitution acknowledges four political powers: the legislative, the moderating, the executive, and the judicial.

The Emperor and the General Assembly are the representatives of the Nation.

All political powers, in the Empire of Brazil, are delegated by the nation.

The Legislative Power.

The legislative power is delegated to the General Assembly, with the sanction of the Emperor.

The General Assembly consists of two Chambers: the Chamber of Deputies, and the Chamber of Senators, or the Senate.

It is the province of the General Assembly to decree the laws, to interpret, suspend and revoke them.

It is the General Assembly that annually fixes the public expenditure and the ordinary and extraordinary naval and military forces; imposes the taxes, resolves any doubts that may arise concerning the succession to the crown; selects a new dynasty in the event of the one reigning becoming extinct; appoints a tutor to the young Emperor in case his father has not done so in his will; upon the death of the Emperor or on the vacancy of the throne, institutes an inquiry about the late administration and reforms all such abuses as may be found out; authorises loans; and exercises, in short, other important attributes, especially reserved for the representatives of national sovereignty.

The initiative of laws belongs, in general, to the members of either chamber. It can, however, emanate from the executive power by means of motions offered to the chamber of Deputies by one or other of the ministers.

All such motions are submitted to the examination of a committee, which subsequently converts them into a bill; this is then discussed and voted in the two chambers, which can either pass it *verbatim* or reform and reject it.

The sessions of the chambers are public, excepting on such occasions as the welfare of the State demands that they should be secret.

Every business is decided by the absolute majority of votes present.

The members of the two chambers are inviolable as to the opinions expressed by them, in the exercise of their functions.

No Senator or Deputy can be arrested by any authority as long as his mandate lasts; excepting *in flagrante delicto*, liable to capital punishment.

The Emperor cannot employ any Senator or Deputy out of the Empire, and no one of these can go and fill any office that will prevent him from being present at the meeting of the General Assembly, either ordinary or extraordinary.

In any unforeseen occurrence whereon the public security or welfare of the State depends, and which renders it indispensable for a Senator or a Deputy to be charged with some special mission, it pertains to the respective chamber to give the permission required.

The Deputies, during the sessions, receive a subsidy, which is taxed at the close of the last session of the previous legislature, and, moreover, they are paid of a certain sum for their voyage expenses. The Senators' subsidy is as much and one half more than is paid to the Deputies.

In cases of an absolute refusal of one of the chambers, the proposal of the other is held as rejected.

In the case, however, of amendments or additions, if the chamber that initiated the proposition does not approve of them, and continues to judge the bill advantageous, it can demand a conference or meeting of both the chambers, and whatever is then decided by the majority of the General Assembly becomes law.

When the two chambers meet together in a General Assembly, the regulation of the proceedings, except a few articles that are common to both, is that of the Senate, the president of which takes the lead, the deputies and the senators sitting and voting indiscriminately.

The *veto* of the moderating power has a suspensive effect for the space of two legislatures following on that in which sanction was refused to any law.

If, meanwhile, the vetoed bill is again presented twice in succession, it becomes law and produces all the same effects as if it had been sanctioned.

If likewise, within one month, the Emperor has neither given nor refused his sanction, it shall be considered as if he had expressly refused it, and then the period above said begins to be reckoned.

The Chamber of Deputies.

The Chamber of Deputies is both elective and temporary.

The elections are indirect and made by the provinces, divided into electoral districts of three deputies each, in the maximum, and of two, in the minimum.

The initiative as to taxes, recruiting, and the choice of a new dynasty, in case of the extinction of the reigning one, constitute its private attributes.

The inquiry about the past administration and the reformation of its abuses should also have its origin in this chamber; as should also the discussion of the propositions of the executive power, and the impeachment of the ministers of State.

The Chamber of Deputies is elected every 4 years, that being the term of duration of each legislature, provided it be not previously dissolved, in which latter case the legislature is considered as terminated, and the new chamber subsists for four sessions.

The Senate.

The Senators are chosen for life, and their election is made by provinces, with special electors who form a triple list of names, from which the Emperor selects one third of the whole.

The number of senators cannot exceed the half of that of the Chamber of Deputies.

The Princes of the Imperial House are senators by right, on their attaining the age of twenty five years.

It is the exclusive attribute of the Senate to proceed to the trial of the members of the Imperial Family, the ministers of State, and senators; of the deputies during the period of the legislature, and of the responsibility of ministers and counsellors of State; in all these cases the Senate acts as a Court of Justice. It is also an attribute of the Senate to convoke the General Assembly, whenever the executive power shall have not done so, within two months after the time prescribed by the Constitution.

The Moderating Power.

The moderating power is exclusively delegated to the Emperor, as being the Supreme Chief of the nation and its chief representative, in order that he may incessantly watch over the maintenance of the independence, and the equilibrium and harmony of the other political powers.

The Emperor exercises this power :

With regard to the legislative power, by choosing the senators; convoking extraordinarily, proroguing or adjourning the General Assembly; dissolving the Chamber of Deputies, whenever the safety of the State requires it; and sanctioning the decrees and resolutions of the General Assembly that they may have the force of laws.

As regards the executive power, by appointing and dismissing, at pleasure, the ministers of State.

As regards the judicial power, by suspending magistrates, pardoning or commuting the penalties of those condemned after legal resources have been employod; and by granting amnisties.

The person of the Emperor is sacred, inviolable, and subject to no responsibility.

The Executive Power.

The Emperor is the head of the executive power, which he exercises through his ministers.

Its principal attributes are:

To convoke the new ordinary General Assembly.

To appoint bishops, magistrates and all civil, military and political functionaries of any rank or condition, created by the general laws.

To provide to ecclesiastical benefices.

To declare war and make peace.

To regulate the political intercourse with foreign nations, and to make treaties of offensive and defensive alliance, of subsidy and of commerce, bringing them subsequently before the notice of the General Assembly, whenever the interest and security of the State will permit so.

If the treaties, concluded in time of peace, involve a cession or exchange of any territory of the Empire, or of possessions to which it has a right, such treaties shall not be ratified without being sanctioned by the General Assembly.

All titles, honours, military orders, or distinctions in reward for services rendered to the State, are also conferred by the executive power ; but all pecuniary recompenses, when they be not determined by law, remain dependent on the approbation of the General Assembly.

It is also an attribute of the executive power: — to grant or deny its consent to the execution of the decrees of the councils and the apostolical letters and any other ecclesiastical constitutions, not contrary to the

Constitution of the Empire, the previous approbation of the General Assembly being required, whenever they contain any general resolutions; to grant titles of naturalization, in accordance with the law—to issue the decrees, instructions, and regulations for the due execution of the laws; and, in short, to provide for all that concerns the home and foreign safety of the State, according to the Constitution.

There are seven ministers, viz: of the Empire and of Ecclesiastical Affairs; of Justice; of Finance; of Foreign Affairs; of Marine; of War; and of Agriculture, Commerce and Public Works. One of the ministers is the Prezident of the council.

Every minister has his office and various departments, which are subordinate to him.

The execution of all the acts of the executive power depends essentially on the countersign of the respective minister of State, in order that may be put into execution.

The ministers of State are responsible for their acts; a verbal or written order of the Emperor in no wise relieving them of this responsibility.

The mode of defining and rendering effective this responsibility is set forth in a special ordinance.

The Judicial Power.

The judicial power is independent, and is composed of judges and juries. The latter pronounce a verdict as to the fact, and the former apply the law.

The judges hold their offices for life, and cannot lose them except by a condemnatory sentence: they can, however, be removed to different places for the time and in the manner prescribed by law.

They possess a privileged jurisdiction, in conformity with the respective laws, and can only be suspended after being previously heard, in order to be legally tried.

No judge can take away from the jurisdiction of another, any causes that are still undecided; nor stop the proceedings, or renew suits once decided.

The judges are responsible for all abuse of power and for any prevarications which they may be guilt of, in the exercise of their functions.

Every one has the right to accuse them before the legal authority for subornation, bribe, peculation or extortion.

In criminal cases all the proceedings are public after the indictment, as are also the audiences of the judges and the sessions of the Jury, except, however, when the council meets for judgement.

In civil cases, and in such penal cases as are tried by civil law, the parties may appoint arbitrators, whose decisions are executed without any appeal, if it has been thus previously agreed upon.

No law-suit can be carried on without the previous declaration that the conciliatory means were attempted in vain.

The Regency of the Empire.

The Emperor' is considered a minor until he is 18 years of age.

During his minority the regency pertains to his nearest relation, according to the line of succession, provided that he be above 25 years old.

In case of non existence of a relation, in the said conditions, the Empire is to be governed by a temporary regent, elected, every four years, by the electoral body of the respective legislature, the acts of the election being opened by the president of the senate and the votes therein contained, summed up before the General Assembly.

Whilst the Regent does not take possession of the office and in his impediments, he shall be substituted by the minister of the Empire, and in the want or impediments of the latter by the minister of Justice.

If the Emperor, either by physical or moral causes, evidently acknowledged by the majority of each of the two Chambers, become unable to govern, the Prince Imperial, if he be above 18 years old, shall govern in his stead, as Regent of the Empire.

The Regent has no responsability for his acts, and the limits of his power are determined by the General Assembly.

Council of State.

The council of State is purely consultative; but it constitutes one of the most important auxiliaries of the high administration.

The hearing this body is. in general, a matter of option, but it is always required by the Emperor when he intends to make use of the prerogatives of the moderating power.

It is also constantly consulted on the most important branches of the public service, under the charge of the seven ministers; on the conflicts of administrative and judicial jurisdiction; on prize claims and others of a quasi-contentious nature; on matters of administrative contentious nature; and on the appeals to the Crown against the excesses of ecclesiastical authorities in those cases no excepted by law.

It is composed of twelve effective members, besides which it may have as many as twelve extraordinary members, all of them appointed for life.

Its proceedings are divided into sections corresponding to the seven ministries, or are carried on in a full meeting, presided over by the Emperor. The Prince or Princess Imperial, on attaining the age of 18 years, has a seat in this council, and so is the case with the other Princes of the Imperial Family, as well as the Prince consort of the Heiress Presumptive of the Crown, when they be appointed. The ministers have also a seat in the Council of State, but they do not vote; nor do they even witness the division when the object of the meeting is to decide about the dissolution of the Chambers or a change of ministry.

Public Ministry (Crown Office).

The public ministry is not yet organized, in Brazil, in all the degrees of the judicial hierarchy.

The important functions of this department, however, are exercised by the Attorney General, a magistrate of high rank; and also by the Crown-proctors, in provinces; the lords advocates, and the solicitors of the public treasury.

The Administration of the Provinces.

The Presidents.

The government of each province is entrusted to a president, appointed by the executive power, that can remove him whenever it is considered advisable for the welfare of the State.

He is the supreme authority in the province, the chief and immediate agent of the central government.

His principal attributes are: to grant or refuse his

sanction to the statutes and resolutions of the provincial assemblies; to suspend, in certain cases, the execution of such statutes; to appoint and dismiss the provincial functionaries ; and to suspend the general functionaries; all of which attributes are regulated by law.

The Provincial Assemblies.

There is also in each province a legislative assembly, charged with the making of the laws, on purely provincial matters, or on those immediately relating to the private interests of the province.

These assemblies are elected, every two years, by the same citizens, who elect the members of the Chamber of Deputies.

Their principal attributes are:

The organization of the budget of provincial and municipal receipts and expenditure, on the proposals of the president of the province and the different town-councils ; — the fixing of the police force according to the informations afforded by the President of the Province ; — the levying of such provincial and municipal taxes as do not interfere with the general revenues of the State; — the creation and extinction of provincial and municipal offices; — the authorization for public works of the same nature ; the issuing of laws concerning public instruction, and those establishments created to spread it, not comprising the high branches of instruction and other literary establishments created by the central government ; — the civil, judicial, and ecclesiastical division of the respective province, provided that in all their resolutions they respect the Constitution, the general laws and interests,

the treaties with foreign nations, the rights of the
other provinces and the municipal economy, according
to the proposals made. on that purpose, by the town-
councils.

Within their respective provinces, they possess together
with the president. the temporary power to suspend any
civil guarantee, in cases and in the manner determined
by the Constitution.

Their laws and resolutions require the sanction of
the president of the province, excepting in very few
cases, expressly declared by the Additional Act, in the
manner and with the solemnities prescribed by it.

Their members are inviolable as to the opinions expressed by them, in the exercise of their functions. They
receive during the ordinary and extraordinary sessions
and even the prorogations, a subsidy fixed by the provincial assembly, on the first meeting of the past legislature.

They likewise receive a sum of money for their voyage
expenses, when they reside far from the place where
the assembly meets. Those expenses are decreed by the
provincial assemblies, in proportion to the length of the
voyage, and in the manner prescribed for subsidies.

The Town-councils.

In every city or town of the Empire a corporation is
chosen every four years, by direct elections, and this
body is charged with the economical and municipal administration of the city or town.

Those corporations have a revenue of their own to
meet their respective expenditures; and a fundamenta

law defines their municipal functions, the organization of their municipal regulations, and the distribution of heir revenue.

They are composed of nine aldermen in the cities, and of seven in the towns; that one who obtains most votes being the president or the mayor.

The town-councils, by the Additional Act, have the right to propose the means of providing for the expenditure of their respective municipalities.

The town-councils are, in the provinces, subordinate to the legislative assemblies and to the presidents; that of the capital of the Empire is subordinate to the General Assembly and the central government.

In each parish there is, at least, a justice of the peace, before whom all parties, disposed to go to law, must previously attempt the conciliatory means.

The Rights of Brazilian Subjects.

The Constitution guarantees the inviolability of the civil and political rights, based on the liberty, the individual safety and the property of Brazilian citizens.

Individual liberty,

No citizen can be compelled to perform or not perform any action but in virtue of a law.

No law can be issued out without public utility, and, in no case soever, it can have a retroactive effect.

Liberty of thought.

Every one can communicate his opinions by words or writing and through the press, without being subject to censure ; but all are responsible for any abuse committed in the exercise of this right, in the cases and in the manner determined by law.

Liberty of conscience.

No one can be persecuted on account of his religious belief.

Liberty of travel and of residence.

Every one can stay in the Empire, or leave it, at pleasure, taking away with him his fortune, provided that he observe the police regulations, and cause no prejudice to third parties.

Liberty of industry.

No kind of labour, cultivation, industry, or trade can be prohibited, as long as there is no offense to morality, to the safety, and to the health of the citizens.

All trade-guilds were abolished by the Constitution.

Right of security.

Every citizen has, in his house, an inviolable asylum. No one can enter it, by night, without his consent, unless it be to protect it from fire or inundation. In every other case, the entry of the domicile of a citizen can only be effected by day, and in the manner determined by the laws.

No one can be imprisoned without judicial inquiry, unless in the cases declared by law, and even then the authority must declare, within a short time, the motive of the arrest, the name of the accuser and those of the witnesses, and deliver a note to this effect to the prisoner. Even after the judicial inquiry, no one can be carried to prison or kept there, if already arrested, if he give sufficient bail in those cases permitted by law, that is to say, in nearly all minor crimes.

Excepting the case of *in flagrante delicto*, no one can be arrested, without a written order from the lawful authority, under penalty of responsibility for the judge, who gave such order, and the party who asked for it.

No one can be sentenced except by the competent authority, in virtue of some previous law, and in the form prescribed by it.

Neither the penalty nor the dishonour of the culprit, however infamous may be the crime, can extend beyond the person of the delinquent : — the confiscation of property is prohibited in every case.

The Criminal Code, in vigour in the Empire of Brazil, is founded on the solid bases of justice and equity ; and neither torture nor any other cruel or dishonourable penalties, expressly forbidden by the Constitution, are found in it.

Capital punishment does not exist for political crimes ; and although only inflicted for the crime of murder and on the leaders of insurrections, it is very rarely put into execution.

In no case can a sentence of death be executed, without the whole proceedings being presented to the moderating power, accompanied by all necessary explanations, in order that the Emperor may decide whether the criminal should be pardoned or the sentence commuted ; the latter course is almost always adopted.

The Right of equality.

The law is equal for all, whether it protects or punishes ; and the Constitution guarantees the recompenses due for civil and military services, in proportion to each one's merit, as well as the right to them, obtained in conformity with the law.

Every citizen can be admitted to public charges, either civil or military, without further distinction than that of his talents and parts.

No one is exempt from a contribution to the expenses of the State, in accordance with his pecuniary means.

There are, in Brazil, no privileges but those based on the public benefit, and connected with the offices held : neither is there any privileged court, nor special commission in civil or criminal cases, with the exception of those misdemeanours, which, from their nature and by law, pertain to a special jurisdiction.

The Right of property.

The right of property is guaranteed in all its plenitude; and if the public welfare, legally verified, requires that the State should dispose of the property of the citizen, the latter is previously indemnified according to its worth.

A regulative law specifies the cases in which can take place this only exception to the full exercise of the right of property; and sets forth how the indemnity must be paid.

The public debt is also guaranteed.

The Right of Inventors (Patent laws).

All inventors have the ownership of their inventions. The law affords them an exclusive, temporary, privilege (patent); or else they are indemnified of the prejudice accruing from the divulgation of their secret.

Inviolability of correspondence.

The secret of letters is inviolable; and the Post-Office authorities are responsible for any abuse of this guarantee, committed in their departments.

The Right of complaint and other guarantees.

The Constitution likewise guarantees to all citizens: — the right of presenting claims, complaints, and petitions, to the legislative and executive powers: — the right to denounce all infractions of the Constitution, and to petition the competent authority to render effective the responsibility of infractors: — the public assistance: — the primary instruction gratuitously: — the foundation of schools and universities.

Even in case of rebellion or foreign invasion, when the safety of the State requires the suspension, for a fixed period, of any one of the guarantees of individual liberty, this can only be done by means of a special act of the legislative power. But if the General Assembly be not sitting at the time, and the country be in imminent danger, the government may take this expedient, as a provisional and indispensable measure; under the obligation, however, of giving an account of their conduct to the said Assembly, at its first meeting.

The like measure, under the same conditions, may be

taken, in the provinces, by their own legislative assemblies, as it was already said.

No article of the Constitution, concerning the limits and respective attributes of the political powers, as well as the political and individual rights of the citizens, can suffer any change by an ordinary statute.

Such a reform depends on essential formalities required by the Constitution. It is only when by one legislature the necessity has been recognised, that a law is issued out for the electors of the deputies, for the next legislature, to confer on their mandataries a special power to make the intended alteration. It is, therefore, in this new legislature, that the question is resolved, which ought to turn exclusively on the article declared reformable by the previous law.

Division of the Empire.

Political division.

The election for the members of the provincial assemblies, of the Deputies, and the Senators, are by the indirect system. Every year a qualification is made of the voters, who are to choose the respective electoral body.

The aldermen and the justices of the peace are, however, directly chosen by the voters.

In accordance with that system, the Empire is divided into electoral districts, each of them electing a fixed number of deputies for the general and the provincial assemblies.

The election for senators takes place at once in the whole province, the electoral districts contributing for the election of the three citizens, from which the moderating power chooses he who is to fill the seat vacant in the Senate.

On the election for the senators by the province of Rio de Janeiro, the electoral district of the capital of the Empire meets with those of the province to make up the triple list.

The electoral districts are divided into colleges, which, in their turn, are subdivided into parish assemblies.

According to the official returns there are 46 electoral districts comprising 408 colleges, and 1,451 parish assemblies.

The number of voters amounts to 1.097,698 ; and that of the electors to 20,020.

There are 578 provincial deputies ; 122 general deputies, and 58 senators.

The number of electors is to that of the voters as 1 to 54,8.

The number of deputies keeps the following proportion :

1 provincial deputy to 34,6 electors, and to 1.899 voters.
1 general deputy to 164 electors, and to 8.997,5 voters.
1 senator to 345,1 electors and to 18.925,8 voters.

Administrative division.

The Brazilian territory, as regards its administration, is divided into 20 provinces, comprehending 642 municipalities, including that of the Capital. The latter contains 209 cities and towns, 433 villages, 1,473 parishes and 28 curacies.

Some peculiar occurrences. so common in new countries like Brazil, drawing constant migrations of the inhabitants from places, the prosperity and progress of which, are owing to transitory causes, almost annually make an alteration in the statistics of the municipalities and parishes, either by the creation of new ones, or by the suppression of others then existing.

Ecclesiastical division.

The ecclesiastical jurisdiction, in the Empire, is exercised in 12 dioceses, one of which is a metropolitan archbishopric; all of them are subdivided into 1,473 parishes, and 28 curacies.

The Metropolitan See, the archbishopric of S. Salvador, comprehends the territory of the provinces of Bahia and Sergipe, divided into 21 ecclesiastical *comarcas* or districts, 1 general vicarage, 201 parishes, and 1 curacy.

This diocese is the seat of a metropolitan Court of Appeal (*Relação*), composed of judges of appeal (*desembargadores*), who decide clerical cases, in final judgement.

It possesses two seminaries, one for the teaching of the Humanities, and another for that of the Ecclesiastical and Canonical Sciences (Divinity College); the courses being attended by those who study for priests.

The diocese of S. Sebastião comprehends the municipality of the capital, the provinces of Rio de Janeiro, Espirito-Santo, Santa Catharina, and the eastern side of Minas-Geraes. It is divided into 28 ecclesiastical districts, 1 general vicarage, 211 parishes, and 11 curacies.

It possesses a petty seminary for the teaching of those who want to be priests, the course of preparatory studies as well as that of theological sciences being lately reorganized.

The provinces of Pernambuco, Alagôas, Parahyba, and Rio Grande do Norte, form the bishopric of Olinda. The religious service is performed in 1 general vicarage, 163 parishes, and 1 curacy. It has a high seminary with courses of preparatory studies, and ecclesiastical sciences.

The provinces of Maranhão and Piauhy are subject to the jurisdiction of the bishopric of Maranhão, which reckons 27 ecclesiastical districts, 2 general vicarages, 82 parishes, and 1 curacy ; and possesses 1 high and 1 petty seminary for the teaching of those who aspire to priesthood.

The amazonic region, comprehending the provinces of Pará and Amazonas, forms the diocese of Belém do Pará.

It is divided into 15 ecclesiastical districts, 3 general vicarages, and 95 parishes. It possesses two petty seminaries, one in the city of Belém, the seat of the bishopric, and the other in the capital of the province of the Amazonas.

The diocese of S. Paulo is formed by the provinces of S. Paulo, Paraná, and the southern side of Minas-Geraes, comprehending under its jurisdiction 48 ecclesiastical districts, 1 general vicarage, 212 parishes, and 12 curacies. It has 1 high and 1 petty seminary.

The province of Minas-Geraes, besides the territory that pertains to the bishoprics of Rio de Janeiro, S. Paulo, and Goyaz, is divided into two bishoprics. That of Marianna, in the central part of the province, with 24 ecclesiastical districts, 1 general vicarage, 214 parishes, 3 curacies; and possessing 1 high and 1 petty seminary.

That of Diamantina, comprehending the northern part of Minas-Geraes, is divided into 8 ecclesiastical districts, with 1 general vicarage, and 67 parishes. It has 1 high and another petty seminary.

The bishopric of Goyaz comprehends the province of the same name, and the western side of that of Minas-Geraes. It is divided into 19 ecclesiastical districts, 4 general vicarages, 82 parishes; and possesses a petty seminary.

The diocese of Cuyabá, consisting of only the province of Mato-Grosso, has 6 ecclesiastical districts, 1 general vicarage, and 16 parishes. It has a petty seminary.

The province of S. Pedro do Rio Grande do Sul constitutes the bishopric of the same name. It is subdivided into 36 ecclesiastical districts, 1 general vicarage, and 73 parishes. A petty seminary will be inaugurated as soon as the edifice destined for it, be concluded.

The bishopric of Ceará is limited to the territory of the same province, and is divided into 57 parishes with 1 general vicarage, the ecclesiastical districts being not created as yet. It has 1 high and 1 petty seminary.

In the Empire there are 23 convents and 1 hospice belonging to the monks of S. Francisco; 13 convents and 2 hospices to the Carmelites; 11 monasteries of Benedictines, besides 6 nunneries. The number of monks and nuns is:

Franciscans.	80 friars and 75 nuns.
Carmelites . . . . . . : .	46 » and 18 »
Benedictines	40 »

There are also 61 Missionary Capuchines, in the most, foreigners, who possess a hospice in the capital of the Empire, it being the seat of the mission and the residence of the prefect. There are more 5 hospices of that community, in the provinces. Besides those, the general committee of the Holy Land, whose object is to get alms for the preservation of the Holy Places, in Jerusalem, owns 7 hospices in different quarters of the Empire for the residence of the respectives monks, the number of which is variable.

The government issued out a decree, in 1855, prohibiting the admission of novices in the regular orders, then existing in the Empire.

In accordance with the law of the 28 th. June, 1870, it was determined that the rural and urban property of the above mentioned orders, should be sold and the product converted into policies of the national debt.

Judicial division.

As to what concerns the administration of justice, the Empire is divided into large judicial districts, each having a Court of Appeals, charged with those civil and criminal causes that cannot be decided by the judges of 1st instance or primary jurisdiction, as also a Court of Commerce, which is about to be reorganized, ceasing to be of a contentious nature.

The courts of appeal are competent to try and judge all crimes perpetrated by the law-judges, and those of responsibility of the military commanders.

Of the sentences of those courts there is but an appeal for redress (revista) to the Supreme Court of Justice, which can only allow it, in cases of notorious grievance and of manifest nullity of the process, and then it designates another court of the same rank and jurisdiction as that one from which it was made the appeal, for the revisal of the law-suit.

The Supreme Court of Justice is the highest rank of the brazilian magistracy, and its members are denominated ministers and, by the Constitution, are Counsellors to the

Emperor. It takes cognizance of the offenses and official errors committed by its ministers, by the judges of appeals, the employés of the diplomatic corps, and the presidents of provinces. It tries and judges the archbishops and bishops, in crimes not purely ecclesiastical.

It decides all conflicts of jurisdiction and the competence of the courts of appeal.

Its members sit and judge together, and they can neither receive more than their salary, nor exercise any other charge, except that of member of the legislative body.

This court consists of 17 members, chosen from among the judges of appeal, according to their antiquity.

The president of the court is chosen, every three years, by the government, from among its members.

According to the lately enacted division, the courts of appeal in the Empire are to be eleven in number, comprising.

The 1ˢᵗ.—the provinces of Pará and Amazonas, the seat being in the city of Belém.

The 2ᵈ.—the provinces of Maranhão and Piauhy, the seat being, as it is now, in the city of S. Luiz do Maranhão.

The 3ᵈ.—the provinces of Ceará and Rio Grande do Norte, its seat being in the city of Fortaleza.

The 4ᵗʰ.—the provinces of Pernambuco, Parahyba and Alagoas, continuing to sit in the city of Recife.

The 5ᵗʰ.—the provinces of Bahia and Sergipe, the seat continuing to be in the city of S. Salvador.

The 6ᵗʰ.—the municipality of the capital where it continues to sit, and the provinces of Rio de Janeiro and Espirito-Santo.

The 7ᵗʰ.—the provinces of S. Paulo and Paraná, its seat being in the city of S. Paulo.

The 8th.—the provinces of S. Pedro do Rio Grande do Sul and of Sta Catharina, the seat being in the city of Porto-Alegre.

The 9th.—The province of Minas-Geraes, the seat being in the city of Ouro-Preto.

The 10th.—the province of Mato-Grosso, with its seat in Cuyabá.

The 11th.—the province of Goyaz, with its seat in the city of the same name.

The organization of those courts is the same for all; the only difference is in the number of the judges, all of them having a president and a crown-proctor.

Both the president of the court and the crown-proctor are appointed by the government, the former from among the members of the court; and the latter from among 15 of the most ancient law-judges.

The court of appeals, in the capital of the Empire, by the new law, is to consist of 17 judges; those of Bahia and Pernambuco of 11; those of Pará, Maranhão, Ceará S. Paulo, Rio Grande do Sul and Minas Geraes of 7; and those of Mato-Grosso and Goyaz of 5.

For the judgement of causes in 1st instance, and those in the 2[d], that do not surpass the value legally determined, the law created *juizes de direito*, law-judges, who minister justice within certain territorial limits, called *comarcas*, districts, and also take cognizance of the crimes of respon- sibility of non privileged officials.

In the whole Empire there are 296 judicial districts, divided into three orders or *entrancias*, besides 30 charges (*varas*) of law-judges, all of the same rank, 11 of them sitting in special districts, for the readiest expedition of civil causes; 5 particularly destined for the affairs of orphans; 5

especially appointed to decide commercial suits ; 4 charged
with the civil jurisdiction upon religious brotherhoods and
unclaimed inheritances ; and 3 for the cognizance of causes
concerning the national treasure ; the remaining special
charges of law-judges are occupied by 2 auditors of war
and 1 auditor of marine (judge-advocates).

No one can be appointed a law-judge unless he has performed the duty of municipal judge, for a period of 4
years ; neither can any law-judge of 1st entrancia (rank)
go up to the 2d, before an equal period, or advance over
to the 3d, before 3 years of uninterrupted service.

The law-judges cannot be removed to charges or districts
of an inferior rank, but at their demand, and neither can
they be appointed to others of the same rank except in
the case:

1st Of rebellion, civil or foreign war, sedition or insur-
rection in any province, or of any conspiracy within
the district.

2d . Upon the demand of the president of the respective
province, arguing the necessity of his removal, by motives
of public utility. In this case the Council of State must
be consulted, as also the magistrate is to be previously
listened to, when possible. At all events, however, he
ought to be acquainted with the motives of his removal.

The new law concerning the judicial organization
created, in the special districts, assistant judges, who,
conjointly with the law-judges, exercise some of their
attributes; the full jurisdiction being imparted to them
only when they substitute the latter, who, in their
turn, assist one another in the same districts.

In the capital of the Empire there are 9 assistant
judges (juizes substitutos); in the province of Rio de

7

Janeiro 2; in that of Bahia 6; in that of Pernambuco 10; and in that of Maranhão 7.

The assistant judges are appointed by the government, from among such doctors or bachelors in law, by the schools of the Empire, as have, at least, 2 years practice of the bar, and they hold their office for 4 years, on the same conditions and advantages as the municipal judges.

As to their rank, the districts are divided into 151 of 1ˢᵗ; 107 of 2ᵈ; and 38 of 3ᵈ, *entrancia* (class).

A district is divided into *termos* (hundreds or boroughs), which may contain one or more municipalities.

In each borough there is a municipal judge, who, besides other attributes, has the criminal jurisdiction on cases of smuggling, except those in *flagrante delicto;* and the judgement of such trespasses as concern private security and good neighbourhood (*termos de segurança e de bem viver*). Their civil jurisdiction is limited to the preparing of the suits, that are to be decided by the law-judges, as well as the trial and judgement of suits from above Rs. 100$000 to Rs. 500$000 (£ 10 to £ 50). In those boroughs where there are not special judges for the orphans affairs, they are likewise charged with that department.

In the whole Empire, there are 418 boroughs and as many municipal judges, appointed by the government, from among such doctors or bachelors of law, by the schools of the Empire, as have, at least, a year practice of the bar. They hold their office for 4 years, but can be reappointed.

The following table points out the number of districts,

charges (varas) of law-judges, and boroughs, actually existing in the provinces and the capital of the Empire.

PROVINCES	DISTRICTS	LAW-JUD-GES SPE-CIAL	BOROUGHS
Amazonas....................		4	5
Pará........................	114	12	15
Maranhão.................	18	23	19
Piauhy...`................	12	12	12
Ceará	21	21	23
Rio Grande do Norte.......	8	8	9
Parahyba.................	14	14	18
Pernambuco...............	27	33	29
Alagôas...................	11	11	14
Sergipe	8	8	17
Bahia	31	36	49
Espirito Santo.............	5	5	6
Rio de Janeiro.............	20	21	33
Municipality of the capital.....	1	11	1
S. Paulo..................	28	28	47
Paraná....................	6	6	7
Santa Catharina...........	7	7	7
S. Pedro do Rio Grande do Sul..	16	18	26
Minas Geraes..............	31	31	61
Goyaz....................	13	13	14
Mato Grosso..............	4	4	6
	296	326	418

In order to plead the interests of society, with regard
to public crimes, there is in every district, at least, a lord-
advocate appointed by the government, in the capital,
and by the presidents, in the provinces; there is in each
borough an assistant, who substitutes the lord-advocate
in his impediments, and is appointed by the respective
law-judge, with the sanction of the president of the province.

The justices of the peace exercise their jurisdiction upon
civil causes, the value of which does not exceed Rs. 100$000
(£ 10), as also on cases of trespasses against the municipal
statutes.

The justices of the peace, actually 1,502 in number, are

elected, every 4 years, by the voters of the respective parishes on lists containing 4 names each.

Each of the 4 most voted upon, holds his office for a year, according to the number of votes, and they all are substitutes to one another.

The judgment by jurors, in conformity with the Constitution, is as yet admitted only on criminal causes. For that purpose, there is in each borough a court consisting of judges of facts under the name of jury, presided over by the law-judge of the district, except at the seats of courts of appeal, for then the presidence of the jury is held by a judge of appeals.

The police, in Brazil, is under the care of the justice department, and has a peculiar organization defined by law.

It is exercised, both in the capital of the Empire and in those of the provinces, by a chief of police appointed by the government from among those magistrates, doctors and bachelors of law, who have 4 years practice either of the bar or of administration.

In the municipality of the capital, there are 3 police-delegates; and in the provinces, there is usually one for each municipality; in every parish or policial district of a parish there is one assistant-delegate (*subdelegado*); and in each ward (*quarteirão*) an inspector.

Public force.

All the Brazilians are bound to take up arms in order to maintain the independence, and the integrity of the Empire.

The public forces consist of the army, the navy, the national guard, and police corps.

The officers, both of the army and of the navy, can only be deprived of their ranks by a legal sentence.

Army.

The army consists of special, movable, and garrison corps, amounting to 15,938 men, including officers. In this number are not reckoned the artillery apprentices, who amount to above 500.

The land-forces were fixed, by the late law, for the year 1873-1874, at 16,000 men, in normal circumstances, and at 32,000, in extraordinary occurrences.

The special corps are: the staff general, the engineers, the 1st and 2d class staff, the medical and the ecclesiastical departments.

The movable corps consist of the three arms.

The garrison corps do duty in the provinces.

The government is authorized to create 2 regiments more of artillery, with 4 batteries of 6 guns each.

In some provinces, besides the garrison corps or companies, there is a force of the movable corps.

The Empire, maintains in the republic of Paraguay, a military division of 1,500 men, of the three arms.

All possible care has been taken to adopt the most improved arms known : for infantry, the type preferred is the improved Comblain musket ; for artillery, the guns Krupp ; for cavalry, the carabine Spencer and the revolvers Lefaucheux, besides the swords used, according to the different corps.

National guard.

The force of the national guard of the Empire, including the reserve is, according to the late official returns, of 741,782 men, that is: 616,596 in active service, and 125,186 in the reserve.

There are 3,343 guards doing detachment duty, as auxiliaries to the army.

The national guard is divided into 274 superior commands, comprising:

The cavalry — 96 squadrons, 112 corps, and 10 companies.

The artillery — 11 battalions, 9 sections of battalion, and 4 detached companies.

The infantry — 278 battalions, 44 sections of battalion, 15 companies, and one detached section.

The reserve — 79 battalions, 144 sections of battalions 97 companies, and 57 sections of detached companies.

Police service in the Capital of the Empire.

This service is performed by a corps of city-guards, which amounts to 560 men.

It is assisted by another corps, under a military organization, called — police corps of the Capital — the effective force of which is 560 men, obtained by enlistment.

The fixing of the police force of each province being under the charge of the respective legislative assemblies, it has a special organization, according to their peculiar circumstances.

Fire-men corps.

For the extinction of fires there is, in the capital of the Empire, a fire-men corps which is very serviceable, and is strong of 109 men, including the commander, the officers, instructors, foremen and fire-men.

The government is about to reorganize it, endowing

it with the most important improvements, actually used
at the chief-towns of Europe, where this kind of service
is perfectly performed. This corps is, to a certain degree,
an auxiliary to the police.

Military legislation.

A Board composed of several competent members, and
presided over by H. R. H. the Comte d'Eu, Marshal of
the Army, is charged with the reformation of the military
legislation, and is to propose whatever it may be thought
necessary to improve it.

As an evidence of its zeal there exist already some'
laborious works, some of which having been submitted
to the examination and disquisition of the general assembly,
it is likely that, in time, they will be converted into law.

Among them deserve a special notice eight schemes on
highly important subjects, such as : 1st, the one for the
recruitment bill, which served as ground-work for that,
approved by the chamber of deputies, and pending from
the vote of the Senate and of the Imperial sanction ; 2d,
that of the penal military code, already sent over by the
government to the above mentioned chamber ; 3d, the
plan for the reorganization of the medical corps, already
forwarded to the said chamber ; 4th, the scheme for a
disciplinary military code ; 5th, that of a bill regulating
the officers's half-pay ; 6th, that concerning the military sa-
laries, upon which was framed the present law, that raised
the pay of the officers and soldiers of the army ; 7th, that
for a new organization of the military ecclesiastical
department; 8th, the one for regulating the service of the
military medical department.

One of its committees has also laid out a scheme of

a code of military prosecutions, still pending of the discussion and approval of the general Board.

Military Arsenals.

Arsenals and Intendancy of War,

The military arsenals of the capital, and of the provinces, have recently been reorganized, and by virtue of the reform that was effectuated, there exist in the capital of the Empire the war arsenal, properly so called, and the intendancy of war.

The arsenal is charged with the manufacturing of arms (which, at present, are repaired and transformed in another establishment, a dependency of the arsenal), of uniforms, equipment, thongs, machinery, apparatus, and other objects necessary to the furnishment of the army, the fortresses and military establishments, as well as in the keeping and preservation of the portable arms and train of artillery.

To it belong the body of military operatives, the company of artisans apprentices, and the military museum.

The intendancy of war has to its charge the commissariat, and the shipping of the arsenal, as well as all that concerns the acquisition, storing, keeping and distribution, of the *materia prima*, and of the products destined to the administrative service of war.

The superintendence of the arsenal of the capital, is entrusted to a director, who must be a superior officer of a scientific arm, and to a subdirector, in the same conditions, having as their assistants, other employés of different military ranks.

Besides these, the war arsenal of the capital gives employment, in its workshops, to about 600 workmen, which number has risen to above 1,000, in extraordinary emergencies.

The body of military operatives is divided into two companies of 100 men each, besides the commander and the subalterns, which number may be increased according to the necessities of the service. The company of mechanics is composed of 200 boys from 7 to 16 years of age, in 4 divisions, each of 50 apprentices and with the teachers required, a chaplain and a physician, who superintends the infirmary,

The apprentice who, after having proved his state of poverty and other conditions required, is admitted into that company, remains there till he is able to pass over to the body of military operatives; those, however, that prefer following the military career are permitted to be transferred to the deposit of artillery apprentices.

They can, however, by special grant, and paying the expenses incurred with their education, obtain their discharge and embrace whatever profession or trade they please.

All the expenses of board, clothing, instruction and treatment, in case of sickness, are defrayed by the government.

Besides the military exercises, they learn primary instruction, geometrical elementary drawing, geometry, and practical mechanics, music, gymnastics, and the trades for which they show capacity and strength, and which are adapted for the manufactory of warlike articles.

In extraordinary circumstances, the government is authorized to create, in the provinces, provisory intendancies.

In each province, where there is no war arsenal, a

deposit exists under the name of store of warlike articles, which is entrusted to an army officer.

These stores serve for the collecting and keeping of all the materiel of the army, sent by the intendancy of the capital or by any of the war arsenals, for the supply of the army corps, fixed companies and fortresses.

Under the immediate control of the war arsenal of the capital is the manufactory of arms, in the fortress of Conceição, which, especially destined for the repairing and transformation of flint lockguns into percussion muskets, is also provided with the necessary instruments for the rifling of smooth bore muskets. It was also a school for primary learning.

The provinces of Pará, Pernambuco, Bahia, S. Pedro do Rio Grande do Sul and Mato-Grosso possess military arsenals, and to the directors of such establishments and to their assistants belong the attributions of chief and assistant of the intendancy of war, besides the direction of the services, which, in the capital, belong to the respective arsenal.

Pyrotechnical Laboratories.

The war office has laboratories of this kind, in the municipality of the capital of the Empire, and in the provinces, where there are arsenals.

The most important is the one in the said municipality, named Campinho, 26,4 kilometers distant from the centre of the capital, and 927 meters from the Cascadura Station, on the D. Pedro II Rail-Road, with which it communicates by a branchroad. It manufactures all the ammunition and warlike articles for the service of the army and the fortresses, and comprises a spacious ground with 36 edifices, including barracks, military infirmary, chapel, station of the branch-road of the rail-way, 14 workshops, powder-magazine, and others more.

It is under the special superintendence of an officer of a scientific arm, and it has the men necessary for the pyrotechnical works and accessory services, as well as for the economy and good management of the establishment.

In normal circumstances, about 100 workmen are employed at the establishment; and they prepare daily:

Percussion caps	30,000
Ball Cartridges	20,000
Friction tubes.	1,000
The same for hollow projectiles .	200

or, in a like proportion, any other kinds of ordnance stores.

The laboratories, in the provinces, have the same purposes as the one at Campinho. They work, however, in a smaller scale, according to the necessities of the service and the remittances of ammunitions from the intendancy of war, in the capital.

Gun-powder and Iron Manufactories.

The powder manufactory is organized with the requisite number of persons and material, and is situated far from the village, at the foot of the Serra da Estrella, in the province of Rio de Janeiro, near a sea-port and at a very short distance from the principal rail-road station, which terminates at that of Mauá.

Solid works are constructed here, in order to canalize the waters for different workshops.

The machines are moved by a Fourneyron turbine and an iron hydraulic wheel.

In the grounds, belonging to the establishment, is to be found excellent and abundant water, that runs down in cataracts from a great height, and also woods, where-from is taken the timber most fit for charcoal.

There is steam apparatus for drying powder, and the coal is prepared in distilling apparatus and by means of the action of steam.

There has been made excellent gun-powder of 5 kinds, to wit :

Powder of 3 different marks for cannon, smooth or rifled, powder for portable arms as well smooth as rifled, and finally powder destined to different artifices of war.

The establishment has the necessary capacity to produce 146,900 Kilograms a year, as was shown during the Paraguayan war, as the manufactory of those 5 kinds amounted, in the year 1869, to than or about 161,590 kilograms.

The government endeavours to carry into effect the establishment of the manufactory, long since projected, in the province of Mato-Grosso ; and from the informations obtained, it may be affirmed, that it will be concluded within a short period.

The iron factory of Ipanema, whereof we spoke length-ly under the head « minerals » , reorganized as it actually is by the Minister of war, besides the incalculable benefices which, in general, it will produce in behalf of the Brazilian industry and agriculture, will prove at the same time qualified to be of great service to the army and navy, in furnishing them all kinds of ordnance stores, iron and steel cannons, white arms, and the works of cast or beat metal, of which the arsenals may stand in need.

Penitentiary and Military Colonies.

Penitentiary Colony in the Island of Fernando de Noronha.

The most important penitentiary colony is that in the island of Fernando de Noronha, in the province of Pernambuco.

It was founded for those sentenced to prison with work, for civil or military crimes.

It is superintended by a superior officer of the army, and is subject to the command of arms, of that province, in the part concerning the materiel, the force and military government. Its means of defense consist in a fortress, 1 artillery park, and 7 forts.

The population, comprising the public force, the employés, the sentenced, and some families, consists of 1,875 individuals.

The sentenced receive here a moral and religious education, and are set to work at any trade they know, or at that occupation for which they are found most apt to.

In order to regulate and reward their service, with equality, pecuniary gratuities are allowed to the prisoners, of which a part is destined to form a peculium, as an aid in the future, for the first expenses of an establishment, when they are restored to society. A company of the sentenced, consisting of 183 men, as well as other inhabitants of the island are employed in the trades of cooper, blacksmith, carpenter, and shoemaker, in the workshops of the colony.

The shoemaker's workshop, which the Minister of war lately ordered to be organized on a larger scale, is to manufacture the greatest part of the shoes, necessary to the soldiers of the army.

It possesses 2 primary schools for the male, and 1 for the female sex ; 2 churches, one of which is the parish, a chaplain for religious instruction and divine services, an arsenal where are established four workshops, store-houses, pharmacy, infirmaries, barracks, prisons, burying-grounds and houses for the whole population of the island.

The fertility of the ground permits that many of the inhabitants may devote themselves advantageously to agriculture, and the ordinary crop is almost sufficient for the consumption.

Military and disciplinary colonies.

For the purpose of facilitating the works of the navigation of the rivers Tocantins and Araguaya, as also to attract population to the margins of the latter, and by means of catechising, call the Indians to civilization, 9 military colonies were founded in the province of G yaz.

They are the following :

The one of Santa Barbara, on the banks of the Macaco river, 46,2 kilometers to the north of the confluence of the river Maranhão with that of Almas, and 330 kilometers distant from the capital of the province.

The population, already numerous, is principal'y occupied in the culture of grains, coffee, sugarcane, mandioca and cotton; and in cattle raising.

The one of Santo Antonio, situated at 12,8 kilometers,

to the south of the passage of the river Ouro, and 429 kilometers, from the capital.

It cultivates tobacco, coton, rice, different grains, and is thriving.

The one of Santa Cruz, founded on the banks of the river Canna Brava, a confluent of the Tocantins, 66 kilometers distant from the hamlet of Descoberto, and 561 kilometers from the capital.

The number of its inhabitants is progressing, there being among them several colonists, that follow the trades of carpenter, shoemaker, tailor, blacksmith, and others.

It has much cattle, and the crop of tobacco is abundant, as also that of cotton, rice, mandioca and grains. The other colonies are considered of second order and though their population is not yet considerable, they will thrive, in a short time, considering the, salubrity of the climate, and the fertility of the lands. They are :

Santa Leopoldina, on the right bank of the Araguaya, below the confluence of the Rio Vermelho and 191,4 kilometers, from the capital, on a plateau of 12,1 meters in height, with the length of 9,9 kilometers, and the breadth of more than 3,3 kilometers.

It contains good pastures, and the ground, fit for the plough, admits of all kinds of culture, whereof the inhabitants already derive good results.

Monte Alegre, established on the line of the Araguaya, 52,8 kilometers, to the South East of the island of Bananal, and 19,8 kilometers to the North West of the lake of Luiz Alves, where the river S. Domingos rises.

It possesses some workshops and its husbandry, which is also very productive, consists in grains, sugarcane and ther plantos.

Santa Maria, situated on the left bank of the Araguaya between S. João das Duas Barras and Santa Leopoldina, is very serviceable to the navigation of that river.

Santa Isabel, created on the upper point of the island of Bananal, on the bank of the Araguaya, offers the same advantages as the preceding one. Finally, S. José dos Martyrios reestablished in 1871, on the confluence of the rivers Canna Brava and Tocantins, with excellent lands for culture and equally promising a hopeful future.

In all these colonies there is a military force corresponding to the development and importance of the colony, a physician, a chaplain and an infirmary.

Military Colonies.

In Brazil these are nucleus of villages subject to military administration and government. They were established for the purpose of protecting not only the civilized people, against the attacks of the Indians, but also the free navigation of the rivers, or, as military posts; to serve as defending centres of the frontier of the Empire, and as a support to immigration on some remote localities.

The most flourishing of the military colonies actually are :

Obidos, in the province of Pará, on the left bank of the Amazonas, with 500 inhabitants of both sexes, including the soldiers of the detachment.

. It possesses a fertile soil and a mild climate. The village is situated on a hill, that arises progressively from the bank to the centre, in an inclined plain, with space for a large city, bathed in front by the river, and having, to the East, the lake Arapicú. The prosperous state of this colony assures it a smiling future, considering the advantages of the locality.

S. Pedro d'Alcantara, in the province of Maranhão, at the place called Boa Vista, on a high and dry ground, on the right bank of the Gurupy, 26,4 kilometers above the village of the same name and nearly 105,6 kilometers from the coast, with a good port for shipping.

In the background runs the Igarapé da Pedreira, 5,5 meters wide, and 6,6 meters deep, in winter. Other rivers cut the grounds of the colony, whose fertility is admirable for culture, and for cattle raising.

The production of coffee, sugarcane, cotton and grains is abundant.

Beautiful timber, excellent whetstones, slate, plastic clay for pottery, and other natural produces, enrich the grounds of this colony. Its commerce progresses and the number of workshops of different trades are every day increasing.

The population is 600 persons, comprising the soldiers of the detachment.

Dourados, in the province of Mato-Grosso, founded at the sources of the river of Dourados, a confluent of the Ivinheima, in order to aid the inland navigation of the Paraná to that province; to defend and protect the inhabitants of that part of the Brazilian territory up to the frontier of the Apa, threatened by the aggression of the Indians, and to try to civilize these.

It is placed in a pleasant spot, on a plateau with very good lands, virgin forests, where the best timber is found, vast fields of maté, much game, excellent palm-tree grounds and pure and crystalline waters.

The war that Brazil sustained against the government

of Paraguay paralized the development of this colony, which, for its position and other advantages, will occupy an important place among other like establishments.

Miranda, also in Mato-Grosso, established at the sources of the Mondego or Miranda river for the same purpose, which caused the foundation of the colony dos Dourados.

Having likewise suffered by the causes, already mentioned, it now receives a new increment, and also promises good results.

Itapura, in the province of S. Paulo, on the right bank of the Tieté, below the great Falls, from which it takes its name, at 13 kilometers from its mouth, in the Upper Paraná.

Its district comprises more than 174,2 kilometers, covered with virgin forests of excellent timber for civil and naval constructions.

There is a great variety of game in these woods and on the banks of the Tieté.

The fish is also very abundant in that river, and in the Upper Paraná.

The population, of more than 300 inhabitants, is exclusively occupied in husbandry.

The lands are extremely fruitful, and its special culture consists in grains, tobacco, coffee, cotton and potatoes.

Avanhandava, also, in the province of S. Paulo, on the right banks of the Tieté and 264 kilometers distant from the village of Araraquara, towards the East, with an area of 43,6 square kilometers.

At 440 meters more or less, above the Avanhandava-Falls, northward, there is a by-path of 6,6 kilometers, that marks the eastern limit of the colony.

On the South it is divided by the said river.

Its lands and those of the neighbourhood are of superior quality.

Culture produces here, in great quantity, the necessary articles for the supply of the population of the Salto and often of Itapura.

The number of inhabitants amounts to 900.

The colony of Santa Thereza. in the province of Santa Catharina, situated on the road that communicates the city of S. José with that of Lages, on the banks of the river Itajahy.

It is destined for the distribution of lands to soldiers, that have been dismissed from the service of the army.

The climate is healthy and the lands fit for all kinds of culture.

Its population amounts to 300 persons of both sexes, excluding the military detachment.

It produces in abundance sugarcane, tobacco, potatoes, grains and all kinds of fruit.

The industry of the colonists consists in raising cattle and domestic fowls.

Besides the colonies, hitherto mentioned, there are others, which, though they are not, by special occurrences, in so advantageous a condition, yet render some services and promise to thrive.

These are:

Dom Pedro II and S. João of Araguaya in the province of Pará: the former, situated on the right bank of the Araguary, 244,2 kilometers above the mouth of the same river, on a dry land, fit for husbandry; the latter, on the banks of the Araguaya, just in the same locality where formerly existed a military post, that gave the name to the colony,

Urucú, in the province of Minas Geraes, founded on the banks of the stream, so called, a confluent of the Mucury, at the place where it traverses the road of Santa Clara.

Nioac and Brilhante, in Mato-Grosso, that one at the point where the navigation of the Nioac begins, this one in the part in which terminates the one of the river that gives it its name, at the foot of the Serra de Maracajú.

Lamare, in the same province, on the right bank of the river S. Lourenço.

Itacayu and Conceição, both also in Mato-Grosso, the first being created in 1871, on the bank of the Aragnaya: the second in 1872 in Albuquerque.

Jatahy, in the province of Paraná, founded at the port of the rivulet Jatahy, in its confluence with the river Tibagy, in the district of Coritiba.

Xagú and Chopim, in the same province, created to defend the frontier and protect the inhabitants of the fields of Palma, Eré, Xagú and Guarapuava, against the incursions of the Indians, and call them to civilization by means of catechising.

Caseros, in the province of S. Pedro do Rio Grande do Sul, situated at the place called Mato Portuguez, in the parish of Lagôa Vermelha, of the municipality of Santo Antonio da Patrulha.

In all those colonies there is a physician, a chaplain and an infirmary for the soldiers, and in some of them a primary school.

The national treasury spends annually with the penitentiary and the military colonies about £ 30,000.

The ancient colony Leopoldina, in the province of Alagôas, was established on the right bank of the Jacuipe, from the Salto up to the mouth of the river Taquara, in front of the place called Riacho do Mato.

It was, not long ago, raised up to the rank of a village; and as such, is now under the respective common regulations.

It is, however, mentioned to prove the good results that, in Brazil, have already been derived from establishments of this description.

Having been formerly established on woodlands which, far from inhabited places and almost out of the reach of the official authorities, served as a shelter to malefactors, it contrived, in a few years, to become an important village of 4,000 inhabitants, in general, of good morals and industrious.

The culture of cotton alone produced already, in the average term of annual exportation, more than 4,000 *arrobas* or nearly 58,760 kilograms.

It produces also in abundance sugarcane, tobacco, mandioca and grains.

The population amounts to 4,000 inhabitants.

The Brazilian Navy.

The naval service of the Empire is under the control of the Minister of Marine, directly assisted by a state office, where the administration is centralized.

It embraces the personnel, the material, and the book-keeping of all naval departments.

The naval council, instituted in 1855, is to a certain

degree organized according to the system of the french admiralty.

Its attributions are to propose whatever may contribute for the advantage and regularity of service, for the development and progress of the navy, independent of any superior orders.

Though the province of the naval council be both the military and civil general inspection of service, there is, however, one of the chief-officers of the navy, known by the designation of adjudant-general, under whose immediate influence lies all that concerns the fighting body, composed of officers of different ranks, the marines and all the personnel of the navy.

As a delegate of the minister, the adjudant-general surveys the behaviour of officers in their respective vessels, maintains the discipline in the naval stations, and takes care that orders and commissions should be duly carried into execution, both in the ships of the navy and in others. Such attributions are somewhat modified in time of war; for then, as the minister's responsibility increases, he sends directly to the admiral, commanding the forces in operation, the orders required by the circumstances.

The adjudant-general, in such a case, has, however, to his charge the surveyance of the garrison in the ships of war, as well as their armament, before they set out the harbour.

The personnel of squadrons comprehends not only the navy officers, known under the particular designation of *combatants*; but even such as pursers, surgeons, machinists, chaplains, mates, and the masters and boatswains that superintend the service of the mariners.

The crews are almost exclusively formed from the corps

of imperial marines, composed of 30 companies, with an effective of 3,000 men, in ordinary circumstances.

This number can be increased, being supplied by the 16 companies of marine apprentices or naval cadets, established in the principal maritime cities of the Empire.

Each company holds 1,200 to 1,300 men, and shall contain a greater number when they be complete. The character of these two institutions is entirely national, not only because the idea was initiated in the Empire, but also because all the soldiers are Brazilian. Their utility is now acknowledged, and they have already been adopted in other countries as the best element for the prompt formation of garrisons. The imperial marine receives, since his apprentisage, a proper training for the profession he has to follow. He knows all the tackling and working on board ship, and at same time he serves as a foot-soldier in occasion of landings and assaults.

To assist him, in this department of the modern tactics, there is also a naval battalion perfectly organized, which consists of 1,000 men, who fulfill on board the duty of gunners. In such a way, independently from the cooperation of the army, it will often be possible to take by storm those fortifications lying on harbours, or on the margins of rivers.

The pursers are 101 in number, and when they are not employed aboard, they are charged with other commissions in the Navy Office.

The legislative power is about to authorize the government to reorganize the medical department of the navy, which contains 69 officers, all medical men. There is in the capital of the Empire a navy-hospital, under the adminis-

tration of a high ranked officer. This i in every respects
a first rate establishment.

The patients who cannot be treated there, find in the
provinces, well dressed infirmaries.

There is besides a house for recovery, lately created at
the island of Governador, in the harbour of Rio de Janeiro.

At the same locality there is in construction an asylum
for the invalids of the navy. A sum superior to £ 36,000
has been already applied to that purpose ; and it yearly
increases by the addition of the interests and of new contributions. That sum has been obtained from the deduction
of one day's pay, in each month, from all the personnel of
the navy.

The military machinists, are in number of 133. A school
of national machinists is intended to be formed, for the
purpose of filling the places actually held by foreigners in
the imperial navy.

The police of harbours, the maritime census, the engage-
ments of sailors, and like concerns, are on the whole
littoral at the charge of a department, called *Capitania do
Porto.*

To that department also belongs the superintendence of
light-houses and harbours.

Navy-Arsenals.

In what concerns the materiel, the progress of the navy
is unquestionable.

There are five Arsenals, besides one, that is about to
be organized, in the province of Mato-Grosso.

The one at the capital of the Empire is in possession

of every means for the construction of vessels and ordenance stores.

It employs about 3,000 workmen, most of them natives.

From its stocks have been launched out most of the vessels of the navy, many of which of great capacity, either sailers or steamers.

It possesses excellent machinery and mighty steam-hammers, and is provided with the necessary means for making plates of the thickness required by any iron-clad ship, as it was plainly demonstrated during the late war against Paraguay.

Brazil is wonderfully abundant of woods fit for naval construction ; they could be exported in a proportion equal to the iron imported, which, however, abounds in the country.

The Arsenal of Rio de Janeiro has a dock, in actual service and another is in way of construction. The former is being enlarged in order to adapt it to modern vessels of whatever length.

A dock is also in construction, in the harbour of Maranhão, where the difference of tides is from 5,^{m}6 to 6,^{m}1.

The river Amazonas in many places, at the vicinity, of the city of Belem, capital of the province of Pará, is proper for the construction of docks capable of holding high tunnage ships.

It would be long to mention the many points on the vast extent of the brazilian sea-coast that might be availed of for the building of stocks for naval construction.

The ships of the Brazilian fleet carry guns of the improved systems.

Many officers and mariners, instructed in the respective

schools, are able to handle and to sight and point the different guns.

The battle of Riachuelo, that bears comparison with that of Lissa, and many other deeds of the fleet in Paraguay, sufficiently prove the military skill of the brazilian navy.

There have been furthermore adopted many other partial improvements, worthy of the attention of professionals.

The steam-corvette *Trajano*, constructed according to the new invention of a clever officer of the brazilian navy, has been launched on 12th July of the current year, and in a short time she will be tried in a sea-going voyage.

Previous experiments made with steam-pinnaces have proved the excellence of the new construction, both in swiftness, and stability.

Experience will decide between this new model and the vessels constructed according to the classic system, that essentially belongs to Great-Britain.

Though in the last five years the service of light-houses has been considerably improved, by the increase of lights and the introduction of new machines, however, the light-houses existing on the coast and harbours of Brazil do not answer yet the claims of navigation.

This service requires a great development and it is to be expected that the legislative assembly will allow a credit of £ 60,000 for such a purpose.

Pyrotechnical Laboratory.

The navy department possesses a Pyrotechnical Laboratory with engine and pyrotechnical work, as well as workshops of gun-smiths and stock-makers. The said laboratory was first established in 1868, on the hill of Armação, in Nictheroy, the capital of the province of Rio de Janeiro.

This establishment, which is under the charge of a navy-officer, contains 10 pyrotechnical workshops, Including those of trituration, of the making of slow burning powder, and of the hydraulic press, which is designed for preparing time fuses for shells.

Every precaution, advised by science, has been taken to protect the workmen in cases of explosion.

The store-houses both for primary matter and for the articles of the laboratory, are placed at a convenient distance from the workshops, that are themselves quite separate from each other.

The engine works, annexed to the laboratory, possess mechanical lathes and 12 capstans, wire drawing iron, mechanical sheers to cut out copper, divers boring tools, circular saws for wood and metals; and engines for making cartridges and friction tubes.

Those of gun-smiths and stock-makers work with mechanical planes for metals, boring machines, grind, and mill, stones to rough-hew and polish.

There is also a black-smith workshop with 4 large and 2 small forges, besides a tempering kiln.

All the machinery works by steam.

The gun-smith workshop makes all necessary repairs in the portable armament of the ships and marine corps, manufactures white arms and, in case of necessity, firearms too.

The engine works not only furnish the necessary articles to the laboratory, but still prepares all the apparatus for tubes and signal rockets and the ordnance appurtenances.

The refining, casting, and brazier's workshops, refine saltpetre, prepare blacking for thongs, and grease for the artillery and armament, prepare case-shots, make zinc and tin caissons to store pyrotechnical products and other like services.

The foundry has 4 ovens for crucibles, and furnishes all objects of metal and lead projectiles.

Near the Armação wharf there exists great stores of projectiles, and workshops for loading and making grape-shot, case-shot wads and other war articles.

In the above mentioned services are employed 155 workmen and 22 servants, a sufficient number for the exigencies of service, in time of peace.

On extraordinary circumstances the number of workmen may be raised to the double, the laboratory being thus enabled to prepare daily sufficient ammunition for a thousand shots, five hundred of which for shells.

It must be observed that every ship has always on board 120 shots for each gun.

Light-houses.

Besides 19 small light-houses that guide navigators approaching the entrance of some ports, and are very serviceable to the river navigation both at Pará and Rio Grande do Sul, there exist 21 first-class light houses along the whole coast of Brazil, not including 2 still in construction, one at the entrance of the river Parahyba do Norte, and the other at Itapoan, in Bahia.

It is to be noticed, with regard to their astronomical position, that all the latitudes are south, and the longitudes referring to the meridian of Rio de Janeiro.

Coming downwards from the North they are situated as follows:

PARÁ.

Floating light-house, on the shoals of Bragança.

Lat. 0° 26' 9" Long. 4° 48' 0" W.
Catoptric, with eclipses; visible at the distance of 8 miles, 14,8 kil. It works since the 24th November 1866.

Salinas, on Atalaia point.

Lat. 0° 35' 3" Long. 4° 13' 15" W.
Dioptric, of 3d class, with flashes, its reach being 17 miles, 31,5 kil.
It works from 8th March 1852.

MARANHÃO.

Itacolumi.

Lat. 2° 10' 0" Long. 1° 18' 0" W.
Catoptr. with eclipses; reach 22 miles, 40,8 kil.
It works since 1st January 1839.

SANTA ANNA ISLAND.

Lat. 2° 16' 30" Long. 0° 28' 0" W.
Catoptr. with eclipses, visible at 24 miles, 44,5 kil.
It works since January 1st 1839.

PIAUHY.

Pedra do Sal.

Lat, 2° 49' 19" Long. 1° 26' 12" E. (not rectified).
Dioptr. 4th class, fixed light, reach 10 miles, 18,5 kil.
It works since the 4th March 1873.

CEARÀ.

Mucuripe, on the point so called.

Lat. 3° 41' 50" Long 4° 39' 0" E.
Dioptr. 4th class, with eclipses, visible at a distance of 10 miles, 18,5 kil.
It works since the 29th July 1872.

RIO GRANDE DO NORTE.

Reis Magos, on the fortress of that name.

Lat. 5° 45' 6" Long. 7° 52' 36" E.
Dioptr. 5th class, fixed light, reach 10 miles, 18,5 kil.
It works since September 27th 1872.

PERNAMBUCO.

Picão, on the northernmost end of the reef (Recife).

Lat. 8° 3' 30" Long. 8° 15' 18" E.
Catoptr ; revolving light, white and red ; reach 15 miles, 27,8 kil.
It works since 1819.

Olinda, on the fort Monte-Negro.

Lat. 8° 0' 49" Long. 8° 16' 48" E. (not rectified).
Dioptr., 4th class, with flashes, reach 12 miles, 22,3 kil.
It works since November 18th 1872.

ALAGÔAS.

Maceió, on the western point of the mountain, lying over the city.

Lat. 9° 39' 50° Long. 7° 25'26' E.
Dioptr. 3.ª class, with eclipses ; reach 22' miles, 40,8 kil.
It works since July 1ᵐ 1836.

Bar of the S. Francisco, on the northern point.

Lat. 10° 29' 0" Long. 6° 47' 23" E. (not rectified).
Dioptr. 4.ᵗʰ class, fixed light; reach 10 miles, 18,5 kil.
It works since 1.ˢᵗ March 1873.

BAHIA.

Santo Antonio da Barra.

Lat. 13° 0' 11" Long. 4° 35' 10" E.
Catoptr. with eclipses, white and red lights ; reach 15
miles, 27,8 kil.
It works since the 2.ᵈ December 1839.

S. Paulo Hill.

Lat. 13° 21' 40" Long. 4° 12' 18" E.
Dioptr. 1.ˢᵗ class, with eclipses ; reach 24 miles, 45,5
kil.
It works since May 3.ᵈ 1855.

Abrolhos, on the island of Santa Barbara.

Lat. 17° 57' 31" Long. 4° 25' 0" E.
Catoptr. with eclipses ; reach 17 miles, 31,5 kil.
It works since the 30ᵗʰ October 1862.

ESPIRITO-SANTO

Santa Luzia, on the hill of that name.

Lat. 20° 18' 0" Long. 2° 49' 30" E. (not rectified.)
Dioptr. 4.ᵗʰ class, fixed light ; reach 12 miles, 22,3
kil.
It works since the 7.ᵗʰ September 1871.

RIO DE JAÑEIRO.

Cape Frio.

Lat. 23° 0' 45" Long. 1° 7' 0" E.
Catoptr. with eclipses; reach 20 miles, 37,1 kil.
It works since 7.ᵗʰ September 1861.

Raza island.

Lat. 23° 3' 30" Long. 0° 1' 20" W.
Catoptr, revolving, white and red lights ; reach 20 miles, 37,1 kil.
It works since July the 31.ˢᵗ 1829.

S. PAULO.

Moela island.

Lat. 24° 3' 0" Long. 3° 9' 0" W.
Catoptr, fixed light; reach 20 miles, 37,1 kil.
It works since 15.ᵗʰ December 1862.

PARANÁ.

Morro das Conchas, on the island of Mel.

Lat. 25° 32' 38" Long. 5° 10' 30" W.
Dioptr. 3.ᵈ class, fixed light, reach 20 miles, 37,1 kil.
It works since the 25.ᵗʰ March 1872.

SANTA CATHARINA.

Point of the Naufragados.

Lat. 27° 50' 0" Long. 5° 27' 0" W.
Catoptr, with eclipses; reach 16 miles, 29,7 kil.
It works since the 3.ᵈ May 1861.

RIO GRANDE DO SUL.

Pontal da Barra.

Lat. 32° 7' 0" Long. 9° 0' 2" W.
Catoptr, with eclipses; reach 25 miles, 46,4 kil.
It works since January 18.th 1852.

Small Light-houses.

PARA.

Chapéo virado.

Lat. 1° 7' 45" Long. 6° 18' 3" W.
Dioptr. 6th class, fixed light; reach 7 miles, 13 kil.
It works since March 25th 1872.

Cotijuba.

Lat. 1° 15' 35" Long. 5° 28' 30" W.
Dioptr. 6th class, fixed light; reach 7 miles, 13 kil.
It works since February 1860.

Capim island.

Dioptr. 6th class, fixed light; reach 7 miles, 13 kil.
It is still in construction.

Panacuera.

Lat. 1° 44' 30" Long. 5° 58' 25" W.
Dioptr. 6th class, fixed light; reach 7 miles, 13 kil.
It works since October 1860.

Goiabal.

Lat. 1° 37' 0" Long. 6° 2' 45" W.
Dioptr. 6th class, fixed light; reach 7 miles, 13 kil.
It works since July 1860.

Jutahy.

Lat. 1° 51' 0" Long. 6° 44' 45" W.
Dioptr. 6th class, fixed light; reach 7 miles, 13 kil.
It works since October 1859.

Marianno.

Lat. 1° 47' 30" Long. 7° 0' 45" W.
Dioptr. 6th class, fixed light; reach 7 miles, 13 kil.
It works since December 1860.

MARANHÃO.

S. Ma cos.

Lat. 2° 29' 0" Long. 1° 9' 25" W.
Catoptr. fixed light; reach 6 miles, 11,1 kil.
It works since March 1831.

Alcantara.

Lat. 2° 24' 0" Long. 1° 17' 0" W.
Catoptr. fixed light; reach 2 miles, 3,7 kil.
It works since February 1831.

Bar.

Lat. 2° 29' 30" Long. 1° 11' 0" W.
Catoptr. fixed light; reach 2 miles, 3,7 kil.
It works since January 1831.

SERGIPE.

Cotinguiba.

Lat. 10° 59' 0" Long. 6° 3' 0" E.
Catoptr. fixed light, white, red and yellow; reach 8
miles, 14,8 kil.
It works since November 1862.

BAHIA.

Forte do mar.

Lat. 12° 58' 16" Long. 4° 43' 10'' E.
Dioptr. fixed light, red; reach, 4 miles, 7,4 kil.
It works since the 30th October 1862.

RIO DE JANEIRO.

Fortress Santa Cruz.

At the entrance of the bay.
Catoptr. fixed light; reach 8 miles, 14,8 kil.
It has been working many years ago.

Cafôfo.

At the Military Arsenal.
Fixed light, red; reach 2 miles, 3,7 kil.
It is working since long.

S. PEDRO DO RIO GRANDE DO SUL.

Ponta do Estreito.

Lat. 31° 46' 14'' Long. 8° 45' 53'' W.
Catoptr. fixed light; reach 6 miles, 11,1 kil.
It has been working since long.

Bojurú.

Lat. 31° 29' 13'' Long. 8° 25' 21'' W.
Catoptr. fixed light; reach 8 miles, 14,8 kil.
It has been working long since.

Capão da Marca.

Lat. 31° 18' Long. 8° 6' 21'' W.
Catoptr. fixed light; reach 6 miles, 11,1 kil.
It has been working long since.

Christovam Pereira.

Lat. 31° 4' Long. 8° 4' 21" W.
Catoptr. fixed light; reach 15 miles, 27,8 kil.
It works since January 8ᵗʰ 1864.

Itapuan.

Lat. 30° 22' 24" Long. 7° 58' 21" W.
Catoptr. fixed light; reach 12 miles, 22,3 kil.
It works since 1ˢᵗ March 1860.

The finances.

The national revenue and expenditure is entrusted to a board denominated the *Tribunal do Thesouro Nacional* (Exchequer), which is composed of high functionaries, and the Minister of Finances presides over its proceedings.

The supreme direction and surveillance of the revenue and expenditure, the collection, distribution and accounts of the public monies are its principal attributes; it also decides administrative questions relating to these matters, and at all times defends the interests of the Treasury.

For this purpose, a treasury-office and sundry bureaux are in each province subordinate to the central board and there are special agents in each municipality.

The Minister of Finances is obliged, at each legislative session, to present to the chamber of deputies, shortly after it meets, a general balance sheet of the revenue and expenditure of the National Treasury during the preceding year, as also the budget of the expenses for the coming year, and of the total amount of the contributions and public income.

The suits or actions of the public Treasury enjoy a privileged jurisdiction.

The payment of the capital and interest of the internal

public debt, funded by law, and represented by bonds,
called *apolices*, is under the charge of an office independent of the National Treasury and denominated the « Caixa
de amortisação » (Sinking-fund office).

It is governed by a committee over which the Minister of
Finances presides, and composed of a general inspector
and five Brazilian capitalists, holders of bonds.

The Treasuries in the provinces where national bonds
or *apolices* have been emitted, are subordinate to this
office, as to all that regards the sinking-fund.

Public revenue.

The public income comprises the municipal, provincial, and general revenues.

The first is decreed by the provincial assemblies on
the proposition of the municipal councils, and collected
by the proctors and agents of the latter bodies, in order
to meet the municipal expenses.

The second is decreed by the assembly of each province, with the sanction of the president, to meet the
provincial expenses, and is collected by the treasury-
offices, collectors and revenue-boards, toll-bars and agencies created, for this purpose, by the said assembly.

The third is decreed by a law of the general legislature, and raised by custom-houses, excise-offices, revenue-
boards, collectors and other fiscal authorities.

The general revenue of the Empire, which, in the financial year 1831—1832 (the first of the present reign),
amounted to £ 1,117,152, (*) and in that of 1840—1841

(·) Each pound sterling is calculated, through this whole work,
at the rate of 10 mil reis in Brazilian money; change at par, however, is 27 pence for 1 mil reis, a pound sterling being thus
equivalent to 8888 reis.

(the first of the majority of the Emperor) to £ 1,631,057 has progressively risen to £ 6,477,684 in 1866—1867, and in 1871—1872 ascended to £ 10,193,075.

The provincial revenue estimated in 1867 at about £ 1,400,000, rose up to £ 1,903,590 in 1870—1871.

The municipal revenue which, in 1867, amounted to £ 350,000 has now risen to nearly £ 500,000.

The number of custom-houses in the Empire, which in 1867 was 16, has risen to 23, including that of the Capital.

The amount of duties collected by them during the year 1871—1872 amounted to £ 7,772,494, without reckoning £ 55,913 proceeding from deposits.

For such a sum the custom-house of the Capital contributed with £ 3,480,198.

During the last three years (from 1869 — 1870 to 1871 — 1872) the average of its collections amounted to £ 3,284,812, not including the deposits, the average of which attained nearly £ 16,200.

Next to this, comes the Pernambuco custom-house with an average of more than £ 1,100,000; that of Bahia with more than £ 900,000; and that of Pará with upwards of £ 400,000.

The fiscal regulations and tariffs of our custom-houses are analogous to those of other european nations, especially to that of France. It is not based on the protecting-system and tends to become more liberal every day, though the facility of smuggling requires more precautions than in other countries.

The government and the legislative assembly are aware that some improvements are required in the fiscal regulations of our custom-houses, and are proceeding to them by degrees, according to what experience points out.

To enable the exchequer to occur to the extraordinary expenses resulting from the war, against the late dictator of Paraguay, new taxes were created, which have almost no influence upon either the imports or the exports.

Such taxes will be diminished as soon as the state of the exchequer will allow it.

The general receipt and expenditure of the Empire are the following :

1870 — 1871

This financial year is definitely liquidated, the respective balances having been distributed to the Chambers, in the present legislature.

Receipts collected, including the sum of £185,128 proceeding from deposits. . .			£	9,773,655
Policies emitted. . .	£	2,614,560		
Produce of the London loan.	»	2,652,174		
Emission of money paper in preceding years, and now liquidated.	»	1,022,043		
Private loan. . . .	»	70,000	»	6,358,778
			£	16,132,434
Expenses paid . . .	»	10,009,351		
Supply to the preceding year.	»	5,147,662	»	15,157,013
Balance forwarded to 1871 — 1872 . . .			£	975,420

1871 — 1872

Though it be ended, this year has not been quite liquidated; a single synopsis of its receipt and expenditure has been made, because the provincial treasuries have not yet sent their definitive balances.

The following figures, however, will not be much altered in the general balance.

General revenue.	£	10,095,490
Deposits (liquidated).	»	269,425
Policies emitted	»	2,426
Nickel coins emitted	»	56,460
Operations of credit.	»	11
Balance of the preceding year, with the deduction of £ 13,067 proceeding from unpaid bills.	»	962,352
	£	11,386,165
Expenditure	»	10,135,627
Balance still unliquidated	£	1,250,538

1872 — 1873

This financial year is neither liquidated nor shut.

In accordance with the system of accounts adopted in the Empire, the financial year begins on the 1st July and finishes on the 30th June of the next year; but the collection of the income, and the expenditure relating to that period are carried on till the end of December, and then the transactions of the financial year are quite closed. From that time forward there is an additional term of 3 months in the provincial treasuries, and of

6 months in the National Treasury for the shutting of accounts.

Thus it is not possible to estimate exactly the revenue and expenditure of the year 1872 — 1873: for its completion a few months are still wanting, during which several receipts are to be collected, and several expenses paid.

In the meantime, according to the official data, afforded by the last report of the Minister of finance and by the synopsis of 1871 — 1872, its revenue and expenditure may be nearly estimated as follows :

Revenue, including the deposits . . .	£	10,804,121
Remaining emission of nickel coins. .	»	56,711
Treasury notes emitted	»	73,090
Balance of the preceding year . . .	»	1,250,538
	£	12,184,461

Expenditure of the several				
State offices . . .	£	9,665,495		
D.º authorized by different special and extraordinary credits, including that for the prolongation of the D. Pedro II Rail-Road.	»	1,307,789	£	10,973,285
Balance probable . .			£	1,211,175

1873 — 1874

This year, which is but in the beginning, the basis for the calculation of the receipt and expenditure cannot be other but that offered by the respective budget-law.

According to the law, that has been just issued under n. 2348 of the 25th August, the valuation is as follows:

General revenne. including only the deposits, estimated at . . .	£	100,000	£	10,400,000
Expenditure voted with fixed sums. . . .	»	9,825,016		
D.º autorized, the importance of which is not possible to prefix exactly	»	74,983	»	9,900,000
Balance of the year, according to the budget			»	500,000
Joined to that of the preceding year . .			»	1,211,175
Total probable . .			£	1,711,175

From this balance is to be abated £ 560,000 sent abroad for defraying expenses made by the war against Paraguay, as soon as be remitted to the exchequer the comprobatory documents of their being paid.

In the receipts of the financial years 1871—1872, 1872—1873 and 1873—1874 are not comprised the sums collected for the Slave-Emancipation-Fund, since they have a special application, by virtue of the law of 1871.

Public-Debt.

The public debt of Brazil is divided into consolidated and floating. Of the first kind are the internal and foreign ones. The latter proceeds from loans negotiated at the London Exchange, in consequence of some legislative authorizations; and the former from the policies emitted, according to the law of the 15th November 1827, and the decree n. 4244 of the 15th September 1868.

The external debt amounted, on the 30th July of the current year, to £ 15,255,200, at change par, that is, 27 pence for 1 mil réis; and the internal is now amounting to £ 28,615,720, of which £ 25,746,870 are from policies authorized by the law of 1827, and £ 2,868,850 from the loan of 1868.

The floating debt consists of the one previous to the year 1827, of different deposits, of Exchequer bills, and paper money. The debt previous to 1827 is reduced to £ 34,453.

The deposits, which are loans borrowed from the coffer of orphans and other sources, ascended, according to the last Report of the Minister of Finances to £ 2,914,668.

The Exchequer bills, which emission can be elevated to £ 2,000,000 by virtue of art. 3[d] of the law n. 1953 of the 17th July 1871, that authorized the prolongation of the D. Pedro II rail-road, amounted on the 30th June 1873 to £ 1,172,890.

Paper-money, on the 30th March 1873, was reduced to £ 14,957,873; but even this figure tends to diminish, since besides the amortization resulting of the change of bronze-coins and by the substitution of paper-money, the government is authorized to apply to the payment of the said debt the balance of the Savings-Bank deposits, as also the excess of the receipts over the expenditure.

The debt of the Empire is then the following:

Foreign debt, change at par. . .	£ 15,255,200
Home funded debt	» 28,615,720
Previous to 1827.	» 34,453
Deposits	» 2,914,668
Exchequer-bills	» 1,172,890
Paper-money.	» 14,957,873
Summing up. . . .	£ 61,255,782

The interests and amortization of the foreign loans, and those of the home loan of 1868, are paid in gold or its equivalent.

MONETARY SYSTEM OF BRAZIL.

In Brazil the monetary unity is the *real*, the existence of which is quite imaginary.

As a basis for the system, was taken a drachm of gold of the touch of 0,97, that is, $\frac{917}{1000}$ of gold and $\frac{83}{1000}$ of alloy, representing the value of 4$000 réis. The gold coin of 20$000 réis has 17,9297 grams weight; those of 10 and 5 mil réis are in equal proportion. They are composed of 0,917 pure gold, and 0,083 copper and silver alloy; the difference of 1 grain being tolerated in the coins of 20$000 réis, and in the others, in an equal proportion.

The relation existing between the gold and silver coins, free from seignoriage duty, is 15 °/₀ silver to 1 of gold of the same touch. By a decree of 1849, the silver coin was charged with a seignoriage duty of 9,863 %, thus becoming an auxiliary coin.

Those coins are worth 2$000, 1$000, and 500 réis. Their composition is 0,097 fine silver; the weight corresponding to that of 2$000 réis is 25,5 gram., and that of the others is proportional; a difference of 2 grains being tolerated in the former, and keeping a like proportion in the others.

The law of 1867 has determined that the silver coins of 2$000 and 1$000 should have 25, and 12,5 grams of silver, of the touch of 0,9; those of 500 and 200 réis, 6,25 and 2,5 grams of silver, with the touch of 0,835.

In 1870 this statute was altered by a law determining that thenceforwards the silver coins should have the values of 2$000, 1$000 réis and 500 réis, the touch of 0,917, and the weight fixed by the decree of 1849; it being also determined that all coins of the touch of 0,9, as well as those of 200 réis should be taken out of the circulation.

In conformity with the said decree, the government resolved to order the manufacturing of small coin, composed of 25 parts of nickel and 75 of copper, their values being 200, 100, and 50 réis; the first weighing 15, the second 10, and the third 7 grams.

The old copper coin of 640 réis, a pound of metal, was substituted by those of 20 and 10 réis of a ternary alloy of copper, tin, and zinc, according to the law of 1867.

In order to fix the values of foreign coins it was agreed that a brazilian pound should contain 4.9 grams, afterwards setting the price of each gram of pure gold, according to what it is worth in the coin of 20$000 réis.

A table of Brazilian coins.

GOLD				
Coins.	Grams.	Standard.	Grams of pure metal.	Remarks.
Pieces of 20$000....	17,9296875	917	16,4415234	} Law of 1847.
» of 10$000.. .	8,9648438	917	8,2207617	

SILVER AUXILIARY.				
Coin of 2$000......	25,500	917	23,38350	} Decrees of 1849 and of 1870.
» of 1$000......	12,750	917	11,69175	
» of $500	6,375	917	5,84587	

ANCIENT SUBSIDIARY.				
Coin of 20 réis....	......	......	......	} Law of 1867.
» of 10 réis.....	......	......	......	

MODERN SUBSIDIARY.				
Coin of 200 réis....	15,000	25 parts of nickel and 75 of copper.	}	Decree of 1870.
» of 100 réis....	10,000			
» of 50 réis....	7,000			
Coin of 20 réis.....	7,000	Copper 95 Fin 4 Zinc 1	}	Decree of 1867.
» of 10 réis.....	3,500			

The Mint.

The first Mint, in Brazil, was established in the year 1694, at the city of S. Salvador da Bahia, whence it was removed to that of Rio de Janeiro, where it began working in 1699. Some time afterwards it was again transferred to Pernambuco, where it stood until 1702.

All the latter establishments were destined for the striking of the coins, then called provincial, for its currency was limited to Brazil. They coined Rs. 3,200:000$ (£ 320,000) in gold, and Rs. 800:000$000 (£ 80,000) in silver.

In 1702 the government ordered the Mint to be removed again to Rio de Janeiro, and so it was, being definitively established in the Capital since January 1703.

It was then that began, in Brazil, the coinage of the general coins, so called because they circulated through the whole kingdom of Portugal. In consequence, however, of the vast production of the gold-mines, a new Mint was founded at Bahia, and afterwards another in Minas; but the latter was shut up in 1735, and the former in 1830.

That of Rio de Janeiro, at first worked in buildings little fit for the purpose.

In 1858 the edifice, where it is now standing, began to be constructed.

Its work-shops are vast, well aired, and in superior conditions to many of the same kind in Europe. From its definitive foundation in 1703 until 1833, the Rio de Janeiro Mint coined Rs. 216,257:629$929 (£ 21,625,762) in gold, and Rs. 16,460:866$319 (£ 1,646,086) in silver;

from 1833 to 1849, by the subsisting standard Rs. 950:684﮷ (£ 95,068) in gold, and Rs. 67:390﮷680 (£ 6,739) in silver ; from 1850 to 1870, by the said standard, Rs. 43,195,250﮷ (£ 4,319,525) in gold, and Rs. 16,812:61﮷﮷400(£ 1,C81,261) in silver.

The Mint comprises seven sections under the superintendence of a governor called *provedor*. Its several departments are the book-keeping and accompt-office, the Cash, the stamping of metals, the casting and allaying of metals, the liming, the coining, the engraving, and machinery, workshops.

Besides the business of coinage, some of the sections take charge of works concerning that art-departement, either for public offices or for private parties, the proceeds being a source of revenue for the Mint.

Thus the casting business comprehends the refining of precious metals, for the account of private parties ; that of the chemical laboratory, the assays and analysis of minerals; and the engraving department, the making of medals and other bespoken works.

To the casting department is adjoined another for the clearing of the earth and ashes proceeding from the workshops, where precious metals have been worked.

The stamping and printing of the policies and other titles of the national debt are a department of the Mint.

The coinage, refining, and other tasks are performed by steam machinery of the most improved and modern system.

All the coining engines, 6 in number, have been constructed in the very establishment, with the exception of some pieces cast at the naval arsenal and private workshops. They are of Tonnelier's system, modified, and strike more than fifty coins, in a minute.

The Mint possesses a precious collection of medals and coins, both brazilian and foreign.

Commerce.

Possessing so many sheltered ports along its vast sea-coast of 9,920 kil, and a great number of rivers navigable to steamers; extensive prairies and forests; most fruitful lands and varied climates, under which thrive numerous plants both of the tropical and the temperate zones; containing, besides, a great deal of mines of gold, silver, lead and other metals and important beds of diamonds, the Empire of Brazil has rapidly progressed, as it was to be expected, since the opening of her ports to all friendly nations, in 1808.

The government has granted important favours to commerce, and regulated the transactions with the utmost liberality, providing for its necessities in proportion as they are pointed out.

With the laudable purpose of facilitating and developing commerce, the government allowed to foreign flags the coasting navigation, as well as that of the principal rivers, the Paraguay, the S. Francisco and the Amazonas to the frontier, an extent of 3,828 kil., and of their respective affluents, thus setting a worthy example to all nations.

The commercial legislation of Brazil, modelled after that of the most refined countries, consists of a code issued out in order to give a greater impulse and security to transactions, as also of legislative acts subsequently decreed to amend the faults pointed out by experience.

On account of such favourable conditions and owing to the steadiness and liberality of legislation, the Brazilian commerce has thriven as much as that of the most prosperous States of Europe.

In 1803 the value of the imports and exports of the foreign commerce was estimated at £ 2,260; during the last five years from 1866 to 1871 the annual average raised up to £ 34,193,200; and in the financial year of 1871 to 1872 this average still went over £ 489,179, notwithstanding the importation having fallen down and the exportation increased to about £ 1,000,000.

The increase of the external commerce is perfectly calculated by the following table, organized after the official returns, comprising the period from 1836 to 1871, in which, for a greater facility, the values are represented by periods of five years.

Years.	Average value in periods of five years.		Increase.
1836 — 1841	£	8,795,300	£ ....
1841 — 1846	»	9,899,880	» 1,104,680
1846 — 1851	»	11,004,560	» 1,104,520
1851 — 1856	»	16,925,880	» 5,921,380
1856 — 1861	»	23,461,500	» 6,535,620
1861 — 1866	»	25,503,508	» 2,042,008
1866 — 1871	»	34,193,201	» 8,689,693

From the first to the second period of five years the commercial movement increased at the rate of 12,5 %, and from 1866 to 1871 at that of 34 %, which proves that the increase is more and more greater, as it is still ascertained with regard to the financial year of 1871 — 1872.

The excess of £ 25,397,900 of the last, over the first period of five years, is corresponding to 288,76 % of increase in the 35 years, or 8,2 % a year.

These results being compared to those of the european trade shows that only that of France, the annual increase of which is 10,2 %, goes, in this respect, more rapidly than that of Brazil; this superiority, however, may be explained by the deficiency and imperfection of the Brasilian statistics.

In a less advantageous position than that of the Empire, there are to be found Norway with 7,4 % of annual increase ; Holland with 7,4 %; Belgium with 7,1 %; Danemark with 6,1 %; England with 5,2 %; the Zollverein with 4,4 %; Spain with 3,6 %; Portugal with 3,6 %; Russia with 1,4 %; and Italy with 0,2 %.

Although the development of the foreign trade be enough to give an idea of the country's progress, in order to render it more perfect, it is convenient to study the proportion of the permutation of commercial articles, during the two last years. That this apreciation may be rendered easier, we shall take the average means of from 1861 to 1866 and from 1866 to 1871.

	Average imports	Average exports
1.ˢᵗ period of 5 years	£ 60,325,476	£ 67,192,055
2.ᵈ » » » »	» 79,246,765	» 91,722,240
Increase	» 18,921,289	» 24,530,184

The result is, therefore, that the importation augmented

from the first to the second period, at the rate of 31,36 %. and the exportation at that of 36,5 %.

The balance of the exports over the imports was during the first said period of £ 6,866,579, and during the second of £ 12,475,474, or 81,7 %. more than the first.

From its commercial transactions with other countries has Brazil, therefore, obtained in the period of ten years, from 1861 to 1871, a total of £ 19,342,053 proportionally greater in the financial year of 1871—72 as well as in that of 1872—73, though it be not yet liquidated.

The constant and progressive increase of trade was also correspondent to the constant and progressive increase of the balance. This result, based on the official returns, greatly proves the development of the public wealth, during the late years, and is the best pledge of the Empire's prosperity.

It was, however, during that period of ten years that the Empire maintained the war against Paraguay, for the space of five years, and its exchanges suffered an extraordinary vexation as well as the markets, that consume a great part of their products.

Notwithstanding all this, the sources of the public wealth were not affected, neither the commerce decreased ; on the contrary, it thrived in a high degree, more by the increase of exportation than by that of importation, a clear evidence of the great productive forces of Brazil.

Upon so solid a basis, rather strengthened by the stability of the institutions, the best guarantee of commerce, of agriculture and general industry, are settled the deserved credits enjoyed by Brazil in Europe.

Of course, the coasting and inland trade followed the same progress, as it may be seen from the adjoined table

with regard to the financial years of 1854, 1863 and
1870.

	FINANCIAL YEARS.		
	1854—55	1863—64	1870—71
Coasting trade. . . .	£ 4,977,200	£ 10,070,200	£ 13,030,000
Inland and fluvial trade	» 1,120,000	» 1,750,000	» 1,900,000
Total. . .	£ 6,397,200	£ 11,820,200	£ 14,930,000

During the 17 years past, from 1854 to 1871, the coasting and inland trade augmented at the rate of 133,4 %,
corresponding to the annual average of 7,8 %, or the same
as the foreign trade.

It is still to be noticed, that the official statistical returns comprised but a very small part of the home trade,
always superior in every country to the foreign one,
since the articles, before their being exported, and after
their importation, go through many transactions.

The total of the foreign trade summed up to that of
the coasting and the inland one, belonging to the last
fiscal year, proves that, in the general balance, the transactions of the brazilian commerce are represented on the
official returns by the figure of £ 49,123,200.

The different nations of the globe have contributed, in
the following proportions, to the result which the commerce of seagoing vessels presents :

As to the imports : Great Britain with 45,73 % ; France
with 17,33 % ; River Plate with 7,26 % : the Hanseatic
Towns with 6,15 % ; the United-States with 5,36 % ;
Belgium with 4,80 % ; Portugal with 3,69 %, and other
countries with 9,68 %.

As for the exports : the United-States, which consume

the brazilian produces in a larger scale, contributed
with a percentage of 45,84 %; Great-Britain with 9,07 % ;
France with 5,62 %.; River Plate with 5,29 % ; Portugal with 3,20 %; Hanseatic Towns with 2,03 %. ;
Belgium with 1,04 %.; other countries with 27,94 %.

For the prosperity of the Empire, during the last years,
much contributed the progress of the transatlantic steam-
navigation, the augment of the banking establishments,
the liberty of coasting navigation, and the development
of the rail-roads and of the coasting and fluvial steam-
navigation, greatly subsidized by the general and provincial governments.

The seagoing navigation in the financial year of 1871
—72, calculated by the entries and sailings, was carried on
by 6,324 vessels of 3,418,412 tons burden or 2,713,691,028
kilogr., and manned by 122,391 men; and the coasting
navigation by 9,893 vessels of 2,402,309 tons burden or
1,905,614,798 kilgr., and manned by 139,235 men.

The progress of navigation, during the financial years
of 1864—65 and 1871—72, may be valued by the following comparative table :

SEAGOING NAVIGATION.

	Vessels.	Tons burden.	Crew.
1864—65. . . .	6,138	2,389,098	89,367
1871—72. . . .	6,324	3,408,402	122,391
Increase	186	1,019,304	33,024

COASTING NAVIGATION.

	Vessels.	Tons burden.	Crew.
1864—65. . . .	6,275	1,283,919	89,822
1871—72. . . .	9,893	2,402,309	139,235
Increase	3,618	1,118,390	49,413

In the increase relating the tonnage of seagoing vessels, was comprised a great number of steamers, which are taking the place of the sailing ships, with notable advantage.

The inland or river navigation had a satisfactory development, and during the year 1872, was carried on by 8,771 vessels, and manned by 16,238 men; being employed in the fishing trade 4,808 boats, manned by 5,301 men.

The provinces of Brazil, which have foreign commercial intercourse, are those of Rio de Janeiro, Pernambuco, Bahia, S. Pedro do Rio Grande do Sul, Pará, S. Paulo, Maranhão, Alagòas, Parahyba, Ceará, Sergipe, Paraná, Santa Catharina, Rio Grande do Norte, Piauhy, Espirito Santo and Mato-Grosso.

There are in the Empire about 53,000 commercial houses, besides nearly 7,000, exempt from taxes, namely: Brazilian 29,000; Portuguese 18,000; other nationalities 6,000.

By the budget law, voted this year, measures were adopted that concern the international trade; the government being authorized:

1.st To reduce, within certain limits, the additional duties of importation.

The official value of the articles of the tariff shall be those of the average prices current in the markets, the additional taxes of 5 % of the value of the articles, and those of 28 and 21 % on the tariff duties, being substituted by a percentage of 30 to 40 %, on the produces of the said duties.

This percentage is to be reduced every year by the legislative power, according to the circumstances of the exchequer, and the increase of the national revenue.

The plan for the new tariff is already being studied.

2.ª To allow, without any limited time, the coasting navigation to foreign vessels, under the conditions actually in vigour, granting to the national shipping a reward not exceeding £ 5 per ton, for each vessel built up in the Empire, as well as the exemption both from the anchorage duty and the excise tax, for the first sale of every vessel built in the national stocks: the exemption from industry and trade taxes to stocks' owners, as well as that from recruitment to Brazilians employed, as sailors, in the national shipping.

3.ª To reduce the anchorage taxes, calculated on the tonnage of foreign vessels, from 500 réis (1 shilling) per brazilian ton to 200 rs. (5 pences) per metrical ton, comprehending all vessels, entered into the ports of the Empire, except those of the navy, those driven into the harbour by stress of weather, those which convey more than a hundred immigrants at a time, those which have a free entry according to the custom-houses' regulations, and finally those which, within the period of a year, have paid the same taxes for six times running.

This statute will put out the doubts and contests of the previous laws, bringing back to trade about 30 °/₀ of the expenses that were formerly paid.

4.ᵗʰ To lessen the taxes and other expenses proceeding from the collecting and sale of the jetsam of vessels, wrecked on the coasts of Brazil, the due charges being reduced to a half of their present cost.

5.ᵗʰ To exempt from export duties the timber and other native articles employed in the fitting out and repairing of foreign ships, lying in the road steads of the Empire.

The principal articles of exportation in Brazil are the following.

Coffee.

This staple, by itself, represents nearly the half of the whole value of the exports.

Its cultivation extends from the Amazonas down to the province of S. Paulo, that is, from 3° E: N to 23° E: S, and from the seacoast to the western boundary of the Empire, the surface favourable to its growth being thus above 15,000 sq. lg. or 683,400 sq. kil.

Both the climate and the soil being so adapted for its culture, it has, of course, rapidly extended itself, though, in the beginning there was not great care in the preparation of the berry, thence proceeding the discredit to which it fell down in the european markets.

During the last 15 years, however, the quality of the coffee has been so considerably improved, by the introduction of machinery and of more perfect processes, that since long more than a half of the brazilian coffee is sold, in Europe, under the denomination of Java, Ceylon, Martinique, S. Domingos and even Moka.

The international Jury of the Universal Exhibition, in 1867, gave a solemn testimonial of this truth, by conferring a gold medal to the brazilian coffee, a reward that was not granted to the similar produces of other countries.

The growth of coffee is increasing, in Brazil, whilst it is either standing still or in little progress, in the East-Indies, Central America, S. Domingos, and other countries.

The following table, organized according to the official returns, shows the increase of its production.

	Quantity.		Value.
1840 — 1841	74,294,689 kilgr.	£	2,000,000
1871 — 1872	243,584,360 »	»	7,164,565
Increase	169,289,671 »	£	5,164,565

In a period of 31 years, the quantity of coffee exported, has raised at the rate of 228 %, and the value to 258 % or 7,35 % and 8, 3 % a year, a sufficient proof of the progress in the cultivation, and of improvement in the quality of the produce.

The production of coffee is, at present, estimated in Brazil at about 260,000,000 kilgr., of which 29,380,000 kilgr. are consumed in the country.

It is calculated that in the Empire there exist 530,000,000 of coffee-trees, covering a surface of about 574,992 hectars.

Cotton.

This staple was always cultivated, in Brazil, chiefly in the northern provinces, but in a small scale till of late, because the price, in the importing markets, did not sufficiently return the expenses of production and conveyance.

The rise in the value of cotton, caused by the United-States war, and by the construction of a few rail-roads, encouraged the planters, and its culture is rapidly spreading even throughout the southern provinces.

The following table shows the amount of its exportation, during the last 11 years.

	Quantity.		Value.
1860 — 1861	9,854,933 kilgr.	£	468,214
1871 — 1872	53,589,838 »	»	3,563,091
Increase	43,734,905 »	»	3,094,877

The exportation, therefore, increased in that period at the rate of 443,8 % or 40,3 % every year, an evidence of the extraordinary progress of the cotton growth, which value, during the same period, rose to 661 % or 60 % in a year.

It should be noticed that this great development, in the cultivation of cotton, did not encroach on the coffee, the sugarcane, and other staples of the country, which is but explained by a better application of the productive forces.

Sugar.

The sugarcane, cultivated in Brazil from the earliest times, constituted its chief staple until the introduction of the coffre-tree, that greatly encroached on it.

Lately, however, the production of this article has rapidly increased as it is shown by the following table, which may be compared to that of coffee, above mentioned.

	Quantity.		Value.
1860 — 1861. . .	65,387,951 kilgr	£	1,090,054
1871 — 1872. . .	141,994,693 »	»	2,627,761
Increase	76,606,742 »	£	1,537,707

Within the last 11 years, the increase of sugar exports, was at the rate of 117 % or 10,6 % annually, and that of the value at the rate of 141 %, which corresponds to the annual increase of 12,8 %, being superior to that of coffee.

The sugar at present produced in Brazil, not comprising a great quantity of treacle and molasses, amounts to 293,800,000 kilgr. Almost a half of this production is consumed in the country.

Dry and salted hides.

Although, throughout the Empire, the raising of cattle may be carried on to a large scale, this trade has been chiefly developed in the provinces of Piauhy, Ceará, Rio Grande do Norte, Parahyba, S. Paulo, Paraná, S. Pedro do Rio Grande do Sul, Minas Geraes, Mato-Grosso and Goyaz. It is calculated that there are at present in the Empire about 15,000,000 of cattle, which represent a stock of £ 15,000,000.

During the financial years already alluded to, the exportation of this article was as follows :

	QUANTITY		VALUE
1860 —1861 . . .	18,883,216 kilgr. £		782,431
1871—1872 . . .	21,748,920 »	»	1,176,571
Increase	2,865,704 »	£	394,140

During the last 11 years the production increased at the rate of 15 %, and the price at that of 50,4 %, or 1,4 % e 4,6 % annually, as it is seen in the table above.

Gum elastic or caoutchouc.

This article, the indus'rial applications of which are constantly growing, is produced for the most part in the valleys of the provinces of Pará and Amazonas, where the *Siphonia elastica*, from which it is extracted, springs up spontaneously and abundantly from the littoral to the distance of 3,300 kilom, towards the interior.

When this plant be regularly cultivated it is likely that the price of caoutchouc will decrease. Even so, however, it will yield a sure revenue superior to that of coffee, since the brazilian kind is the best known.

The following table points out the quantity and value of its exports during the years, that have been taken for our comparative study.

	QUANTITY	VALUE
1860—1861 . . .	2,412,612 kilgr.	£ 285,395
1871—1872 . . .	4,798,921 »	» 750,949
Increase	2,386,309 »	£ 464,554

The increase was, with regard to quantity, of 99 %. and to price of 162,2 %, or 9 to 14,7 % a year.

Tobacco.

The soil of Brazil is perfectly suited to the culture of tobacco which growth has increased, chiefly in the provinces of Bahia, Minas, S. Paulo, Pará and several localities of Rio de Janeiro.

During the period referred to, the exportation was as follows :

	QUANTITY	VALUE
1860—1861 . . .	4,608,987 kilgr.	£ 237,643
1871—1872 . . .	12,835,126 »	» 674,803
Increase.	8,226,139 »	£ 437,160

The total rise of the quantity amounted to 178.5 %., that of the value to 184 %. The annual average was 16,2 % with regard to quantity, and 16,8 % with reference to value.

Mate (Paraguay Tea).

This article, as an object of exportation, is exclusive to the southern provinces of Rio Grande, Santa Catharina and Paraná.

The wild produce is still availed of, some attempts have, however, been carried on for its cultivation. From the good methods employed, it will result an increase in the production and, of course, great advantages to the country, attending to the therapeutical and alimentitious uses of the plant.

The exportation was as follows:

	QUANTITY	VALUE
1860—1861. . . .	6,803,056 kilgr.	£ 142,975
1871—1872. . .	9,507,086 »	» 227,581
Increase.	2,704,030 »	£ 84,606

The increase was, as to quantity, of 39,7 %, and as to the value of 59,1 %. The annual average is with regard to quantity 3,6 %, and to the value 5,4 %.

Cacáo.

It is likewise from the valleys of the Amazonas and the Tocantins that proceeds most of the cacao, exported from Brazil. Its culture is greatly increasing in the provinces of Bahia and Ceará.

Next to the gum elastic this is the article, that yields more profits to the producer.

It grows up abundantly and spontaneously in the forests of the Amazonas, being chiefly cultivated in the province of Pará; but it yields well throughout the country, extending southwards as far as Rio de Janeiro.

The exports were as follows:

	QUANTITY		VALUE
1860—1861 . . .	3,481,324 kilogr.	£	147,671
1871—1872 . . .	3,181,471 »	»	150,929
Difference	299,853 »	£	3,237

There was a fall, in the quantity, of 8,6 %, and a rise of 2,2 % in the value, or 0,8 % to 0,2 % in a year.

Rum.

After the financial year of 1860—61, in which the official value attained £ 59,744 and the quantity 3,599,636 litr, the exports of this article, which may take a great development, increased considerably, its value rising up in the year 1871—72 to £ 124,336, and the quantity to 5,652,908 litr., as it is shown in the following table:

	QUANTITY		VALUE
1860—1861	3,599,636 litr.	£	59,744
1871—1872 . . .	5,652,908 »	»	124,336
Increase	2,053,272 »	»	64,591

The increase was 57 % in the quantity, and 108,1 % in the value, the annual proportion of the former being 5,2 %, and of the latter 9,8 %.

Manioc flour.

When the alimentitious uses of this article be better known and valued, its exportation is likely to increase.

During the financial year of 1860 to 1861 were exported 3,269,963 litres, officially estimated at £ 10,283. Since that time the foreign consumption of this staple has rapidly increased.

The following comparative table of the year referred to, and that of 1871—1872 shows out the total augment.

	QUANTITY.	VALUE.
1860—1861. . . .	3,269,963 litr.	£ 10,284
1871—1872. . . .	7,087,620 »	» 35,813
Increase.	3,817,657 litr.	£ 25,529

The increase is correspondent to the total percentage of 116,7 % and of 10,6 % annually, with regard to quantity, or 248,3 % and 22,6 % annually, with regard to the value.

Jacarandá (Rosewood.)

In the last financial year the official value of its exports was £ 105,100.

The richest forests containing this wood, are to be found in the provinces of Rio Grande do Norte, Pernambuco, Alagôas, Espirito-Santo, Rio de Janeiro and Minas Geraes, from which it is exported by the rive. Mucury and the ports of Bahia.

Hairs and wool of animals.

In the export tables of 1860—1861 these articles are represented, in the official statistics, by the quantity of 370,012 kilogr., and the value of £ 25.794; in the year 1871—1872, however, the quantity exported was 543,387 kilogr., with the value of £ 42,893, as it is seen in the table at foot.

	QUANTITY.	VALUE.
1860—1861. . . .	370,012 kilogr.	£ 25,794
1871—1872. . . .	543,387 »	» 42,893
Increase.	173,375 kilogr.	£ 17,098

The increase was 46,8 %. in the quantity, and 66,2 %. in the value; or annually 4,3 %. to the former, and 6 %. to the latter.

Gold and diamonds.

There was a fall in the exportation of those articles, the value of which in 1860—61 was £ 540,159. In the year 1871—72 it fell to £ 301,054: this fall is explained by the discovery of more abundant diamond mines, in other countries.

Sundry articles.

The exportation of other articles not referred to, in this work, amounted in value to £ 389,394.

The production of cotton was that which had the greatest increment within the period of the last ten years, compared to that of tobacco, rum, sugar, caoutchouc, hides, coffee, and maté.

The cacao fell down in quantity, but rose in value. The exportation of the latter article is liable to many changes, because of the overflowings of the Amazonas, which very often destroy the crops.

Exchanges.

In virtue of a regulation, sanctioned by the government, the merchants of Rio de Janeiro, who constitute the commercial association, elect every two years a committee composed of 15 members of different nationalities, to whom it pertains: 1st to deliberate on all matters which concern commerce generally; 2d to make the necessary representations to the powers of State and to the authorities, either in behalf of themselves or of other merchants.

The directory or committee of the Exchange, that was elected for the years 1872 and 1873, is composed of 3 Brazilian, 2 Portuguese, 2 English, 2 French, 1 German, 1 Danish, 1 Spanish, 2 North–American and 1 Argentine members.

From amongst the members of the directory is chosen the respective president as well as a committee of three members, who are the arbitrators on commercial and industrial questions, when consulted.

The Exchange is maintained at the expenses of a great many subscribers, who have free entrances and seats in it, and enjoy many other immunities. The number of the subscribers is actually 951.

In 1872 they had a capital of £ 6.835 ; their income was in the same year £ 5,283, and the expenditure £ 3,677.

The commercial association acknowledging that the respective edifice was not capacious enough, has lastly resolved to build another on the same place, with larger and more commodious proportions, by means of subscriptions amongst the merchants. The plan of the new building is drawn according to the architectonical rules, and it shall be one of the most important in the Empire.

In the newly projected palace, the commercial board intends, according to an agreement made with the government, to let rooms for the sitting of Banks, and other anonymous banking companies, and also for the instalment of the Post-Office and the Sinking-fund Department, which are at present standing near it, and which by their intimate connexion with trade, must be kept in the centre of the commercial movement.

The above said plan being led to execution, a third part
of the edifice will be left to the disposal of the government, the other two parts being occupied by the Exchange and counting houses.

The new building shall measure 4,554 square meters,
in surface, and be bounded by 4 commercial streets: a
space actually occupied by 34 houses, the dispossessing
of which was declared to be of public utility.

There are likewise similar committees in the capitals
of the Provinces of Pará, Ceará, Pernambuco, Bahia and
S. Pedro do Rio Grande do Sul, appointed to the same
purposes; but the number of the members is less.

In 1872 the commercial court of the capital registered
8 commercial firms, and 154 merchants; of which 76
are Brazilians and 78 foreigners.

Since the Commercial Code has been put into execution,
in 1851, till the 31st last December, 443 social firms and
2,928 merchants were registered, of which 1,372 are Brazilians and 1,556 foreigners.

During the same year the commercial court of Bahia
registered 60 merchants: 39 Brazilians and 21 foreigners.

That of Pernambuco 13 merchants: 7 Brazilian and 6
foreigners.

That of Maranhão 18 merchants: 6 Brazilians and 12
foreigners.

The commercial committee of Rio de Janeiro grants
pensions, deduced from their receipts and capital fund,
to their associates or to the widows and orphans of the
latter, when they fall into poverty.

The pensions, which are regulated according to the
number of successive annuities paid by the aforesaid
associates, vary from £ 36 to £ 84 a year, for the

associates, and from £ 24 to £ 72, for their widows and orphans.

The committee actually spends £ 588 with those allowances.

Banking Institutions.

In the Capital of the Empire.

BANK OF BRAZIL.—Founded in 1853 with a capital of £ 3,000,000, divided into shares of £ 20 each, this bank of deposits and circulation acquired by the desisting of the Banks Commercial e Agricola and Rural e Hypothecario, the exclusive right of emitting bank-notes, raising up, on this account, its fund to £ 3,300,000, and the number of the shares to 165,000.

Deprived of the right of emission in 1866, after the commercial crisis of 1864, it was compelled to reduce its circulation, recoiling its notes for a sum of, at least, 5 % of the emission, every year; and within the period of 20 years.

The law of 1867 that determined so, created in the said establishment a Mortgage Cash, for the purpose of coming to the assistance of husbandry, and on that account organized it, so as to enable it for performing such operations.

Till last June, its circulating notes had been reduced from £ 4,560,000 to £ 3,192,000.

It exists only one of the branches once founded in several provinces, namely, that of S. Paulo. The others have been dissolved.

RURAL AND HYPOTHECARY BANK. — Founded in 1853 with the purpose of making loans on mortgages of rural and land property, with a capital of £ 800,000, the latter was raised up to the double when, in 1858, it became a bank of circulation, of which advantage, as it was already said, it desisted in behalf of the Bank of Brazil.

Thus becoming a simple bank of deposits and discounts, only 50 % of its social fund has been realized to the present time.

To the board of directors is entrusted the administration of the Life-Insurance company called « Protectora das Familias » (Aid to Families).

COMMERCIAL OF RIO DE JANEIRO BANK.— It was created, in 1866, for deposits and discounts, with a capital of £ 1,200,000, in shares of £ 20 each, being half of them already emitted, and scarcely the amount of £ 1,800,000 paid up. Lastly this bank demanded to be allowed to make loans on mortgages.

NATIONAL BANK. —Destined as the preceding one, to be a bank of deposits and discounts, its operations began, in 1871, with the capital of £ 1,000,000 divided into 50.000 shares, already emitted. The stock realized is £ 200,000.

INDUSTRIAL AND MERCANTILE BANK.—The capital with which it began its operations in 1872, is of £ 2,000,000, distributed into shares to be emitted in 2 series of 50,000 each.

Of the first series scarcely a sum of £ 250,000 has been realized.

It will also comprehend in its transactions the operations of hypothecary credit.

ECONOMICAL AND HELPING ASSOCIATION. — Its statutes being approved by the government in 1872, it has realized a capital of £ 50,535 for account of £ 200,000, its nominal fund, of which only 7,040 shares of £ 10 have been emitted.

ENGLISH BANK OF RIO DE JANEIRO.— Formerly called— London & Portuguese Bank— it has got branches in the cities of Santos and Recife, and a capital of £ 1,000,000, divided into 50,000 shares.

NEW LONDON & BRAZILIAN BANK.—In 1862, under the title of London and Brazilian Bank, it began its operations, being destined for deposits and discounts, with a nominal capital of £ 1,000,000, raised up to £ 1,500,000 in 1863, divided into shares of £ 100 each. Its realized fund is £ 520,000

BANQUE BRÉSILIENNE-FRANÇAISE.— It was authorized, in 1872, to make operations of credit in the Empire, its capital being 10,000,000 francs, divided into 20,000 shares. Half of its capital is realized.

SAVINGS BANK AND MOUNT OF PIETY (LOMBARD HOUSE). —These institutions have been created by the government, in 1861.

The former receives, under a guarantee of the government, sums not exceeding £ 5 every week, and the maximum £ 400 of each person, at an interest of 5 % a year. If the amount entered goes above £ 400, the excess will not perceive any interest at all.

The interests are, every 6 months, added to the capital, though it be not required by the depositors. The capital and interests may be retired, after a previous advertisement of 8 days.

The latter, called Mount of Piety, lends on the pledging of precious objects.

A moderate interest is paid when the term of the debt expires, according to the borrower's will, who can renew the transaction after having paid the interests due. It is but when the 2nd term is over, that the object given on pledge is put to auction, in order to defray the debt, and when there is any balance in favour of the borrower, it is deposited to be delivered to him within the term of five years, after which he loses all claims to it.

HOUSE-BUILDING COMPANY.—Established since 1871 for the purpose of purchasing and building houses, and forwarding the required amounts on mortgage, in 1873 it obtained the permission to act as an establishment of real credit. Of the capital of £ 400,000 divided into 10,000 shares, £ 31,535 have been paid up. Actually it is called «House-Building Bank. »

BANK OF TERRITORIAL CREDIT.—Destined to operations of credit; its encorporation was authorized, with a capital of £ 2,000,000, in shares of £ 20 each.

MORTGAGE BANK.—Its encorporation was permitted just with the same capital and conditions, as the preceding one.

THE POPULAR FLUMINENSE.— Established in 1871 as a branch of the «Popular Argentina» of Buenos-Ayres, it was, in 1872, authorized to exist by itself, after obtaining the concession granted to this company of mutual assistance. Its statutes have been lately altered.

BANK MAUÁ & Cº. — Founded in 1853 by a joint stock-company, with a capital of £ 2,000,000, of which £ 1,000,000 only have been realized: it possesses 7 branches in the Empire of Brazil, 1 in London, and 6 in the River Plate. It makes discounts and other banking operations between Rio de Janeiro, Europe and South America.

In the Provinces.

The banks of Bahia and Maranhão are the only banks of circulation now existing in the provinces. They both continue to reduce annually the circulation of their bank-notes.

BANK OF BAHIA.—It has a capital of £ 400,000 or 50 °/₀ of its authorized stock. In January 1872 its emission amounted to £ 157,397.

The balance of cash existing was £ 41,316.

BANK OF MARANHÃO.—It was established, in 1857, with the capital of £ 100,000 in 10,000 shares, and with the right of issuing notes to the bearer, suffering an annual sinking of 6 °/₀, whilst they be not paid in gold. The said fund was elevated, in 1871, to £ 300,000, a third of which is applied to mortgages; and of the 30,000 shares into which it is divided, 13,100 were already paid up.

COMMERCIAL BANK OF PARÁ.—Founded in 1869 with a capital, already paid up, of £ 100,000, in shares of £ 10, it is a deposit and discount Bank.

COMMERCIAL BANK OF MARANHÃO.—Of the 20,000 shares of £ 10 each, into which its fund is distributed, it has issued 15,000, which are already paid up. It exists, since 1869, as a bank for loans, deposits and discounts.

£ 121,000 of its capital are already paid up.

COMMERCIAL BANK OF ALAGÔAS.—It is also for loans, deposits and discounts, and exists since 1861, with a capital of £ 50,000 in £ 10 shares.

MERCANTILE BANK OF BAHIA.— It was called « Mercantile Reserve Bank », when it began its operations in 1859; in 1872 it changed to the present denomination.

The capital-fund is £ 400,000 divided into 40,000 shares already paid up.

SAVINGS BANK OF BAHIA (*Caixa de Economias*). — According to its statutes, approved in 1860, its fund cannot rise above £ 300,000, in shares of 2 sh. each.

SAVINGS BANK OF BAHIA (*Caixa Economica*). — Founded with a capital of £ 600,000 divided into shares of 6 sh. each, of which only the sum of £ 382,412 was paid up in May 1873.

COMMERCIAL SOCIETY OF BAHIA. — It exists since 1848, with a nominal capital of £ 800,000, and a real one of £ 559,410.

HYPOTHECARY BANK OF BAHIA. — Formerly called « Caixa União Commercial. » Of a capital of £ 120,000 divided into shares of £ 10 each, only £ 35,620 have been paid up.

BANK OF CAMPOS. — It was authorized, in 1863, and has realized £ 50,000 of its capital which is, in the whole, £ 100,000 divided into shares of £ 20 each, already issued out.

COMMERCIAL AND HYPOTHECARY BANK OF CAMPOS. — Its existence dates from 1872. Its capital being £ 100,000 in shares of £ 20 each, scarcely £ 15,820 are paid up to the present time.

MERCANTILE BANK OF SANTOS. — Founded in 1872, with a capital of £ 400,000, in shares of £ 20 each, which have been issued in two series. Only 10,000 shares have been distributed, and £ 50,000 paid up.

AGRICULTURAL AND COMMERCIAL BANK OF CAMPOS. — For deposits and discounts. It began its operations, in 1872, with a capital of £ 200,000 distributed, into shares of £ 20 each.

BANK OF RIO GRANDE DO SUL.—Founded in 1857, as an issuing bank, it desisted of this privilege, limiting its operations to discounts and deposits.

BANK CONFIANÇA DO RIO GRANDE DO SUL.—Its operations on deposits and discounts began since July 1869, with a capital of £ 150,000, divided into 7,500 shares.

There also exists a commercial bank at Campos, and another at Santos, both founded in 1857.

The Banks Rural and Hypothecary, Commercial, National, Industrial and Mercantile, created in the municipality of the Capital, and in that of Campos, in the province of Rio de Janeiro, summing up a realized capital of £ 1,500,000, employed an amount of £ 4,033,432, on loans to merchants and industrials, represented by discounts and cautioned bills, current accounts, with and without interests, and mortgages.

In order to be enabled to effect such important transactions, this capital was reforced with the product of deposits belonging to private parties.

The total amount of the deposits raised up to £ 4,174,211

They all obtained considerable benefits.

Insurance and other Anonymous Companies.

At Rio de Janeiro, there are 10 national companies for maritime and terrestrial insurances against fire, on life, on inheritances, on furniture and other objects. Some of them are of mutual assistance, and they all represent a capital, partly paid up, of nearly £ 4,600,000 : there are also several agencies of foreign insurance companies.

There exist several companies and agencies of the same description, in the capitals of the principal provinces.

At Bahia there are 3 insurance companies and 7 agencies.

Numerous are the Anonymous Companies, now existing in the capital of the Empire, viz: 9 first class banks, with a fund of £ 12,100,000 ;—16 street rail-way Companies either organised or duly authorized, the former possessing a capital superior to £ 1,900,000 ; — 6 rail-road Companies with a capital of £ 1,800,000 ; — 10 steam-navigation Companies including 4 of ferry-boats, employed in their traffic within the bay, all of them representing a stock superior to £ 1,000,000 ; — 2 of highways with a capital of £ 348,000 ;— 3 Gas Lighting Companies with a capital of £ 700,000; and 24, for different purposes, with a capital superior to £ 3,100,000.

Some of them, having their head-offices in the Capital, are established to carry on important undertakings out of the Empire, as for instance, the Brussels, Lisbon, Montevideo street rail-way Companies ; or in the Provinces, such as the Paulista and Sorocabana rail-road Company, the Santos street-railway Company, and likewise those of the Capitals of S. Paulo, Rio de Janeiro, Ceará, Maranhão, S. Pedro do Rio Grande do Sul and several others.

The chief towns of the provinces also possess some anonymous, industrial, mercantile Companies.

Docks.

Since the law of 1871, by which the government was authorized to grant some favours to such companies as would undertake the construction of docks, and other improvements, in the commercial ports, on the coast of Brazil, the construction of the following docks has been contracted :

That of D. Pedro II, in the inlets of Saude and Gambôa, in the harbour of Rio de Janeiro. The respective company, created with a capital-fund of £ 1,000,000 has already begun their important works.

That of Maranhão, in the harbour of S. Luiz do Maranhão.

That of Bahia, in the port of the city of S. Salvador. An english company has been raised to carry on this work, its capital being £ 90,000.

That of Santos, in the harbour of the same name, in the province of S. Paulo. The grantees sent an English engineer, whose opinion is respected in those matters, to rectify the studies already made.

Those of Imbitiba and Concha, in the municipality of Macahé, and that of Grajahù, in the municipality of Campos, all of them in the province of Rio.

That of Paranaguá, in the port of the same name, in the province of Paraná.

Weights and measures.

Since the first of January 1874, the law of which the object is to render the weights and measures uniform throughout the Empire, by the adoption of the french metrical system, will be put into execution.

The government has issued several ordinances for its execution; it has acquired models of the metrical system duly stamped, and has entrusted competent parties with the conversion to this system of the weights and measures now in use in the Empire.

Metrological system of the Empire of Brazil used in commercial transactions. compared with the french metrical system.

EXCHANGE AT PAR.

1$000 rs. in Brazil = 27 pence sterling=2 francs 84 cent.

BRAZIL.   FRANCE.

MEASURES OF SPECIFIC QUANTITY.

Grain	Equal to	4,981 Centigrams
Drachm, equal to 72 grains . .	Equal to	3,586 Grams.
Ounce, equal to 8 drachms. .	Equal to	28,691 Grams.
Mark, equal to 8 ounces. . .	Equal to	229,526 Grams.
Arratel (pound)	Equal to	459,053 Grams.
Arroba equal to 32 pounds . .	Equal to	14,690 Kilograms.
Quintal (Cwt) equal to 4 arrobas.	Equal to	58,759 Kilograms.
Ton equal to 54 arrobas . . .	Equal to	703,243 Kilograms.

MEASURES OF CAPACITY.

DRY.

Selamin	Equal to	1,136 Liters
Maquia, equal to 2 selamins .	Equal to	2,273 Liters
Quart, equal to 4 maquias . .	Equal to	9,091 Liters
Bushel, equal to 4 quarts . .	Equal to	36,334 Liters
Moio equal to 60 bushels . .	Equal to	21,818 Hectoliters

LIQUID.

Quartilho or pint	Equal to	0,667 Liters
Canada, equal to 4 quartilhos.	Equal to	2,667 Liters
Almude. equal to 12 canadas. .	Equal to	16,000 Liters
Pipe, equal to 25 almudes . .	Equal to	1,007 Hectoliters
Ton, equal to 50 almudes . .	Equal to	8,000 Hectoliters

MEASURES OF LENGTH.

LINEAL.

Line	Equal to	0,00229 Meters
Inch, equal to 12 lines . . .	Equal to	0,0275 Meters
Palm, equal to 8 inches. . .	Equal to	0,22 Meters
Ell, equal to 5 palms. . . .	Equal to	1,1 Meters
Fathom, equal to 2 ells. . .	Equal to	2,2 Meters
Mile, equal to 843 fathoms . .	Equal to	1.854,625 Meters
League, equal to 2,529 fathoms (20 degree each)	Equal to	5.563,875 Meters

Table showing the relations of the measures of length of Brazil and England with the corresponding ones in the metrical system.

UNITIES.	BRAZIL.				ENGLAND.					
	Inches into centimeters.	Fathoms into meters.	Centimeters into inches.	Meters into fathoms.	Inches into centimeters.	Feet into meters.	Miles into kilometers.	Centimeters into inches.	Meters into feet.	Kilometers into miles.
1	2,75	2,2	0,3936	0,4545	2,54	0,305	1,609	0,3937	3,281	0,622
2	5,50	4,4	0,7273	0,9091	5,08	0,610	3,219	0,7874	6,562	1,243
3	8,25	6,6	1,0909	1,3636	7,62	0,914	4,828	1,1811	9,843	1,865
4	11,0	8,8	1,4545	1,8182	10,16	1,219	4,437	1,5748	13,123	2,487
5	13,75	11,0	1,8182	2,2727	12,70	1,524	8,047	1,9685	16,404	3,100
6	16,50	13,2	2,1818	2,7273	15,24	1,829	9,656	2,3622	19,685	3,730
7	19,25	15,4	2,5455	3,1818	17,78	2,134	11,265	2,7559	22,966	4,351
8	22,00	17,6	2,9091	3,6364	20,32	2,438	12,875	3,1496	26,247	4,973
9	....	19,8	3,2727	4,0909	22,86	2,743	14,484	3,5433	29,528	5,595
10	....	22,0	3,6364	4,5455	25,40	3,048	16,093	3,9370	32,808	6,216

BRAZIL

Fathom.	= 10 palm.	= 2,2	meters.
Palm.	= 8 poll.	= 0,22	»
Inch.	= 12 linh.	= 0,0275	»
Line.	= 12 point.	= 0,00229	»
Ell.	= 5 palm.	= 1,1	»
Cubit.	= 24 3/4 poll.	= 0,68	»

ENGLAND

League bas	= 3 miles.		
Mile	= 1,700 yards.	= 1608,640	meters.
Yard	= 3 feet	= 0,914	»
Foot	= 12 inches	= 0,3048	»
Fathom	= 2 yards	= 1,829	»
Cubit.	= 1 1/2 foot	= 0,4572	»

To convert 247 fathoms, 3 palms and 6 inches into meters.

200	fathoms =	440	meters.
40	» =	88	»
7	» =	15,4	»
247	»	543,4	»
3	palms =	0,66	»
6	inches =	0,165	»
Total		544,225	

To convert 164,6 meters into english measures of length.

100	meters =	328 08	feet.
60	» =	196,85	»
4	» =	13,12	»
0,6	» =	1,97	»
164,6	» =	540,02	»

Table showing the relations of the weights of Brazil and England with the corresponding ones in the metrical system.

UNITIES.	BRAZIL						ENGLAND.			
	Grains into grams.	Drachms into grams.	Pounds av. du p. into kilograms.	Grams into grains.	Grams into drachms.	Kilograms into pounds av. du p.	Pounds av. du p. into kilograms.	Tons into metrical tons.	Kilograms into pounds av. du p.	Metrical tons into tons.
1	0 0498	3,586	0,459	20,076	0,279	2.178	0,453	1,0157	2,206	0,984
2	0,0996	7,173	0,918	40,153	0,558	4,357	0,907	2,0313	4,411	1,9692
3	0,1494	10,759	1,377	60,229	0,836	6,535	1,360	3,0469	6,617	2,9538
4	0,1992	11,315	1,836	80,305	1,115	8,714	1,814	4,0626	8,822	3,9384
5	0,2191	17,932	2,295	100,381	1,394	10,892	2,267	5,0782	11,028	4,9234
6	0,2989	21,518	2,754	120,458	1,673	13,070	2,720	6,0939	13,233	5,9075
7	0,3487	25,104	3,213	140,534	1,952	15,249	3,174	7,1095	15,439	6,8921
8	0,3985	28,691	3,672	160,610	2,231	17,427	3,627	8,1252	17,644	7,8767
9	0,4483	32,277	4,131	180,687	2,509	19,606	4,081	9,1408	19,850	8,8613
10	0,4981	35,863	4,591	200,763	2,788	21,784	4,534	10,1565	22,056	9,8459

Brazil
Pound av du p.=	2 marcs	= 459,053 gram.
Mark	= 8 ounces	= 229,526 »
Ounce	= 8 drachms	= 28,691 »
Drachm	= 72 grains	= 3,586 »
Ton	= 13 ½ cwt	= 793,24 kilog.
Cwt	= 4 arrobas	= 58,76 »
Arroba	= 32 pounds	= 14,69 »

England
Pound av. d. p.	= 16 ounc	= 453,4 gram.
Ounc	= 16 drachm	= 28,3 »
Drachm		= 1,77
Ton	= 20 quint.	= 1015,65 kilgr.
Cwt		= 50,78

Suppose 3 pounds, 2 ounc., 8 drachms to be converted into metrical weights

$$3 \text{ pounds} = 1,377 \text{ kilogr.}$$
$$2 \text{ oz} = 2 \times 0,02869 = 0,057 \text{ »}$$
$$5 \text{ drachm} = 0,018 \text{ »}$$
$$\text{TOTAL } \overline{1,452} \text{ »}$$

To convert 245 kilograms into english weights.

$$200 \text{ k.} = 441,1 \text{ pounds av. d. p.}$$
$$40 \text{ k.} = 82,2 \text{ » av. d. p.}$$
$$5 \text{ k.} = 11,1 \text{ » av d. p.}$$
$$\overline{245} \text{ k.} = \overline{540,3} \mid \frac{112}{4}$$
$$92,3 \mid \frac{14}{6}$$
$$8,3$$

or 4 cwt, 6 stones and 8,3 pounds.

Table of the measures and weights of Brazil and their corresponding values in the metrical system.

NAMES OF THE MEASURES.	VALUES.	METRICAL SYSTEM.
Itinerary measures.		
League of sesmaria	3,000 fathoms	6,600 meters.
» of 18 each degree	2,810 »	6,182 »
» of 20 »	2,529 »	5,564 »
» of 25 »	2,023 »	4,451 »
Of length.		
Fathom	2 ells = 10 palms	2,2 meters.
Geometrical step	5 feet = 7 1/2 palms	1,65 »
Foot	12 inches = 1 1/2 palm	0,33 »
Palm	8 inches	22 centimeters.
Inch	12 lines	2,75 »
Line	12 points	0,229 »
Point		0,191 millimeters.
Agrarian measures.		
Alqueire of Minas–Geraes.	10,000 square fathoms	484 ares =48,400 square meters.
» of Rio-de-Janeiro	10,000 » »	484 ares = 48,400 square meters.
» of S. Paulo	5,000 » »	242 ares=24,200 square meters.
Small measures of surface.		
Square fathom	100 square palms	4,84 square meters.
Square foot	2 1/4 » » = 144 square inches	0,1089 » »
Square palm	64 square inches	484 square centimeters.
Square inch	144 square lines	7,56 square centimeters.
Of volume.		
Cubic fathom	1,000 cubic palms	10,648 cubic meters.
Cubic foot	3,375 » » =1728 cubic inches	0,03594 of the cubic meter.
Cubic palm	512 cubic inches	10,848 cubic centimeter.
Cubic inch	1,728 cubic line	20,797 » »
Dry.		
Moio	60 alqueires	2181,8 liters.
Alqueire or bushel	4 quart	36,36 »
Quart		9,09 »
Selamim	1/4 quart	1,14 »
Liquid.		
Tun	2 pipas	800 liters.
Pipe	25 almudes	400 »
Almude	6 canadas	16 »
Canada or medida	4 pints	2,667 »
Pint		0,667 »
Weight.		
Ton	13 1/2 quintaes	793,243 kilograms.
Quintal (cwt)	4 arrobas	58,759 »
Arroba	32 pounds	14,690 »
Arratel or pound	2 marks	0,459 »
Mark	8 ounces	229,526 grams.
Ounce	8 drachms	28,691 »
Drachm	3 scruples or 72 grains	3,586 »
Grain		0,0498 »
Pound troy	12 ounces	344,292 »

A metrical ton is equal to 1,000 kilograms and, corresponds to 1,2606 of the brazilian ton.

A metrical league is equal to 4 kilometers, and represents 1,818,2 fathoms.

Agriculture.

The greatest part of the population is employed in agriculture, that constitutes the chief source of national wealth.

Nature seems to have destined Brazil to be one of the most agricultural countries in the world.

Still covered, in its greatest extent, with majestic native forests its soil preserves its primitive luxuriance, which largely and generously repays the toil of man. Wheat and rye that yield in Europe 20 °/, and in Asia 8 to 12 for 1, produce in Brazil 30 to 60 for 1. There are lands, in which 19,36 ares may give any of the following results in the indicated proportions :

Of cotton, 826 to 918 kilograms ; of coffee 688,5 kilograms ; of manioc 3,636 liters ; of maize 1,818 liters.

In general, maize produces 150 for 1, beans 80, rice 1,000 ; and when in the United States an acre of land (36,3 ares) yields 925,5 kilograms of clean cotton, the poor lands of Brazil produce 1,469 kilograms, the better ones 4,407 kilogr., and the best 8,814 kilogr.

The topographical formation, the varied climate, the abundance of water, the almost general and constant strength of the vegetation make its lands adapted, in larger or smaller scale, to the cultivation of all the plants of the globe.

Thus in almost all the southern provinces whilst in some places coffee, sugarcane, cotton and tobacco thrive, as in the most advantageous countries and while tea, cacao, vanilla and all asiatic plants, also flourish, other zones of the same provinces are favourable to the planting of fruit trees, grain, and vegetables of Europe. Indeed, in some provinces they cultivate coffee and sugarcane and plant also with good result, wheat, barley, rye, vineyards, pear, apple and peach-trees.

Many produces of Brazilian agriculture supply already the markets of the northern and southern provinces, as for instance, excellent cheese, butter, bacon, a great variety of fruit, different qualities of potatoes and other bulbous plants.

Even the real potatoe, commonly known by the name of English potatoe, as good as the one imported, is already cultivated in great quantity.

Gardening, properly said, fruit and vegetable culture, have made since some years remarkable progress, in the capital of the Empire, and in those of Bahia, Pernambuco, S. Pedro do Rio Grande do Sul and others, as well as in the colonies.

The same occurs with the acclimatization of exotic plants, of grafting and transplantation.

The advantages of the culture of the coffee-tree are obvious to all in the Empire, having even only a slight knowledge of the results obtained by it. One hectare may contain 918 coffee-trees, which, on inferior lands, produce 674 kilograms; on those of second quality, 1,384 kilograms; and on the best lands 2,022 kilograms. An active man, working regularly, can take care of 2 hectares planted with coffee, his annual income being therefore in the first case £ 36,7 sh., in the second £ 74, 15 sh, and in the third £ 109, 2 sh, calculating at the lowest price of 270 réis a kilogram. On a regular coffee farm the average production per head, including women, children, and old people, is £ 60,000.

Nearly the whole Brazilian soil, from the Amazonas

down to S. Paulo, is perfectly fitted to the culture of sugarcane, offering real advantages ; but in the provinces of Pernambuco, Bahia and Rio de Janeiro it is cultivated on the largest scale.

Many of its varieties are acclimated, and the Imperial Agricultural Institute of Rio carefully cultivates, on the normal farm, which it created, 17 varieties of it, viz: the green one from Penang or Solangor, rose, violet, cayenne, red of two qualities, cayenne rose, S. Julião, black, creole, iron, soft, 'striped with green and black, green and red, green and yellow or imperial, Egyptian, yellow and red, ubá indigenous, ubá improved.

Of these varieties the same Institute is used to distribute annually a great quantity of specimens amongst the planters.

The great agriculture prefers the Otahiti cane to the green Penang, and to the violet of Batavia ; because the former, planted in lands fertile and rich of calx, produces more abundantly. In some agricultural districts, however, the Otahiti cane, on account of different diseases, that attacked it, was substituted by the violet.

Even in silicious lands, less adapted to culture, the cultivation of sugar cane is remunerating; whereas, if the plant does not develop itself so much, it furnishes in return a juice of 12 to 14 degrees Baumé and a much purer one. In the new lands, in which scarcely some correctives such as lime and marl are used, one can gather in 1 hectare of plantation, 100 to 120,000 kilograms, at the end of 15 months, with the addition, that the labour for its plantation and tillage benefits the vegetables, that may be planted in the same ground.

An active workman, making use of the cultivator, may

take care of 2 hectares planted with sugar cane, and will gain at least annually £ 60,10 sh. deducting half the value of the sugar for the expenses of manufacturing.

The expenses with the culture of sugar cane, in Rio de Janeiro, where wages are high, regulate £ 13 for each hectare, including the interest of 8 °/o of the sums employed.

The product, however, amounting to £ 70, in 1 hectare, the liquid profit will be £ 57. This result is greater yet, when after preparing the ground, the plough may be used. In the manufactory of sugar, excellent results have been obtained by the use of steam to boil the sirups in low temperature, and of the turbines for the forced clarification of the crystallized masses.

Excellent results have also been obtained in the culture of the cotton-tree, that interests the small farmers; chiefly because it does not require investment of capital with machines and engines. Its production has much increased, thanks to the remunerating price, which it obtains at present in the markets, and the facility of transport, which our railways offer.

It is to presume, that it will develop itself still more, as soon as our lines of rail-ways are prolonged in the direction of the central points.

In 1 hectare there is space for 4,545 cotton-trees, that give 2,160 kilograms of cotton in pod, according to the quality of the ground. A workman takes easily care of 3 hectares planted with cotton and grains; he has, therefore, an annual income of £ 81, supposing at the rate of 125 réis a kilogram, the regular price, in the interior of the country.

The culture of the vine is another new branch of agricultural industry, that promises to develop itself in a larger scale, and shows itself already in animating conditions in the provinces of S. Paulo, and S. Pedro do Rio Grande do Sul.

It has also been tried in the district of Nova-Friburgo, in the province of Rio de Janeiro, and in some districts of the South of Minas Geraes.

The number of American and European varieties of the *vitis vinifera*, acclimated in S. Paulo, is very great. It is calculated at 320,000 liters, the wine made there last year, sold at £ 13 to £ 40, and it was observed in many places that 1,000 vines might produce 4,000 liters.

In the province of S. Pedro do Rio Grande do Sul, only on the Island of the Marinheiros and in the colonies, 400,000 liters were annually made, using in preference the American grape. Though this produce cannot as yet be considered of first quality, it is however, all consumed in the provinces, that make it, and in view of its purity compared to many of the imported wines, it is much sought for. Persevering endeavours are made, principally in the district of the capital of S. Paulo, in order to improve it, by introducing new specimens of vines, and bettering the process of its manufactory.

Another branch of export, whereof may result advantages, superior yet to its consume in the Empire, is the *tapioca*, already known and appreciated in Europe.

Up to this time it has been exported thither, especially from the provinces of Maranhão and Pará. Provenient from the roots of the manioc (*Manhiot utilissima*, family of the *euphorbiacea*, of which there are 30 varieties in Brazil, it consists in the pulverized matter, that is deposited, when the mass of these roots, grated or smashed, is left some time in water.

The manioc produces well in almost all lands of the temperate intertropical regions, with preference, however, in the dry and loose, and especially sandy lands.

It is one of those cultures that, comparatively, require the least attention of the farmer. From it excellent flour (farinha) is extracted, that serves to auxiliate the food in almost all provinces, and also starch, *carimã*, and other masses of extensive and varied use.

The tapioca is prepared with much facility and even if there were in its actual price a fall of 50 °/₀, it would still give a considerable gain, provided it be prepared carefully.

It suffices, in order to acknowledge it, to consider that 220 square meters, of good ground, planted with sugar-cane, produce as a rule, 4,690 kilograms of sugar that are sold at £ 300, whereas it is demonstrated by the experiments of an intelligent farmer from the district of Campos, in the province of Rio de Janeiro, that in an equal space of ground, even of inferior quality, 40,000 plants of manioc produce regularly, 36,720 kilograms of tapioca. At the lowest price of 60 réis a pound, 0,459 kilograms will give £ 480.

Besides this advantage the manioc has yet that of not requiring, in its culture, so much care and lands so fertile, nor the making of the tapioca so costly machines, and agricultural apparatus, as the other plants, with which it has been compared.

One may add in its favour other reasons for preference, as for instance its serving for the food of man, and various and important applications, and its fibres and roots being, independently of any preparation, used as nourishment for domestic animals.

The culture and preparation of coffee, sugar, cotton and tobacco has improved considerably by the introduction of important machines, and application of perfected processes.

As to coffee, the principal article of national production, it can be assured, that no country produces so much, or of better quality.

The first of these truths is generally acknowledged ; the other will be so by unprejudiced minds, that give themselves the trouble to examine it.

For the progress of the culture of our first articles, the agricultural societies, established in the capital and in some provinces, have greatly contributed, and the individual interest, awaked by the example and experience of the most intelligent husbandmen and farmers. Rivaling with those societies, agricultural institutes, created by the government and with] sufficient property, are destined to promote by themselves and by means of municipal commissions, the development of agriculture.

This, together with the construction of new roads, the improvement of those existing, the greatest amplitude, that is always given to the coast and river navigation, the professional instruction, for which attempts are made in the city of Rio de Janeiro and in different provinces, and the introduction of moralize l and industrious colonists, which the authorities of the State incessantly promote, will, doubtless, cause the best distribution of rural property, and set it on other basis, thus elevating agriculture in Brazil to the state of perfection, to which it is entitled.

For this purpose will also concur with valuable aid

the national and international exhibitions, and above all
the partial ones, that the agricultural institutes aided by
the government, are to inaugurate in certain periods,
for determined agricultural produces, and in which there
will be prizes awarded to the planters, that distinguish
themselves most in these contests of intelligent labour.

A proposal of the Imperial Agricultural Institute of Rio
about these expositions in the capital, is actua'ly submitted
to the examination of the government.

Agricultural Institutes.

Agricultural Institutes have been created in the capital
of the Empire and in the provinces of Bahia, Pernambuco, S. Pedro do Rio Grande do Sul and Sergipe.

The three first have already commenced their task,
the Imperial Institute of Rio being under the inspection
of the Minister and Secretary of State for the Affairs of
Agriculture, and the others under that of the presidents
of the respective provinces.

IMPERIAL AGRICULTURAL INSTITUTE OF RIO.—This one is
charged to maintain and improve the Botanical Garden
of Lagôa de Rodrigo de Freitas, and receives for this
purpose from the government an annual contribution of
£ 240.

It possesses a stock of more than £ 30,000.

To its foundation its members contributed with different offers, and the Chief of the State with the sum
£ 10,800 from his civil list. The sessions of the Institute
have almost always been honoured with the August presence of His Majesty the Emperor.

Close by the Botanical Garden the Institute founded a

normal farm, that dates of a few years, but where are already found those workshops, of which agriculture stands most in need, and carts for the service of the farm are made, as also engines and agricultural instruments adapted to the nature of the soil of Brazil, which are also sold to the farmers and husbandmen for prices inferior to those imported.

Here are nurseries of thousands of indigenous and exotic plants, and improved culture of many, the produces of which constitute the principal national exportation, or are most generally used by the population.

It contains 17 varieties of sugarcane, 27 kinds of manioc, many of aipim, tobacco Djebel, Havanna and other procedencies, cotton of the most appreciated qualities and a great number both of fructiferous plants and of simple ornament.

It possesses also a chimical laboratory conveniently organized, where lands and rural produces are often analyzed.

The Institute founded also a hat manufactory imitating those of Chile, some of which so beautifully made, that they were considered worthy of the Universal Exhibition of Vienna.

The substance employed in the fabrication of these hats, is extracted from the Bombonassa straw, a plant brought out some years ago, from Peru and cultivated in great quantity in the normal farm.

To this factory, in which poor boys, almost all from the Santa Casa da Misericordia of the city of Rio de Janeiro, serve as apprentices and workmen, there has been just annexed a practical school for teaching, not only the breeding of the silkworm of the Asiatic species

Bombix mori, and of the national one, named *Saturnia*, but also the process of the extraction of the silk.

The Institute created an agricultural asylum on the system of the most modest ones in Switzerland, for indigent boys, that, whilst they apply themselves every day to practical agriculture in its different branches, cultivate their intellects and receive religious education.

This asylum is situated in a vast edifice, containing a closed yard for gymnastical exercises and recreation, a chapel for divine service, school and sleeping rooms, a workroom for rainy days, horse stables, pens and hedges, made according to the rules of art for the animals, that exist here ; ponds for bathing and swimming, agricultural machines and implements, culture grounds, and plantations made by the scholars, the produces of which are already used to assist and vary their alimentation.

The asylum purposes to enable the scholars to be some day excellent overseers or administrators of great rural establishments, and very good auxiliaries of the farmers and cultivators, for the progress and perfection of husbandry.

Of late the Institute proposed the foundation, by means of the aid of the government, of a zoological garden and of a veterinary school, inside the Botanical Garden, and to take gratuitously charge of the superintendence of the forest service, at present under the care of the General Inspection of Public Works.

With those measures they have in view the future establishment of practical courses of zoothechnics and sylviculture.

The Institute promotes, besides this, the means to realize, on a large scale, the culture of certain textible plants, lately discovered in the forests of the provinces of Rio de Janeiro and Minas Geraes, which furnish fibres of first quality, the excellence of which was acknowledged in London and Manchester, in the examinations made there by order of the government.

It is already determined that not only the acclimatization and culture of these plants, but also the preparation of the materia prima they furnish, are easy and of little expense.

According to the opinion of the persons charged with the examination in England, those fibres may be worth more than £ 84 per 793,243 kilograms or 11,7 pence 0,459 Kilograms, that is, 9 pence more than flax, and as much or nearly as much as cotton.

The Institute publishes an illustrated review of practical agriculture, that is in the 4th year of its existence, and is assisted by the legislative assembly of the province of Rio de Janeiro.

Imperial agricultural institute of bahia.— Founded in the capital of the province of Bahia, it is about to open a normal course of agriculture, with a boarding school for the scholars that wish to frequent it.

It constructed, at its own expense and aided by the national and provincial treasuries, a vast edifice, especially adapted for that purpose, in which it spent more than £ 25,000.

Agricultural implements bespoken by the Institute have of late arrived from Europe.

It possesses a small library, a laboratory, seeds, some animals and other objects necessary to the wants of agriculture and the industries concerning it.

It has already a small cabinet of physics and chemistry,

an industrial museum, and has already submitted the regulation of the agricultural school to the approbation of the government. The course of agriculture is to be theoretical and practical.

The farm of Lages, where the establishment is situated, has already roads, indispensable for-the traffic, plantation of different kinds of sugarcane, that are distributed amongst the farmers, and a great quantity of cattle in its fields.

IMPERIAL AGRICULTURAL INSTITUTE OF PERNAMBUCO. — The work to its charge has not commenced, since it is yet collecting the necessary elements.

It was endowed by the respective legislative assembly with the sum of £ 10,000 for the purchase of lands, on which a normal farm or model plantation is to be founded.

It is also annually subsidized by the provincial treasury.

In the capital of the province of Pernambuco endeavours have been also made to organize a society for the purpose of promoting the development of agriculture.

Societies of the same description exist in the district of Campos, province of Rio de Janeiro, where a company intends founding engines with the most perfected machinery, exclusively for the making of sugar, in return of a pecuniary compensation from those farmers, who may choose to grind there the sugarcane of their crop. From the good success of this company must result great advantages, proceeding from the separation of the culture of the plant, and the fabrication of the sugar, in behalf both of little husbandry and the improvement of the produce.

In Maranhão and other provinces, agricultural societies and courses are, likewise, about to be organized.

In the district of the Capital, besides the Imperial Institute there is the «Society for the Aid to National Industry» which founded in 1830, has rendered, by means of the greatest perseverance and constant efforts, important services to agriculture and to all branches of National Industry.

Its meetings are frequently honoured by the august presence of the Emperor.

Not only it has introduced many machines and agricultural implements, but it has also been infatigable in promoting, by every means in its power, the development of fabrile industry.

In the «Auxiliador da Industria Nacional», a review, that is published monthly, important articles respecting industry and agriculture, are to be found.

To it is yet due an evening, and an industrial school frequented by numerous pupils.

Very recently a society of acclimatization was founded in the city of Rio de Janeiro, that may also render many services to husbandry.

Its principal object is to acclimate plants and animals, to improve, domesticate, and multiply species, races or varieties of native animals or vegetables, and the useful application of those recently introduced, acclimated or propagated, and of their products.

To accomplish its purpose the society intends founding zoological and botanical gardens of acclimatization, a special library and a scientific review, prizes and exhibitions of the products it may obtain.

Industry.

In Brazil there is a complete liberty of industry, guaranteed by the Constitution, as long as it does not offend the public morals, safety and health. Industry can be exercised either individually or by means of associations.

No law or privilege restrains it, unless in the exceptional cases of an exclusive privilege in favour of invention, or the introduction of a new branch of trade.

Although Brazil is not in reality a manufacturing country, still on this account its different manufactories have none the less increased and extended themselves.

Numerous and important manufactories exist in the capital and in many of the provinces ; some of them are worked by steam and they employ a large number of hands.

Some of them can compete, as to their machinery and products with those of the countries most advanced. The proof of this assertion is found in the large number of manufactured objects sent to the international exhibitions, and there rewarded.

The State has occasionally subsidized some of the most important manufactories and has always assisted them with its protection.

The hands employed in the manufactory of cotton goods are exempt from recruitment, that is up to a certain number set down by the government.

The products of these same manufactories are exempt from all duties in the transport from one province to another, as also from all export duties when shipped to foreign countries.

The machinery or pieces of machinery, imported for the use of manufactories, are generally allowed to pass free of import duty,· by decision of the government.

These favours, however, are only granted for the space of 10 years.

Privileges of invention (patents) cannot be granted by the government for more than 20 years. Beyond this period the concession requires a legislative act.

The government has on some occasions conceded, as a recompense, an exclusive privilege to the introducers of branches of useful and important trades, but this concession requires the approval of the legislative power.

The effects of the patent cease:

When it is proved that the patentee presented false statements or concealed essential points in the explanation or declaration given by him with a view to obtain the patent.

When it is proved to the party stated to be the inventor, that the invention which he has presented as his, has already been the object of a previous decree.

If the patentee has not put his invention in practice within the space of two years from the date of the concession of the patent.

If the inventor has obtained a patent for the same invention in any foreign country.

If the article manufactured has been recognised as prejudicial to the public, or contrary to the laws.

If it be proved that the patentee used his invention previous to the concession of privilege.

The capital of the Empire possesses many manufactories and workshops, which produce and prepare many articles for its consumption, which were formerly imported in a large scale, viz: Laboratories of chemical products, manufactories of optical, nautical, surgical and engineering instruments, of shoes, oil cloths, carpets, Russian and Morocco leathers, of glass, carriages, varnishes, Italian pastes, hanging and writing paper, asphaltum, artificial marble, pasteboard, different kinds of snuffs, of cigars and cigarrettes ; many of them having obtained different prize medals and honourable mentions, that attest the perfection or the excellence of their manufactory.

Amongst these, 17 founderies deserve special mention on account of their improved machinery and the perfection of their products.

Eleven of them, not taking into consideration those belonging to the arsenal and other public establishments, are for iron engine works and casting, and six are for copper, brass and bronze castings; not including in this classification no small number of workshops on a smaller scale.

The former give employment to 700 workmen, and produce in different sorts of iron articles the sum of £ 214,00 .

The total products of the others amounts to £ 32,000.

One of them is at present occupied in forging important pieces of machinery for the hoisting engines, which are to be fixed in the vast iron store-houses of the Custom-house docks of Rio de Janeiro.

All agricultural implements can be manufactured by them, as in general most of them actually are. They are a great improvement on those imported, as they are more adapted to the special circumstances of the grounds, where they are to work at.

There are also many breweries, as well as several soda, tonic, and mineral water manufactories, where a large number of hands are dayly employed. Nearly 400 persons are employed in the former, which produce from 90 to 100 millions of bottles or from 60,030,000 to 66,700,000 liters of beer, per annum; consuming from 6 to 7 thousand barrels of barley, and 20 thousand kilgr. of hops.

There is also a great number of hat manufactories, some of them very important establishments, the products of which are so perfect that, for some years past, they have supplied the market and home consumption so as greatly to supersede the foreign importation of this article.

Twenty three of the most important manufactories of silk, felt, straw, and fancy hats, occupy nearly 500 workmen, independent of steam engines employed by some of them, annually producing in an average term 34,000 silk, 406,000 felt, 30,000 straw and fancy hats, in the value of £ 160,000. In almost all the cities of the Empire there are manufactories of soap, oil and candles, not only stearine, of which there is an important establishment, in Rio de Janeiro, but also common tallow candle; most of the provinces have manufactories of wax candles; at Ceará and the margins of the river S. Francisco there are many of carnauba candles.

In 25 of the principal ones, established in Rio de Janeiro, more than 260 persons are employed, besides some of them using steam engines. They produce an average of 850,000 boxes of candles, with the value of £ 575,000, nearly 430,000 boxes of soap, in the value of £ 170,000, and 412,000 liters of oil, in the value of £ 14,000.

In many of the capitals of the provinces are found

work-shops where watchmakers, saddlers, shoemakers, brass founders, tinmen, tailors, and different other branches of industry, exercise their trade, comprehending in this number a class of men in the provinces of Rio Grande and Paraná, and in some of the municipalities of S. Paulo and Minas Geraes, who work with the greatest artistic taste and delicacy in raw-hides and leather ; gold and silver smiths occupy a proeminent part in that branch of industry for the excellence of their workmanship.

The cotton manufactories of S. Aleixo and Sta Thereza, in the province of Rio de Janeiro, of Todos os Santos, Nossa Senhora do Amparo, S. Antonio dos Queimados, Modelo and Conceição in Bahia; Fernão Velho in Alagôas; Canna do Reino in Minas Geraes; S. Luiz, and others in S. Paulo, gave employment in 1871 to more than a thousand operatives, and worked with 84,875 spindles and 460 looms.

The water-power used for the machinery is equiva-lent to 400 horse. They produce annually 4.510,000 me-ters of cloth, which, including the thread and twist balls, form a total value of £ 250,000.

The new manufactory called « Brazil Industrial » which is at present in construction, in the capital of the Empire, is made to work with 400 looms.

The capital of the province of S. Paulo has 20 manu-factories, including 4 for hats, a saw mill worked by steam, and many others of different trades.

A spacious and an excellent cotton manufactory, which is now in construction, will soon be finished, where the owners intend to employ machinery of the most mo-dern and approved system.

The principal municipalities also possess different es—tablishments applied to more or less important industries, such as iron and brass foundries in the cities of Campinas, Itú, Pindamonhangaba; and in the second of these cities, a cotton manufactory for spinning and weaving cloth, two stories high, occupying 52 workmen, and 62 looms worked by steam, which produce 880 meters of cotton cloth per day; the hat manufactories of Sorocaba, Campinas and other places, the marble sawing-mill of S. Roque, the wax-candle manufactories of Itú, Guaratinguetá and S. Roque, where they have the advantage of the raw material being produced by the bees of the country; and several establishments, the greater part of which use steam power to card cotton and press it into bales, to prepare coffee, and saw-timber, and also to make soap, prepare tobacco, to press oil, and for several other purposes.

The capital of the province of Bahia possesses eight manufactories, including four of cotton weaving, besides three more in different municipalities, four saw mills worked by steam, important sugar refineries, one by Derasne and Cail's system, a great number of soap, carnauba, and tallow candles manufactories, some for ice, soda water, different sorts of snuff, cigars, and workshops of other branches of manufacturing industry.

Besides those of S. Aleixo in Magé, already mentioned, and Santa Thereza, established last year in the city of Paraty, which weaves dayly 1,650 meters of plain and drilled cloth, white and of different colours, occupying 100 workmen, the province of Rio de Janeiro possesses a chemical laboratory, several foundries and other industries, the most important among the latter being the cigar and snuff manufactories in the Capital. Shortly will be installed at Petropolis, in the province of Rio de Janeiro, two large cotton spinning manufactories.

The provinces of Pernambuco and Minas-Geraes have also important foundries and other industrious pursuits.

It is worthy of a special notice, in the province of Alagôas, not only the cotton weaving manufactory of Fernão Velho, already mentioned above, but also the important oil pressing factory in the city of Penedo.

In the other provinces and particularly in the capitals, there are industrial establishments of different descriptions, which the limits of a work like this will not allow being more amply treated of.

In the period of 1867 to 1872, 85 patents were granted either for invention or introduction, in conformity to the law of 28th August 1830, viz:

Patents concerning agriculture................... 16
     »   city cleanliness............... 6
     »   public works................ 10
     »   locomotion.................. 14
     »   navigation 5
     »   public lighting............... 3
     »   manufactories................ 17
     »   other industries............. 14

Post-Office.

The general land and maritime postal service, with its head office in the city of Rio de Janeiro, extends its branches through the whole Empire, by means of partial administrations, in the capitals of the provinces, and by agencies in the towns, and in almost all the villages and parishes, and in some important districts.

The business of the post-office, both maritime and fluvial, is transacted by means of companies, that receive a subsidy from government and by 6 English, 4 French, 1 German and

1 Italian navigation companies, that carry the transatlantic mails from the port of Rio de Janeiro to Southampton, London, Liverpool, Falmouth, Bordeaux, Havre, Marseille, Antwerp, Hamburg, Genoa, Naples, Barcelona, Lisbon, St. Vincent, Pernambuco, Bahia, Santos, River Plate, Valparaiso, Saint-Point, Arica, Islay, and Callao de Lima.

To the steamers of these lines the government allows certain favours and privileges, with the intention of giving them every facility in clearing from the ports to which they call, in the Empire.

In general the favours are as follows :

1" Immediately to charge and discharge independent of the custom's regulations on any day of the week, even in holydays.

2ᵈ To have the liberty of keeping on board the provisions, without putting on them the government stamp·

3ᵈ To substitute the manifest of the intermediate ports they are to touch at, by a register of the cargo and merchandise received in the said Brazilian ports, with destination to the River Plate.

4ᵗʰ Dispensing the term of responsibility, on the part of the captains or commanders of steamers, for transhipment and exportation of goods dispatched to the ports of the River Plate, or to those of the South of the Empire.

The steamers can leave the Brazilian ports at any hour of the day or night, by observing the government regulations of the port, and by the agents of the said navigation companies being responsible for any fines that the captains may incur on.

The passengers are allowed to land, on the same day of their arrival, till seven o'clock in the evening.

Thus Brazil mantains an immediate civil and commercial intercourse with most of the civilized nations of

Europe and America, from whence they receive almost weekly news.

The Brazilian post-office has postal conventions with France, Spain, Belgium, the United-States and Perú, and endeavours to celebrate the same with other States.

The amount of the revenue of the post-office, in the year 1871 to 1872, was £ 81,285, and its expenses £ 93,29s.

If it cannot, at present, be considered as a source of public revenue as it happens in other countries, the proceeds are undoubtedly quite satisfactory, if we attend to the peculiar circumstances of so large and extensive a country and to a population so disseminated.

The service of the post-office, however, is constantly improving, and the government is using all its efforts to give it the necessary development.

Electric Telegraph.

It is but fourteen years since the first small telegraph lines were constructed in Brazil, for the service of the government, in the capital of the Empire.

In the year 1863, by means of a submarine cable, the city of Rio de Janeiro was put in communication with the fortresses at the entrance of the bay; shortly afterwards a line was taken to Cabo-Frio, which is used to give ready dispatches to commerce.

At the end of the year 1865, the government determined upon the construction of a double line, from the capital of the Empire to the province of S. Pedro do Rio Grande do Sul, passing along the coast of Rio de Janeiro, to the important commercial harbour of Santos,

Imperio do Brazil
Linhas
da Repartição Geral dos
TELEGRAPHOS

Linhas construidas
" projectadas

OCEANO ATLANTICO

from there to S. Paulo and Santa Catharina, the extension of this line being above 1,450 kil.

It was necessary to cross 16 mouths of rivers and
inlets, and during the erection of the line to vanquish
difficulties of all sorts, crossing over mountains, covered
with thick forests, without any civilized inhabitants and,
many a time, without resources of any kind.

The same difficulties, or still greater, are encountered
in the maintenance and conservation of this line, in
consequence of great distances being completely uninha-
bited, and because of the scantiness of transports, and no
help to be had at those localities. But these obstacles
are being overcome, and in the year 1867, the line rendered already valuable services.

From that time forward the electric telegraph lines
are increasing rapidly.

At the principal points and important cities, such as
Rio de Janeiro, Paraty, Santos, Iguape, Paranaguá, Des-
terro, Laguna, Porto Alegre, Pelotas, Jaguarão and Rio
Grande, the lines are worked with Morse's double key
apparatus, and the intermediate stations are worked with
Siemens magneto electric dial instruments.

The electric telegraph department is decisively organized,
and best use is made of the experience of other nations
that have had more advancement in this branch of public
service.

The telegraph lines constructed at the expense of the government extend up to 3,469 kil., with 5,180 kil., of
aerial telegraph and 64 stations, besides 36,743 meters
of submarine cable.

They are divided into three sections :

The first line, called the *urbana*, or belonging to the

city, with 24 kil., 13 stations, and 1,200 meters of submarine cable, between the arsenal of war and the fortress of Villegaignon, was laid down for the services of different government departments.

The second section or the northern, has 907 kil. in length, with 1,026 kil. of aerial telegraph and 20 stations.

The city of Rio de Janeiro is in communication with the province of Espirito-Santo, by the first part of this line already constructed; and the capitals of Alagôas and Pernambuco communicate between themselves by the extremes of the sections. The intermediate portion from Itapemirim, in the province of Espirito-Santo, up to Maceió, in that of Alagôas, will be concluded in a few months, and the capital of the Empire will be in communication by telegraph correspondence with the cities and intermediate towns down to Pernambuco.

Of this intermediate portion there is erected 400 kil., that are only waiting for the personnel and instruments, in order to be worked at the provinces of Espirito-Santo, Bahia and Sergipe.

Thirdly, that of the south : it has 2,538 kil. in extension, with 32 stations, and 4,130 kil. of aerial telegraph, and it is erected, in a great part, with two conducting wires.

This line, the trunk of which starts from the capital of the Empire and terminates at the borders or frontiers of the Oriental State of Uruguay, contains 4 branch lines : the first, from Santos to São Paulo, with a station in that city ; the second, from Paranaguá to Coritiba, capital of the province of Paraná, joining at Morretes for the city of Antonina, and having 3 stations : the third from Porto Alegre, capital of the province of São Pedro do

Rio Grande do Sul to the city of São Gabriel, which will in a short time arrive at Uruguayana, and having 5 stations: the fourth, from the city of Pelotas to the bay of Rio Grande, in the same province, having 2 stations.

At first the telegraph lines belonging to the State were erected with wooden posts, but the rapidity of their decay caused them to be changed into iron posts, what is successively being done on the South line and in a large scale is employed in the construction of the North telegraph lines.

Besides the electric telegraph lines, under the administration of the general government's telegraph department, there are others that have 113 kil., accompanying the different railways, satisfying the necessities of the respective traffic, and also that of the public, that are charged according to tariffs approved by the government.

There is also, in the Capital, a company of telegraph lines to the interior, with a central station at the Constituição square, and others at different parts of the provinces of Rio de Janeiro and Minas Geraes up to Ouro Preto.

This company has to open other stations in the province of Rio de Janeiro, in Porto Novo, Cantagallo, Macahé, Campos and São João da Barra.

For transatlantic communication there is an important company already organized.

The submarine cable that connects Pernambuco with the city of Belém, in the province of Pará, is already laid down up to the port of the same city.

It is expected that about the end of this year, Brazil will be connected with Europe by the cable that starts from thence in direction to Pernambuco, coasting the Brazilian littoral up to Pará where by S. Thomas, it may be connected with the United States line.

The works are now going to be carried on along the coast of Pernambuco to Rio de Janeiro, where they should reach by the beginning of next year.

Another company will not be long before they lay a submarine cable between the capital of the Empire and the Platine republics, that are already in communication with Chili.

Thus a great part of the South American territory, in a short time, will be endowed with a telegraphic correspondence with Europe.

The produce of the telegraph stations on the government lines has been increasing in proportion to its development.

In the financial year 1861 — 1862, when there was but one line from the Capital to Petropolis, there was but an income of £ 32, going up to about £ 300 when the South line was initiated. It went on advancing, and by the time that all the line was working, though irregularly, the produce was up to above £ 2,600 in the year 1866 — 1867.

From that date the progressive increase continued, and in the year 1872 — 1873, the telegraphic receipts produced £ 15,750.

The stations are yet few in comparison to the length of the lines, keeping between them an average distance of 68,5 kil.

It is to be mentioned that there are only 12 stations established in the principal towns, that make more use of the telegraph, and that give the greatest produce.

From July 1866 to June 1867, in which was concluded the south line from the capital of the Empire up to Porto Alegre, the produce has been: 1866 — 1867,

25 % of the expenses; 1867—1863 21 % ; 1868—1869
26 % ; 1869 — 1870, 32 % ; 1870 — 1871, 39 % ; 1871
— 1872, 34 %

Adding to the expenses of stations those that are provenient of the conservation of the lines, the produce represents a considerable percentage.

In the year 1866 — 1867 the expenses with the construction and maintenance of telegraphic lines was £ 22,168,
and in 1871 — 1872 they went up to £ 109,056.

Fluvial and maritime communication.

Steamship navigation.

Eighteen lines of steamships make the chief part of the
service of maritime and fluvial navigation of the Empire,
and are subsidized by the government with the annual
sum of £ 343,000.

The Government also assists with the annual amount of
£ 20,000 the north american company — United States and
Brazil Mail Steamship — which, by a contract, makes a
round monthly voyage between Brazil and the United
States, calling at the ports of Belém, Pernambuco and
Bahia.

Besides the line for the United States, and the companies, almost all Brazilian, charged with the service for
the navigation of 17,160 kilometers along the coast of
the Empire, and between the several provincial ports,
the general and provincial governments allow pecuniary aid
to steam navigation along the river Paraguay, from Montevidéo as far as the capital of the province of Mato-Grosso,
in the extent of 4,620 kilometers, as also to the navigation

of the Lagôa dos Patos, in the province of S. Pedro do Rio Grande do Sul; of the lakes of Manguaba and Jiquiá, in Alagôas; of the rivers Pardo, Ribeira de Iguape, Mucury, Jequitinhonha, Maragogipe, Paraguassù, S. Francisco, Parahyba do Norte, Parnahyba, Itapicurú, Mearim, and Pindaré, comprehending 4,620 kilometers, the extent of those rivers which is navigated by steamers.

In the Amazonas, in its chief affluents, and other rivers of the province of Pará, packets of subsidized and other steam companies navigate through an extent of 9,900 kilometers. We have, then, 36,300 kilometers of steam navigation, almost entirely carrying on their trade with the pecuniary aid of the general and provincial governmens, that is 17,160 kilometers along the sea-coast, and 19,140 kilometers through the interior of the country.

The province of Bahia has launched out, on the river S. Francisco, the steamer *President Dantas*, which, with many sacrifices and difficulties was conveyed to, and fitted out on its banks.

The rich and important production of the fertile valleys of the S. Francisco and that of its mighty tributaries, calling the attention of commerce, awaken the hope that, within a short time, a regular service of steam navigation will be established along the above said rivers.

Rail-ways.

It having been recognized, by most of the capitalists of the Empire, how advantageous is this means of transport, they eagerly choose to lay out their money on undertakings of this description.

In 1867 the Empire had only six lines of rail-ways, in an extent of 683,2 kil., but at present it possesses the following ones: 15 carrying on their traffic along an ex – tent of 1,026,596 kil ; 17 in course of execution with 1,575,64, kil. in length ; 12 already in studies, which are calculated at 2,421,90 kil ; and finally 26 already granted, comprehending an average extent of 5,505 kil

If we compare the progress of rail-ways before 1867, with that effected at a later date, particularly since 1869, we find that there have been established 9 rail-ways more, with a development of 343,396 kil ; which gives an yearly average of 57,2 kil., in actual service from 1867 ; and 85,9 kil., if we calculate from 1869, in which period these important works received a greater impulse.

This progress becomes yet more evident by the larger sums allowed in the budgets, for this purpose.

Whilst the construction, expenses, guarantee of inte- rests upon the sums invested, projects and surveys for their construction, absorbed in the financial year of 1866 to 1867, the annual sum of £ 426,327; in the year 1871 to 1872, the treasury spent with the same item the sum of £ 1,167,528.

The government has, in project, three great lines of com- munication, which are designed to give a greater impulse and encouragement to the commerce of Brazil and, in general, to that of all the South American States, taking advantage of the navigation of the rivers Amazonas, S. Francisco, Tocantins, Paraguay and other important ones.

The first trunk-line already begun, starts from the metropolis of the Empire and proceeding through the provinces of Rio de Janeiro and Minas Geraes, to the point where the river S. Francisco begins to admit of free navigation, will continue from thence to the valley of the Tocantins, in the province of Pará.

This line comprehends the D. Pedro II rail-way, the construction of which is in active prosecution, the surveys and plans being already contracted, and in execution, for its prolongation, through the valley of the river Paraopeba to the river S. Francisco, and for the construction of another rail-way, in search of the valley of the rivers Carinhanha and Paraná, or of the rivers Grande, Preto and Somno, intended to connect the navigation of the said river S. Francisco to the point where the river Tocantins begins to offer a free navigation, at a distance of 600 kil. from the city of Pará.

The completion of this system of rail-ways will be the means of placing the capital of the Empire at a few days distance from the greater part of the central and northern provinces, as far as the province of Pará.

The second trunk-line is intended to cut Brazil in two through its centre, extending itself from the mouth of the Amazonas to the River Plate, through the valleys of the rivers Tocantins, Araguaya and Paraguay in an extent of 6,798 kil., which is already navigated by steamers, although in different sections.

To complete this trunk-line it will only be necessary to open a rail-way, in communication with the two navigable extreme points of the rivers Guaporé and Jaurú, in a distance of 165 kil., in the maximum.

The third trunk line, already partly executed, will also begin in the city of Rio de Janeiro, and terminate in the southern frontier, passing through the capitals of the provinces of S. Paulo, Paraná, the central part of Sta Catharina, and the city of Porto Alegre, the capital of the province of S. Pedro do Rio Grande do Sul.

The three trunk-lines cross, in general, vast and yet

uncultivated territories, for want of population, but which are very fertile, healthy, and fit for the cultivation of cotton, coffee, tobacco, sugar cane, cocoa, wheat, different sorts of grains, and many valuable products, covered, in a great extension, with virgin forests, abounding with the best building timbers or possessing excellent pastures.

The government made a contract with some Brazilian engineers for the surveys and plans for the prolongation of the rail-ways of Joaseiro, in the province of Bahia, and of Recife, in Pernambuco.

They have already begun their explorations in the first of these provinces, between the Alagoinhas station and the most advantageous position in the Joaseiro district, on the right bank of the river S. Francisco, with a branch from Soledade to Casa Nova, above the falls of Sobradinho, comprehending about 500 kil.

In the second province, they began at the Una Station, coasting the valley of the Pirangy, and passing by Garanhuns, Aguas Bellas and Mata-Grande, or by any of the tributary streams of the Moxotó as far as Jatobá, also on the banks of the river S. Francisco, with almost the same extension.

The surveys for the continuation of the rail-way from Santos to Jundiahy are also entrusted to Brazilian engineers.

They are ordered to choose the most convenient position between the cities of Limeira and S. João do Rio Claro, towards the banks either of the Paraná or the Parnahyba.

In order to complete the system of rail-ways that the government intends to construct at its own expense or by means of subsidized companies, it has been contracted with a company composed of Brazilians and foreigners, the surveys for a rail-way between Corifiba, in the province of Paraná, and Miranda, in the province of Mato Grosso, through the valley of the Ivahy, and along the banks of the rivers Ivinheima ˜ and Brilhante, taking advantage of the localities that afford easy navigation.

The government specially authorized by the legislature, is going to issue orders for the study, the estimate, and the definite tracing of a rail-way, which connecting the sea-coast to the frontiers of the province of S. Pedro do Rio Grande do Sul, may better avail to the commercial interests and the strategical conditions of that important province.

This rail-way is to meet the D. Pedro I railway, as it will be hereafter mentioned.

In accordance with this authorization, the government can spend £ 4.000,000, independent of £ 40,000 allowed for surveys; and also can grant a subsidy for each kilometer, or a guarantee of 7 °/₀ interest to any private entreprises, which shall undertake the construction of the sections that may best answer the commercial advantages of the province.

There is pending of the legislature another authorization, which enables the goverment to guaranty an interest of not more than 7 °/₀. for the period of 30 years, in the maximum, to those companies that shall undertake the construction of rail-roads, and show by their definite plans and statistical calculations that they expect to obtain a net revenue of 4 °/₀.

Whenever the companies have obtained any guarantee from the provinces, the government is merely to act as standing security to the parties.

It is also pending of the Chambers the concession of favours petitioned for the construction of a rail-way between the coal-mines of Tubarão, in the province of Santa Catharina, and the navigable river of the same name.

In short, many other preparatory studies for the construction of rail-road lines are in course of execution.

Rail-roads at the charge of the central government.

D. PEDRO II RAIL-ROAD.— Destined to be the principal trunk of the general system of improved locomotion in the Empire, by being the means of giving to the provinces easy access and intercourse to its metropolis, this grand undertaking has already its traffic along an extent of 374,7 kil., besides 11,64 kil., in the fourth section, and 89 kil., in the central line, which await but for the completion of some complementary works, to be traversed by steam locomotives.

The works are being executed along an extent of 159 kil. ; 398,2 kil. of surveys having been made last year.

With the execution of all these works the government has spent, to the present time, the sum of £ 5,043,334, having expended with the prolongation, only during last year, a sum of £ 667,732. The construction of the 374,7 kil., already working, cost £ 4,477,883.

. The D. Pedro II rail-way is divided into sections.

The first occupies the whole space between the metropolis and Belem, being 62,7 kil., in extent.

The second, built up on the slope of a steep ridge of mountains, is considered a monumental piece of work.

It contains 16 tunnels, one of them with 437,33 meters, another with 654,47 meters, and a th'rd one with 2.237,51 meters, in length; all cut in rock more or less hard, and principally in granite.

The total extension of these tunnels amounts to 5.189,38 meters, of which 2,000 meters were lined.

The enormous cuttings and embankments, in this line, attract the notice, as also some of its bridges that attest the difficulties to be surmounted : one of them being 20 meters high, another, over the Pirahy river, with three arches having a span of 12 meters each, and two with spans of 6,15 meters each.

The whole of this section is 46,2 kil., long.

The third, following the course of the Parahyba, reaches Porto Novo do Cunha, with a route of near 151,7 kil.

The fourth, taking an ascending direction along the river Parahyba, ought to terminate in the town of Cachoeira, being 154,7 kil. long, a small extent of which being already open to traffic as far as the parish of Campo Bello, at a place called Major Corrêa, near the Serra of Picù, which divides, on this side, the province of Rio de Janeiro from that of Minas Geraes.

The central line ought to extend from the Entre-Rios Station, through the province of Minas Geraes, as far as Lagôa Dourada, after surmounting the steepy mountain range of Mantiqueira. Eighty nine kilometers on this part of the road are already completed.

The traffic of the road, last year, gave the following results : passengers, 1,013,621, the corresponding receipts amounting to £117,802; merchandises, 162,879,702 kilgr., producing the total receipt of £ 436,213.

Coffee contributed to this result with the weight of 78,963,682 kilograms.

The total income of the road amounted to £ 573,193, the expense to £ 322,053, and the net balance £ 251,139, corresponding to the interest of 5,6 %, on the capital invested on the working line.

It is, however, to be remarked, that only in the end of last year some stations were inaugurated, their receipts, therefore, being much reduced, whilst the cost of them was additioned to the capital laid out, but for what the percentage would be much higher.

RAIL-WAY FROM SANTOS TO JUNDIAHY.—Next to the D. Pedro II rail-way, this is to be considered the most important one, in the Empire, on account of the development of its traffic, which accompanies the progressive production of one of the richest provinces of the Empire.

Constructed and managed by an English Company, with a guaranteed interest of 7 % per annum, it commences in the city of Santos, which has an excellent sea-port in direct communication with Europe, and crossing the Cubatão mountains, which form a part of the extensive range of mountains that run parallel to the sea, has its terminus in the city of Jundiahy, serving in its passage, as an intercommunication between important districts, amongst which is the capital of the province of S. Paulo.

The well combined plans and direction of this rail-way allows it to accumulate the produce of the culture of this rich and thriving province, whose richest soil, principally adapted to coffee and cotton plantations, even where its condition is less favourable, abundantly repays the labour of the husbandman.

To Jundiahy it has an extent of 139 kil.; but, owing to the spontaneous efforts and to the activity of its inhabitants, it was carried on as far as Campinas, 49 kil., more in extent, and will in a short time extend along the 86 kil. more, which separate that city from S. João do Rio Claro, because the provincial government has already contracted the construction of this part of the road.

The receipts of the rail-way from Santos to Jundiahy were last year £ 201,261 ; the road would have dispensed the guarantee of 7 %, if the expense of maintenance, which amounts to £ 98,227, had not been overcharged with the extraordinary disbursements proceeding from the repairing of damages caused by the torrential rains, that fell at the Cubatão mountains, on the beginning of the same year.

The liquid profit summing up to £ 103,034, is corresponding to 4 % of the capital invested. Every thing tends to make us believe, nevertheless, that in the financial year of 1872 to 1873 the receipts will be sufficient to occur to the payment of the 7 % interest.

The principal source of its revenue consisted in the transport of 76,412 passengers, and of 70,938,790 kilogr. of goods, charged by weight, besides small parcels, baggage and merchandise, that pay by cubic meter or by waggons load.

BAHIA RAIL-WAY.—An English company was also the contractor of this line, with the obligation of constructing the 123,5 kil., now in active service, with a guarantee of the annual interest of 7 %, on the capital expended on its construction, according to the agreement entered into.

The line begins in the city of S. Salvador, the capital of the province of Bahia, and terminates at Alagoinhas, in the same province.

Its receipts have to the present time, been inferior to its expense. Last year the former did not exceed £ 41,556, and the latter amounted to £ 44,061, leaving a deficit of £ 2,504.

This inconvenience, which is owing to the competition of the small barges of the coasting trade, which absorb the transport of great part of the goods destined for importation and exportation, will disappear as soon as the rail-way shall be prolonged to the important centres of production, which are situated beyond Alagoinhas.

The explorations are finished, and the engineers are actively employed in surveys to carry the line as far as the river S. Francisco, either for the normal or the narrow gauge, 92 kilometers of the road having already been approved.

During last year 78,132 passengers frequented this road, and 19,206,399 kilogr. of goods were transported along its rails.

PERNAMBUCO RAIL-WAY.— Intended to connect the port of the city of Recife with the upper part of the river S. Francisco, this railway has at present, in active operation, 124,9 kil. of road, which connect the station of Cinco Pontas, in the suburbs of Recife, with that of Una, on the border of the river of the same name.

The surveys for the prolongation of this rail-way to Jatobá, on the left bank of the S. Francisco, which is an extent of more than 500 kil., are actively progressing, and ought to be finished by September 1874 ; the first 55 kil, being already approved of.

The company, that undertook it, is in a prosperous condition, and the government has not been obliged to pay the whole interest guaranteed.

The receipts last year amounted to £ 93,434, being superior to that of 1871 by £ 21,362, and the managing and working expenses were £ 44,979, that is, £ 467 less than in the former year. The net profits amounted to £ 48,454 or 3 % of the guaranteed capital.

The circumstances of this enterprise will yet become more favourable when, after its complete development, it shall traverse vast regions of a most fertile territory, which for want of commodious and cheap means of transport cannot send their produces to market at a remunerating price.

This rail-way, by taking the direction of the S. Francisco, will be the means of turning to useful purposes large tracts of land which are apropriate to the culture of the principal productions of the country, such as coffee, sugar and cotton.

Madeira Rail-way.—In 1870 the government contracted the construction and management of a rail-way that, starting from the district of S. Antonio, should pass the falls of Guajará-mirim, on the right bank of the river Madeira, and also might carry a branch to some point opposite to the mouth of the river Beni.

This rail-way, which is considered to be 396 kil. long, is projected with the intention of avoiding the falls of the rivers Madeira and Mamoré, and to join their navigation with that of the Beni, Guaporé and other rivers, giving to the commerce of the republic of Bolivia an easy and free access to the Atlantic Ocean.

The English company that undertook it, after having obtained the approval of the government to the plans of the line, has already begun its construction.

The extraordinary importance of this rail-way cannot

fail to impress on the mind of those who reflect that, independent of the great difficulties of navigation, a great quantity of the productions of Bolivia, and all the articles imported by that republic, are conveyed through the river Madeira.

The above mentioned company has no interest guaranteed, but it obtained the grant of 4,356 square kil. of land, on the banks of the river, besides other very valuable favours.

BAHIA CENTRAL RAIL-WAY. — It was formerly called Paraguassú, and starts from the city of Cachoeira, taking the direction of the Chapada Diamantina, in the same province, having a branch to the town of Feira de Santa Anna, with a concession to extend to the river S. Francisco.

The concession was granted by a law which also conceded several other favours.

The construction of the main road having been suspended, the works were carried on at the branch above mentioned, which ought to have at present 44,6 kil., in extent. The whole length of the line when concluded, will be 244 kil.

D. PEDRO I RAIL-WAY. — Authorized by law, the government made a contract for the construction and management of this rail-way between the provinces of Santa Catharina and S. Pedro do Rio Grande do Sul.

An English company is already formed with £ 50,000, of capital, and has already begun the necessary surveys.

The rail-way between the cities of Parahyba do Norte and Alagôa Grande, and the towns of Ingá and Independencia, the extent of which is calculated at 202,6 kil., has received the authorization of government; and likewise another one that, branching from the station of Alagoinhas, on the Bahia rail-way, shall have its terminus at Itabaiana, in the province of Sergipe, which ought very nearly to have 140 kil., in extent.

In the municipality of the metropolis, there was a concession obtained for a rail-way from Andarahy-Pequeno to Boa Vista, on Tijuca mountain. It is calculated at 9 kil., long.

In addition to these railways, the following ones are worthy of notice :

The Leopoldina rail-way, a branch of the D. Pedro II, which starting from its last station in Porto Novo do Cunha, in the 3.ᵈ section, is to terminate at the parish of Santa Rita de Meia Pataca, in the province of Minas Geraes.

A company was formed, and the capital of £ 240,000 subscribed, to construct and manage the rail-way : the structure of the first 28 kil. is almost finished.

The total extension of the line, according to the surveys already made, is nearly 100 kil.

The location of the road work is already estimated at 65 kilometers.

The following rail-ways are also branches of the D. Pedro II rail-way, and have already the concession of government.

One from Itajubá, starting from the most convenient point of the fourth section of D. Pedro II rail-way, near the district of Cachoeira in the province of S. Paulo, to Itajubá, a village in the province of Minas Geraes ; its extent is calculated at 75 kilometers.

Another from the Chiador Station in the D. Pedro II rail-way, in the province of Rio de Janeiro, to the city of S. João Nepomuceno in Minas Geraes, 80 kil., long.

The province of Minas Geraes has granted to some of

these rail-roads the guarantee of interest on the capital laid out, or a subsidy per each kilometer.

A third from Barra Mansa, a city in the province of Rió de Janeiro, to Bananal in the province of S. Paulo, 30 kil. long.

A fourth from Rezende, a city in the province of Rio de Janeiro, branching from the D. Pedro II rail-way, to Arêas, a city in the province of S. Paulo, 33 kil., distant from the former.

Provincial rail ways.

PARÁ.

The capital of this province communicates with Nazareth, one of its most charming suburbs, through a railway belonging to a joint stock company « The Pará City Rail-way Company » with a fund of £ 50,000 and receiving from the province the annual subsidy of £ 1,000. Its receipts in 1871 were £ 9,205, and its expenses £ 5,963.

It conveys passengers and goods, and is worked by locomotive engines.

MARANHÃO.

A rail-way, between the capital and the city of Caxias which is to have 340 kil. in extent, has been contracted for; and the surveys for the rail-way tract, authorized by a provincial law, between Caxias and S. José de Cajaseiras opposite to Therezina, a city in the province of Piauhy, are terminated; — as also for another rail-road between the capital of the province and S. José, which lies beyond the rail-way between Barra da Corda and Chapada.

PIAUHY.

The president of the province is authorized by law, to grant a privilege for 30 years, with an annual guarantee of 3 %, upon the maximum capital of £ 30,000, to any company that shall undertake the construction and management of a rail-way between the city of Parnahyba and the bank of the river Iguaraçú, opposite to Amarração. Its length will be about 8 kilometers.

CEARÀ.

The railroad, between the capital of the province and the city of Baturité, is in construction and will be more or less 120 kil. long, which will be the means of giving free access to the opulent and fertile centre of its produce.

The company that contracted its construction has a fund of £ 80,000 which it is thought sufficient to complete the first section of 39,6 kil., in length.

The province has granted an annual guarantee of 7 % upon the sum of £ 260,000 limited.

There are also concessions for the following rail-ways.

One from Acaracú to Ipú, which ought to be 220 kil. long.

Another from Mundahú to Itapipora, having in length 45 kil.

A third from the capital of the province to Soure, 22,8 kil. long.

PERNAMBUCO.

The following railways either are in active service or under contract :

From Recife to Caxangá.— It is 12,87 kil.,,long. In 1872 its receipts were £ 24,841, and its expenses £ 23,367 ; leaving £ 1,474 profit.

From Recife to Olinda and to Beberibe.— There are in operation 8 kil., on this line. In 1872, the company receipts were £ 18,506, and the expenditure £ 13,178; having a balance in their favour of £ 5,327.

Limoeiro.— This railway commences in the capital of the province and, passing along the district of S. Lou-renço da Mata, terminates in the city of Páu d'Alho, with a branch to Nazareth.

This line will be 100 kil. long.

Leaving the sea-shore, it immediately begins to cross fertile lands, where more than 500 sugar manufacturing plantations are established. This judicious tracing, which has become so important to the planters by the economy it has produced, will soon be the means of dispensing the guarantee of 7 % which the provincial government granted to the Company.

The construction of the road has already been inaugurated.

Victoria.— It is intended to establish a communication between the capital and the city of Victoria, passing through Jaboatão.

The surveys are already made, and the expenses of construction are estimated at £ 360,000. The line will be 54 kil., long. The province granted a guarantee of interest on the capital spent in the construction.

According to the laws approved by the province, contracts have been made for the construction of the railways between the city of Goyana and the district of Timbauba, 54 kil. long ; from Una to Jacuipe, and Agua-

Preta to Bebedouro, the former 20 kil., and the latter 54 kil. long.

ALAGÔAS.

This province contracted the construction of two railways, one between the city of Maceió, the capital of the province, and branching on the Recife railway, which by a proximate calculation is estimated at 120 kil.; the other from the port of Jaraguá to the city of Imperatriz, with the extension of 114 kil., this last with the obliging clause of connecting it to the capital of the province and to the districts known by the name of Bebedouro and Fernão-Velho.

SERGIPE.

A rail-way is contracted, in this province, between Maroim and Propriá, which is to be 282 kil. long.

BAHIA.

This province has the following railways :

« The Nazareth Rail-way » between the capital of the province and the city of the same name, with an extension of 126 kil., of which 46 kil. are actually in construction.

« The Santo Amaro Rail-way » between the capital of the province and the city of Santo Amaro, having already 33 kil. in construction.

« The Jequitinhonha Rail-way » between Cachoeirinha on the border of the Jequitinhonha river, and a point where the said river meets the province of Minas-Geraes; the distance being calculated at 80 kil., long.

ESPIRITO-SÁNTO.

The provincial assembly has given several authorizations for the construction of rail-ways. But the most important of the projected ones, are those that, starting from the city of Victoria, the capital of the province, take their direction to the port of Souza in the Rio Doce, and diverging from its trunk, one will branch to Diamantina or Serro, in the province of Minas-Geraes, crossing Cuyethé and Pontal, and the other is to follow to Queluz where it will meet the grand trunk of the D. Pedro II rail-way, crossing the valleys of Manhuassú, Ponte Nova and Ouro Preto.

It will have an extension of 135 kilometers.

RIO DE JANEIRO.

The rail-way system has of late received great encouragement from its inhabitants, who have given it a great impulse.

Independent of the D. Pedro II rail-way, which crosses the greater part of its territory, it has in full operation already four others, which are exclusively confined to this province, with an extent of 103,5 kil. The carrying on of the construction of two of the above ones is nearly coming to a completion and also two others, which altogether make up the total sum of 317 kil.; the surveys and plans of 70 kil., being very much advanced.

The rail-ways in operation are the following ones :

The Mauá, with	19,0	kilometers.
The Cantagallo.	48,5	»
The Valença	25,0	»
The Campos to S. Sebastião. . . .	11,0	»

Are nearly ready :

The Cantagallo, in continuation . . 101,5 kilometers.
The Campos to S. Sebastião, idem. . 9,0 »
The Nictheroy to the parish of Neves
  in Macahé, 1ˢᵗ Section . . . . 107,5 »
The Macahé to Campos. . . . . 99,0 »

Sixteen others are projected, the privileges having already been granted by the province ; the length of them cannot be exactly fixed, as the surveys and plans are not yet finally completed. But there is every reason to calculate that the total extension of them will not be less than 800 kilometers, viz :

			Probable length.	
1ˢᵗ	From	Nictheroy to Maricá.	31,0	kilom.
2ᵈ	»	Piedade to the mountains of Theresopolis	31,0	»
3ᵈ	»	the Serra da Estrella to Petropolis	23,1	»
4ᵗʰ	»	Itaborahy to Capivary. . . .	61,0	»
5ᵗʰ	»	Paquequer to Cantagallo rail-way.	31,0	»
6ᵗʰ	»	Friburgo to Sᵗᵃ Maria Magdalena.	71,0	»
7ᵗʰ	»	Sᵗᵃ Maria Magdalena to Macahé.	55,0	»
8ᵗʰ	»	Macahé to Campos.	99,0	»
9ᵗʰ	»	Campos to Tombos	133,0	»
10ᵗʰ	»	Campos to Gragahu, nearly . .	60,0	»
11ᵗʰ	»	Gragahu to Itabapoana . . .	66,0	»
12ᵗʰ	»	S. Fidelis to S. João da Barra. .	71,0	»
13ᵗʰ	»	S. Fidelis to S. Antonio de Padua.	45,0	»
14ᵗʰ	»	S. João do Principe	39,0	»
15ᵗʰ	»	Pirahy to Rio Preto.	39,8	»
16ᵗʰ	»	Vassouras to the Station of Mendes	11,0	»

866,9

The Cantagallo rail-way, 150 kilometers long, issues from Villa Nova, and will soon effect a junction with one whose construction is progressing, between the capital of the province and the parish of Neves, in Macahé.

It is almost ready to Nova Friburgo whence it will proceed to Santa Maria Magdalena, passing through the city of Cantagallo, important centres of the coffee plantations.

Its present traffic is confined between Villa Nova and Cachoeira. The second section has required important works of art to cross the steep mountain ridges of Friburgo or of Orgãos, one of the ramifications of the ridge of mountains that accompanies the sea-coast.

This section is divided into three parts, each having its different type.

The first, from Cachoeira to Boca do Mato, with an extent of 6.336,15 meters, is divided into:

Level lines . . . . 973,44 meters.
Acclivity lines . . . . . . 5.364,371 »
With the average declivity of . 0,025 inches.

The second, being 13.393,32 meters long, extends from Boca do Mato to the Alto, having the following extent :

Level lines . . . . . . 857,48 meters.
Acclivity lines . . . . . . 12.535,84 »
Average declivity . . . . . 0,071 inches.

The third finally reaches Nova Friburgo, being 15.797,86 meters long, divided into

Level lines . . . . 6.477,16 meters.
Declivity lines . . . . . . 9.320,70 »
Average declivity . . . . . 0,025 inches.

Proper and appropriate engines can run on the first and third section of this road ; as the strongest declivity gradient does not exceed relatively 0,033 and 0,27 inches.

Although in many places there are sharp curves with radii of 60 meters, the Fairlie engines overcome them with facility.

In the second section, however, of this line, taking into consideration that the maximum of the declivity was 0,083 meter, 3,02 inches, equal to the celebrated rail-road over Mount Cenis, it was found convenient to employ the system Fell. The perfection, however, and pro-ficiency with which the works were executed, offer greater security than the above mentioned line, not only because it has only half of the extension of the former, but be-cause the declivity is in average less ; for in Friburgo line it is of 0,071 meter, 2,58 inches, whereas on Mount Cenis it is of 0,074 meters 2,69 inches, the maximum declivity being in both the same.

And it must here be added, that 50 °/. of the European line, in a distance little more than 14 kil., is construct-ed in a curve, a disadvantage which in the Brazilian line is solely limited to 40 °/. of the same where the acclivity is greatest, 13 kil. in length, the limits of the radii of th ecurves of both rail-roads being of 40 meters.

Finally, important improvements in the superstructure, increase the probability and almost certainty of a safe and regular traffic.

Those which are more worthy of special mention are the following : in 60 °/. more the number of sleepers employed ; in the greater power of resistance given to the chairs, that were fixed 0,50 meters distant from each other, instead of 0,80 meters as in the rail-road that serves us, as a point of comparison ; in having alternate struts driven obliquily on either side; and finally in the outward rails, nailed on each sleeper with four spikes, being substituted in every three sleepers by screws, the heads of which are made to sink in iron wrought plates, made fast in the whole breadth of the rail, on its under side.

This strong superstructure, says a respectable authority, has just past through a decisive and experimental trial, by making engines of 28.557,36 kilogr. weight, run over the rails several times, without causing the least damage to the central rail.

The province contracted this section for £ 180,000 each kilometer.

The Mauá rail-way deserves special mention, and if it at present does not maintain a constant traffic, at least it is deserving being named for the benefits the public has received from it, and for being the first in essaying this system of locomotion.

Its length does not exceed 19 kil. distance, from the port from which it took its name and whence it starts and the foot of the Serra da Estrella where it terminates.

Although its receipts have diminished in a most extraordinary manner, from the period when the centres of production, that made it their vehicle, began to make the D. Pedro II rail-way supply their wants of transport, yet it still carries the produce of the neighbourhood; its principal item of receipts being nevertheless the passengers traffic in the hot season of the year, who retire to, or make of Petropolis their habitual residence.

The President of the province lately made a contract for its continuation to Petropolis, the distance being 23,1 kiloms.

S. PAULO.

This rich province counts nearly 1,000 kil. of railways either in operation, in construction, or under survey.

Amongst the former above mentioned are the following :
Paulista, between the cities of Jundiahy and
Campinas, length . . . . 49 kil.
Ituana, between Jundiahy and Itú, length. . 67 »

Total. 116 »

The following are in construction :

Sorocabana, between the cities of S. Paulo and the
Ipanema iron manufactory, crossing the city
of Sorocaba . . . . 111 kil.
From Itú to Piracicaba . . . . 85 »
From S. Paulo to Rio de Janeiro, between the
city of S. Paulo and Cachoeira Station,
in the D. Pedro II rail-road . . . . . 286 »
From Mogymirim to Amparo . . . . . . 85 »

Sum total. . . . . 567 »

There were lately contracted : a rail-way that, in continuation to the « Paulista », is intended to connect the
city of Campinas to Rio Claro, 86 kil. long, according
to the surveys and plans already made ; and the Mogymirim between Rio Claro and the city of that name, 88 kil.
long. A grant has been made by the provincial government
to a company that undertakes its construction, with a
guarantee of 7 °/₀ upon £ 300,000 limited, and which
also received from the same, £ 3,000 to help the preliminary works.

PARANÁ.

The surveys for the rail-way between the cities of
Antonina and Coritiba, in the extension of 83 kil., are
terminated. The company that shall be formed for the
construction and management of the same, will receive

from the province a guarantee of interest, as stipulated.

Another line was also authorized to be constructed, between Paranaguá and Morretes, with 15 kil. long.

S PEDRO DO RIO GRANDE DO SUL.

There is already, in this province, a rail-way in operation called S. Jeronymo: it begins in the city of the same name, which has an excellent port on the River Jacuhy, and terminates at the coal-mines, on the border of Arroio dos Ratos. It is 19,9 kil. long. The works for the construction of the rail-way of Hamburg-Berg are progressing; which issuing from the capital of the province, terminates at the point where trunk colonial lines of the municipality of S. Leopoldo meet together, an extent of 66 kil, long. It is expected that it be inaugurated this year. The company that undertook its construction received a guarantee of 7 % from the provincial government upon the limited capital of £ 170,000.

Another grant is made of a railway between Rio Grande and the coal-mines of Candiota, with near 170 kil. of extension.

MINAS-GERAES.

The following rail-ways are either projected or contracted by the president, authorized by the provincial assembly:

OURO PRETO.— It is to issue from the city of the same name, capital of the province, and join the trunk line of D. Pedro II rail-way. Its approximate extension is calculated at 140 kilometers.

ITABIRA.— It also starts from Ouro Preto and terminates at Itabira, 151 kil. long.

Manhuassu. — It is intended to connect the capital with Manhuassú in the confines of the province of Espirito Santo, at the point where the rail-way that is to start from the capital of that province must terminate.

Caldas. — Starting from the municipality of that name, it is to meet the Mogymirim line, a branch of the railway from Santos to Campinas. This rail-way will be the means of giving greater facility to travellers who go in demand of the hot springs of its environs.

Ubá. — This rail-way is intended to be a prolongation of the Leopoldina line to the city of Ubá, and passes by S. Paulo de Muriahé, thus connecting that city to the D. Pedro II rail-way.

Farpão. — Taking the direction of the locality of that name, on the confines of Bahia, it is to make a junction with another line projected from that place to Cachoeirinha.

Sapucahy. — This prolongation of the branch line of Itajubá, is intended to be carried to the point where the river Sapucahy begins to be navigable.

Diamantina. — Although this rail-way ought to terminate on the confines of the province, in the valley of the river Doce, yet it will form a communication between Diamantina and the capital of the province of Espirito Santo, by the Souza rail-way, which follows the borders of the river of the same name, in direction to the capital.

Piumhy. — The construction of this rail-way will connect S. João d'El-Rei with Piumhy.

The following table shows out the rail-ways of the empire, specifying their names, the progress of all the general and provincial rail-ways, in operation, in construction, under surveys, or projected.

RAIL-ROADS.

| NAMES OF THE RAIL-ROADS. | INITIAL AND TERMINAL STATIONS. | KILOMETRICAL EXTENSION IN EXPLORATION. | KILOMETRICAL EXTENSION IN CONSTRUCTION. | KILOMETRICAL EXTENSION IN STUDIES. | TOTAL KILOMETRICAL EXTENSION (NEAR CALCULATION.) | KILOMETRICAL DISTANCE BETWEEN THE INITIAL STATIONS OF THE LINES AND THE CITY OF RIO DE JANEIRO. | | PROVINCES. | CLASSIFICATION OF RAIL-ROADS. | NAMES OF THE DA |
						In a straight line.	By the common roads.			
Pará City rail-way............	From Belém to Nazareth........	K 9,132	K	K	K 9,132	K 2,463,0	K 4,292,0		Gener	Leopoldina.........
									Prov.	Cantagallo ....
From the capital to Caxias......	From the capital to Caxias......				346,0	2,321,0	3,566,0			
From Caxias to Therezina.......	From Caxias to Therezina.......				126,0	2,037,0	3,889,0		»	Santa-Maria Magdal
From Caxias to S. José.........	From Caxias to São José........				156,0	2,037,0	3,689,0			
From Barra do Corda to Chapada	From Barra do Corda to Chapada				130,0	1,870,0	¡3,650,0		»	From Paquequer ...
									»	Valenciana.........
From Parnahyba to Iguarassú..	From the mouth of the river Iguarassú to the town of Parnahyba...........				6,0	2,418,0	3,156,0		»	From Nictheroy to Section) ....
"	From the capital to Soure..				22,8	2,256,0	2,014,0			
From the chief town to Soure..	From the capital to Baturité....			39,6	120,6	2,167,0	3,656,0		»	From Macahé to Ca
Ccarense......................	From Aracacu to Ipú...........				220,0	2,250,0	3,050,0		»	From Macahé to Magdalena ....
From Ipú......................	From Mundahú to Itapipora ...				45,0	2,422,0	3,400,0			
From Itapipora................									»	From Itaborahy to
From the capital to Alagôa-Grande and to the villages of Ingá and Independencia,...........	From the capital to Alagôa-Grande and to the villages of Ingá and Independencia.				303,6	¡2,056,0	2,167,0	Rio-de-Janeiro.	»	From Mauá.........
									»	From Campos to S
São-Francisco	From the capital to the province of Jatobá on the river São Francisco	124,9		54,0	692,0	1,944,0	2,056,0		»	From São João do
Caxangá......................	From Recife to Caxangá........	12,872			12,852	1,944,0	2,056,0		»	From Campos to G
From Recife to Olinda........	From the capital to Olinda......	8,0			8,0	1,941,0	2,054,0		»	From Graçulai to I
From Olinda to Beberibe.....	From the capital to Beberibe....				6,0	1,846,0	1,951,0		»	From São Fidelis da Barra........
From Una to Jacuipe.......	From Una to Jacuipe.........				20,0	1,820,2	2,1·8,0			
From Agua-Preta to Bebedouro	From Agua-Preta to Bebedouro.				54,0	1,990,0	2,189,0		»	From São Fidelis l
From the capital to Limoeiro..	From the capital to Limoeiro...				100,0	1,941,0	2,056,0			tonio de Padua..
Central......................	From Recife to Victoria				53,82	1,944,0	2,056,0			
From Goyanna to Timbaúba..	From Goyanna to Timbaúba...				54,0	1,993,0	2,056,0		»	From Magé........
									»	From Pirahy to Ri
From Maceió to rail-road São Francisco	From the capital to the São Francisco				129,0	1,729,0	1,833,0		»	From Nictheroy to
					114,9	1,722,0	1,833,0		»	From Serra-da-Estr polis...........
From Jaragua to Imperatriz...	From Jaragua to Imperatriz....	8,8		89,2	104,5	1,700,0	1,900,0		»	From Campos to T
From Pirauhas to Jatobá......	From Pirauhas to Jatobá.......			104,5						
									»	Vascouras.........
From Maroim to Propriá........	From Maroim to Propriá........				282,0	1,558,0	1,764,0		Gener	From Santos to Jur
									Prov.	Paulista..........
Joaseira.....................	From the capital of the province of Bahia to Joaseiro on the river São Francisco............	123,46		446,0	571,40	1,278,0	1,444,0		Gener	Sant'Anna do Parna
Central rail-road	From the town of Cachoeira to Chapada Diamantina.........		44,6		944,0	1,278,0	1,444,0		Prov.	From Campinas to Rio-Claro......
From Alagoinhas to Itabayana Sergipe	From Alagoinhas to Itabayana Sergipe				140,0	1,380,0	1,508,0	São Paulo.	»	Mogyanna.........
Nazareth.....................	From the capital to Nazareth...		46,0		126,0	1,278,0	1,444,0		»	Ituana ....
Santo-Amaro.................	From the capital to Santo-Amaro.		33,0		33,0	1,278,0	1,414,0			
Jeqoitinhonha................	From Cachoeirinha on the banks of Rio Jequitinhonha to the frontier of Minas Geraes......				80,0	1,008,0	¡1,217,0		»	From S. Paulo and I
Tocantins	From Villa da Barra of Rio Grande (Bahia) to Barra do Sonsho (Goyaz)				800,0	1,200,0	2,840,0		»	From Itú to Piracic
									»	From Mogy-mirim Sorocabana......
From Victoria to the port of Soura......................	From the town of Victoria to the port of Soura, on the Rio-Doce.				135,0	436,0	700,0	Paraná.	Gener	From Coritiba to Mato-Grosso.....
									Prov.	From Antonina to Paranaguá t
From Andarahy-Pequeno up to Tijuca mountain............	From Andarahy-Pequeno to Alto da Boa-Vista..............				9,0			S.ta Catharina.	Gener	D. Pedro I.......
									»	From Tubarão....
D. Pedro II principal line......	From the capital to the valley of São Francisco................	197,635	150,0	106,2	640,0			S. Pedro do Rio Grande do Sul.	Prov.	From the coast to Hamburg-Berg...
» embranchment of Porto-Novo do Cunha.	From Entre Rios to Porto-Novo do Cunha.................	63,158			63,158	69,0	197,0		»	Candiota..........
» embranchment of Cachoeira......	From Barra do Pirahy to Cachoeira (S. Paulo)........	95,47	24,44	36,0	155,91	77,5	102,1		»	São Jeronymo....
» embranchment of Macacos........	From the bicurcation to Macacos.	4,719			4,719	56,0	65,1		»	From Santo Amaro
» embranchment of Rio Verde......	From the central line to Rio Verde			356,0	356,9				»	Ouro Preto........
Barra Mansa.................	From the town of the same name to that of Bananal, province of S. Paulo								»	Inabira...........
									»	Munhuassuú.......
Itajubá......................	From D. Pedro II to Itajubá (Minas-Gerses).			80,0	80,0	109,0	153,87	Minas Geraes.	»	Caldas........... Ubá..............
					75,0	190,0	218,24		»	Farpão...........
São-João-Nepomuceno	From D. Pedro II Rail-road, to São João Nepomuceno (Minas Gerses)................				80,0	95,0	216,8		»	Sapucahy .... Diamantina. ......
Rezende to Areas.............	From the town of Rezende to that of Areas (S. Paulo)...........				85,0	133,0	190,39	Mato-Grosso	»	Piumby........... Madeira and Mam
									Gener	

IL-ROADS.

TOTAL KILOMETRICAL EXTENSION. (REAL CALCULATION.)	KILOMETRICAL DISTANCE BETWEEN THE INITIAL STATIONS OF THE LINES AND THE CITY OF RIO DE JANEIRO.		PROVINCES.	CLASSIFICATION OF RAIL-ROADS.	NAMES OF THE RAIL-ROADS.	INITIAL AND TERMINAL STATION.	KILOMETRICAL EXTENSION IN EXPLORATION.	KILOMETRICAL EXTENSION IN CONSTRUCTION.	KILOMETRICAL EXTENSION IN STUDIES.	TOTAL KILOMETRICAL EXTENSION (REAL CALCULATION.)
	In a straight line.	By the common roads.								
K	K	K					K	K	K	K
8,132	2,462,0	4,292,0		Gener	Leopoldina	From Porto Novo do Cunha to Santa Rita de Meia Pataca, Minas-Geraes		80,0	20,0	100,0
345,0	2,721,0	3,556,0		Prov.	Cantagallo	From Villa-Nova to Nova-Friburgo	48,5	101,5		150,0
136,0	2,677,0	3,889,0								
156,0	2,057,0	3,889,0								
130,0	1,870,0	13,650,0		»	Santa-Maria Magdalena	From Nova-Friburgo to Santa-Maria-Magdalena				71,0
				»	From Paquequer	From the Cantagallo rail-way to Paquequer				31,0
				»	Valenciana	From D. Pedro II rail-way to Valença	25,0			25,0
8,0	2,418,0	3,156,0		»	From Nictheroy to Campos (1st Section)	From Nictheroy to Neves, (Macahé with embranchment at Villa-Nova		107,5		150,5
22,0	2,250,0	2,014,0								
120,0	2,145,0	3,056,0								
200,0	2,220,0	3,050,0		»	From Macahé to Campos	From Macahé to Santa-Maria Magdalena		99,0		99,0
45,0	2,422,0	3,400,0		»	From Macahé to Santa-Maria Magdalena	From Macahé to Santa-Maria-Magdalena				55,0
			Rio-de-Janeiro.	»	From Italorahy to Capivary	From Italorahy to Capivary				64,0
202,6	2,056,0	2,167,0		»	From Mauá	From the port of Mauá to Serra da Estrella	19,15			19,15
				»	From Campos to São-Sebastião	From Campos to São-Sebastião	11,0	9,0		75,0
				»	From São João do Principe	From São João do Principe to D. Pedro II rail-way				20,04
692,0	1,944,0	2,056,0		»	From Campos to Gragahú	From Campos to Gragahú				60,01
12,852	1,941,0	2,056,0		»	From Gragahú to Itabapoana	From Gragahú to Itabapoana				60,0
8,0	1,944,0	2,056,0		»	From São Fidelis to São-João da Barra	From São Fidelis to São João da Barra				71,0
6,0	1,848,0	2,0640								
20,0	1,848,0	2,1840								
64,0	1,880,0	2,189,0		»	From São Fidelis to Santo-Antonio de Padua	From São Fidelis to Santo Antonio de Padua				45,0
100,0	1,944,0	2,056,0								
53,82	1,944,0	2,056,0		»	From Magé	From Magé to the Serra of Theresopolis			31,0	31,0
54,0	1,999,0	2,056,0		»	From Pirahy to Rio-Preto	From Pirahy to Rio-Preto			39,0	39,0
				»	From Nictheroy to Maricá	From Nictheroy to Maricá				31,0
170,0	1,722,0	1,893,0		»	From Serra-da-Estrella to Petropolis	From Serra-da-Estrella to Petropolis				23,31
114,0	1,722,0	1,893,0		»	From Campos to Tombos	From Campos to Tombos				120,0
194,5	1,700,0	1,950,0								
282,0	1,556,0	1,764,0		»	Vassouras	From Vassouras to Mendes, D. Pedro II rail-way				14,0
				Gener Prov.	From Santos to Jundiahy	From Santos to Jundiahy	139,0			139,0
				Paulista.		From Jundiahy to Campinas	40,0			40,0
571,40	1,278,0	1,444,0		Gener	Sant'Anna do Parnahyba	From São João do Rio-Claro to Sant'Anna do Parnahyba			650,0	650,0
244,0	1,278,0	1,441,0	São Paulo.	Prov.	From Campinas to São João do Rio-Claro	From Campinas to São João do Rio-Claro				80,0
146,0	1,360,0	1,508,0		»	Mogyanna	From Campinas to Mogy-mirim		35,0		88,0
120,0	1,276,0	1,441,0		»	Ituana	From Jundiahy to Itú	67,0			43,0
35,0	1,278,0	1,441,0								
80,0	1,008,0	1,217,0		»	From S. Paulo and Rio de Janeiro	From the town of S. Paulo to Cachoeira, D.Pedro II rail-way				285,0
800,0	1,200,0	2,840,0		»	From Itú to Piracicaba	From Itú to Piracicaba		45,0		45,0
				»	From Mogy-mirim to Amparo, Sorocabana	From Mogy-mirim to Amparo		86,0		86,0
				»		From S. Paulo to Ypanema		111,0		111,0
135,0	136,0	790,0	Paraná.	Gener Prov.	From Coritiba to Miranda, in Mato-Grosso	From Coritiba to Miranda				1.800,0
				»	From Antonina to Coritiba	From Antonina to Coritiba			69,0	83,0
				»	From Paranaguá to Morretes	From Paranaguá to Morretes				15,0
9,0			S.ta Catharina.	Gener	D. Pedro I	From Santa Catharina to São Pedro do Rio Grande			384,0	384,0
				»	From Tubarão					50,0
649,0			S. Pedro de Rio Grande do Sul.	Prov.	Hamburg-Berg	From the coast to the Uruguay. From the capital to New-Hamburg				1.700,0
				»	Candiota	From the town of Jaguarão to Candiota		66,0		66,0
				»	São Jeronymo	From the village of São Jeronymo to Arroio dos Ratos	19,8			170,0
48,158	89,0	197,0		»	From Santo Amaro to Jacuhy	From Santo Amaro to Jacuhy				19,8
135,91	77,5	168,1		»	Ouro Preto	From D. Pedro II rail-road to Ouro Preto				165,0
4,719	56,0	85,1		»	Itabira	From Ouro Preto to Itabira				140,0
				»	Manhuassú	From the port of Souza, on Rio-Doce and Ouro-Preto				151,0
336,0			Minas Geraes.	»	Caldas	From Mogy-mirim to Caldas				380,0
				»	Ubá	From Leopoldina to Ubá				165,0
										160,0
30,0	102,0	153,67		»	Farpão	From Farpão at the confines of Bahia and Jequitinhonha				283,0
75,0	190,0	216,21		»	Sapucahy	From Itajubá to Sant'Anna de Sapucahy				125,0
				»	Diamantina	From the port of Souza to Diamantina				430,0
80,0	95,0	216,9		»	Plumby	From São João d'El-Rei to Plumby				363,0
			Mato-Grosso.	Gener	Madeira and Mamoré	From Santo Antonio to Guajará-Guassú		363,0		363,0
85,0	133,0	190,59					1.026,590	1.575,64	2.423,90	10.478,4

Tram-ways in the metropolis.

There are two companies of tram-ways, in the city of Rio de Janeiro, whose object is to' transport passengers through the streets of Rio de Janeiro, on rail-ways, to the suburbs; the whole extension of their lines is calculated at 58,763 kilometers.

There are also grants made for three more companies, which cars will run along the extension of 40 kilometers.

Of those already in operation, the North American Botanical Garden's Rail-way is established for the traffic of passengers to the suburbs of Gloria, Cattete, Botafogo, São Clemente, Jardim Botanico, Larangeiras and the adjoining localities. Their lines extend along 20,84 kilometers.

Last year (1872), it made 117,773 passages carrying 4.966,523 passengers.

The second « Rio de Janeiro Street Rail-way Company », maintains six lines that branch along different streets of the city and the suburbs, comprised in their privilege, viz: São Christovão, Pedregulho, Tijuca, Sacco do Alferes, Catumby, Cajú and Rio Comprido, comprehending 37,92 kilometers.

In the same space of time, as the first, it made 195,437 passages carrying 5.816,388 passengers : it also transports heavy articles.

The « Villa Isabel Tram-way Company » has already commenced the construction of its line, having opened to traffic 4,114 kilometers of road. The object of the company is to carry passengers to the districts of São Christovão, Engenho Velho, Engenho Novo and Andarahy Grande.

It comprehends 28,576 kilometers of extension.

In construction :

There is a tram-way about to be constructed, that will be the means of promoting welfare and comfort to a great part of the city and particularly to those that dwell on the hills of Santa Thereza, Paula Mattos and Neves, where the sick find a healthy and mild climate in their convalescence, and the population, in general, finds a refreshing breeze, in the hot season of the year. Its whole extension is calculated at 12,87 kilometers.

Another line was also granted between Pedregulho, a suburb of the city, and Nossa Senhora da Penha, in the parish of Irajá, being considered to be 9,9 kilometers long.

There is yet another tram-way called « Locomotora », for the transport of goods and merchandises to the central station of the D. Pedro II Rail-way, and the most commercial streets in Rio de Janeiro.

All its lines measure 18,14 kilometers in extension.

A small urban line has, for some time past, been in operation, which is intended to carry passengers from the «Fluminense Steam-boat Company's wharf» to the end of Hospicio street at the entrance of the Campo da Acclamação. It is nearly 1,650 meters in length.

Provincial tram-ways.

MARANHÃO.

There is a tram-way, in the capital, with different branches, one of which goes as far as Cutim, where it will soon be in connection with the rail-way between this point and Itibiry, 11,21 kilometers in extent. It belongs to the entreprize called São Luiz do Maranhão, and has a guarantee of interest upon £ 80,000, capital limited.

CEARÁ.

In the city of Aracaty, there is a privileged company to lay down a tram-way.

PERNAMBUCO.

This province has the following tram-ways:

Boa Viagem. — The contract for this line is still pending on the approbation of the provincial assembly.

Tram-way to Torre, Estrada Nova, Caxangá and Varzea. — This, although very promising, is merely projected. The president sent the contract to the assembly for its approval.

Tram-way to Goyanna. — The contractor has not yet began the structure of the road.

Pernambuco tram-way. — This company having been organized originally in New-York, lately established its board of direction in Recife, with a fund of £ 120,000. Its lines carry passengers to Magdalena, Afogados, Santo Amaro, and Fernandes Vieira making its route through different streets of that city. Its lines have an extension of 21,600 kilometers.

The average number of passengers per month is 150,000.

ALAGÔAS.

There is a tramway in the capital.

BAHIA.

There are the following tram-way companies, in that city:

Central rail tram-way. — This line branches from Barraquinha to Fonte Nova in one direction, and to the lower part of the city at Soledade, in the other, being 11 kil, long. During last year the traffic of passengers reckoned 264,997.

Economical carriages. — This line commencing in Riachuelo has its terminus in Itapagipe, being 9,66 kil., long. As far as Bomfim the cars are drawn by horses, the rest of the road is then served by engines. In 1872 it conveyed 665,192 passengers.

City tram-way. — The line traverses the streets between Palacio Square and Graça. It is to be continued to Barra. The company contracted the construction of a hoisting machine, which is nearly completed, to transport passengers and merchandise from the lower part of the city to the higher one and vice versa.

Bahia Locomotive. — It has been organized to transport passengers and merchandise between the higher and lower part of the city. The rail-way is calculated to have 6,6 kil. in extension, and ought to be inaugurated next December.

RIO DE JANEIRO.

This province has three concessions for tram-ways; one for its capital, another for Macahé, and a third for Campos.

The first is nearly 12,9 kil. long, and has already three stations in operation. Inaugurated in 1871, its traffic of passengers to June of 1872 amounted to 1,349,718.

S. PAULO.

There are two lines, one in the capital, and another in Santos, having both the extension of 6 kilometers.

S. PEDRO DO RIO GRANDE DO SUL.

There are several tram-ways projected in the capital and in the city of Rio Grande.

The following table shows out the number of tram-ways either in traffic, in construction, or merely granted, which are existing in the Empire.

TRAMWAYS.	NUMBER OF METERS IN TRAFFIC.	NUMBER OF METERS IN CONSTRUCTION.	NUMBER OF METERS IN SURVEY.	NUMBER OF METERS OF THE PROJECTED LINES.	TOTAL.
	k	k	k	k	k
Botanical Gardens..	20.845	....	....	....	20.845
S. Christovão, etc..	37.918	....	....	....	37.918
Villa Isabel........	4.114	24.462	....	....	28.576
Santa Thereza.....	....	12.870	....	....	12.870
From Praça de D. Pedro II to Campo	1.650	....	....	....	1.650
From Pedregulho to Penha...........	....	....	9.900	....	9.900
Locomotora	18.143	....	....	....	18.143
S.Luiz do Maranhão	11.210	....	....	....	11.210
Aracaty (Ceará)....	....	....	....	....	....
Boa-Viagem (Pernambuco).......	....	....	....	....	....
Torre and Varzea (Pernambuco)....	....	....	....	....	....
Goyanna (Pernambuco)...........	....	....	....	....	....
Iron rails (Pernambuco)...........	21.600	....	....	....	21.600
Maceió (Alagòas)...	....	....	....	....	....
Central-rails (Bahia)	11.000	....	....	....	11.000
Economical carriages (Bahia)......	9.660	....	....	....	9.660
City rails (Bahia...	....	....	....	....	....
Bahia Locomotive..	6.600	....	....	....	6.600
Nictheroy (Rio de Janeiro)........	12.900	....	....	....	12.900
Macahé (Rio de Janeiro).........	....	....	....	....	....
Campos (Rio de Janeiro).........	....	....	....	....	....
Capital of S. Paulo.	4.000	....	....	....	4.000
City of Santos (S. Paulo)..........	2.000	....	....	....	2.000
Porto Alegre (S. Pedro do Rio-Grande do Sul)	....	....	....	....	....
City of Rio-Grande (S. Pedro do Rio-Grande do Sul)..	....	....	....	....	....
	161.640	37.332	9.900	....	208.872

Macadamized Roads.

The road *Union and Industry*, which goes from Petropolis to Juiz de Fôra, in the province of Minas-Geraes,
is macadamized and constructed with the utmost perfection :
it is remarkable for its well drawn tracing and for artistical
works of great merit.

It has an extent of 146,8 kilometers.

The company that made it takes to its charge the conveyance both of passengers and merchandise.

In the year 1872 its traffic consisted of 3,626 passengers, and 50,425,035 kilgr. of merchandise; 30,495,945
kilgr. belonging to exportation, and 19,929,090 kilgr.
to importation.

The receipts were £ 157,397 , and the expenses
£ 115,803 ; the balance in favour £ 41,594.

Graciosa Road.—It connects the port of Antonina, in
the province of Paraná, with Coritiba, the capital of the
same province.

It is not wholly terminated, but it is already much
frequented by cars.

Serra da Estrella Road.—It is a monumental work, in
the province of Rio de Janeiro, constructed at a very
steepy point of the Serra do Mar. It offers a free access to the city of Petropolis, where the Emperor has a
beautiful country palace, and a great many of the
wealthiest inhabitants of the capital of the Empire spend
the hot season, called forth by the mildness of the climate.

This city is pretty important as it contains a great number
of elegant edifices and chalets.

The road is 10 kil., in length.

There are still other roads, more or less important, in the different provinces, the extent of roads of that description being calculated at 450 kilometers.

Canals.

Brazil possesses, as yet, very few canals to transport to market the products of its vast territory.

RIO DE JANEIRO.

The canal that joins the municipalities of Campos and Macahé is 100,56 kil. long, running for an extent of 17,6 kil., through rivers and lakes.

It has its commencement in the lake Ozorio, now extinct, 230 meters distant from the right bank of the Parahyba, and, in continuation, it reaches the left bank of the river Macahé, opposite to the city of the same name, making a junction with the rivers Ururahy, Macabú, Carrapato, and Macahé, and the lakes Piabanha, Jenuez, Paulista, Carapebús, Jentahiba and different others.

The province spent with this work £ 200,000, and at last made a lease of it to a company, to which it granted certain favours with the obligation of keeping up a steam navigation line.

The Nogueira Canal made to communicate the virgin forest tracts of Nogueira and Imbury with the river Parahyba, in the municipality of Campos; it is 1,097, 8 metres, long.

The *Cacimbas Canal*, which discharges its waters into the left bank of the river Parahyba, on the north of the city of S. João da Barra. It is 32 kil. long, and is chiefly employed in transporting timber during the wet season of the year.

The *Magé Canal*, having 2,596 meters of extension, from the city of Magé to the port of Piedade, in Nictheroy bay.

Before the construction of the D. Pedro II Rail-way, this canal was of extraordinary advantage to the municipalities of Cantagallo, Nova Friburgo, Parahyba do Sul, Magé and also to different other localities of the province of Minas Geraes, in transporting their produces, that came down the Sapucaia road.

The province spent in its construction the sum of £ 6,400.

It is now sailed by small vessels that carry sundry commodities and products from different places in the neigbourhood of Piedade port.

The *Itaguahy Canal* between the city and river of the same name, is 2,552 meters long.

The products of the municipalities of Rezende, Barra Mansa, Pirahy, Itaguahy, and part of S. João do Principe were formerly exported to the market of Rio de Janeiro, through the port of Itaguahy.

Actually the interest of these municipalities is better served by the D. Pedro II Rail-way ; but the canal is still of use to the neighbouring planters.

PARANÁ AND S. PAULO.

Varadouro Canal. — It is intended to join the bay of Paranaguá, in the province of Paraná, to Iguape and Cananea, in the province of S. Paulo, by the coast of the isthmus that separates them.

According to the plans approved, for the execution of which active measures are being taken, the canal ought to be 2,700 meters long, 1,65 meters deep, and 2,8 meters broad at the bottom, and 8,8 meters broad at the water's edge. The cost of its excavation was estimated at about £ 6,000.

SERGIPE.

In the construction of the canal, that ought to join the two rivers Poxim and Sta Maria, difficulties supervened in the execution of the works, so that only 4,241 cubic meters were excavated.

MARANHÃO.

There are, in this province, the following canals:

Coqueiros, with 1,650 meters, in length, and 22 meters, in breadth ; it communicates the two rivers Mosquitos and Coqueiro, and shortens the voyage between the capital, the Itapicurú, and Mearim, avoiding the shallows of the islands Taná Redondo and Taná Mirim.

It is regularly kept, and is navigated by steamers drawing 3,05 to 3,66 meters.

Arapapahy, with which the provincial treasury has spent large sums of money. The excavations that now exist were made in the years 1848 to 1858.

When finished, the canal will be 2,200 meters long, and will make a junction of the waters of Bacanga and Arapapahy with the bays of Arrayal and S. Marcos.

The *Mearim Canal*, which is not yet finished, but is projected, as the means of avoiding the shallows of Lage Grande in the river of the same name ; it allows only the navigation of small vessels of not much draught.

Immigration and Colonization.

It being universally acknowledged that one of the first requisites for Brazil, is an increase of its population, the powers of the State continue to make every effors to obtain it, not only by affording every facility to laborious and well moralized immigrants, by granting them valuable privileges, but also by taking every precaution, in order that nothing may be wanting to them on their arrival, where they will find every comfort and redress, and meet persons to direct their first steps and give them every protection.

In order to promote these views, besides the facilities granted to colonists and immigrants to be naturalized, as is explained in its proper head, regulations have been issued for their conveyance, that nothing should he wanting to them, on their voyage to the Empire.

These regulations are, in the whole, a copy of those adopted in most of the ports of Europe. They fix the proportion that there ought to exist between the number of passengers and the tonnage of the vessel that carries them, the space allotted to every passenger, the quantity and quality of the provisions on board, the accommodations under deck, the sanitary and police precautionary measures, and the penalties incurred by captains that transgress the established orders.

A law on lands has been published, in harmony with the system followed in the United-States, and adapted to the peculiar situation of Brazil. Amongst other provisional regulations it only permits the acquisition of spare lands by purchase, except on the frontiers of the Empire;

establishes and discriminates public from private property, and regulates the surveying, the description, and the demarcation of the lots of land to be purchased.

The lowest price is from 1/2 *real* to 2 *réis* for each square fathom; 4,84 meters square. The sale of the lots of land in the colonies of the State, is, however, made according to the prices hereafter mentioned.

The aforesaid law is still to be modified by complimentary measures that ought greatly to aid its execution.

An Official Agency has been appointed since 1864 to put into execution, in the port of Rio de Janeiro, what is prescribed and ordained for the transport of immigrants; to superintend the service of the asylum of the new settlers ; to provide for their landing and conveyance to their settlement ; to give directions to those that intend to establish themselves in the colonies of the State; to encourage spontaneous immigration ; to act as an intervening agent between individuals that intend to import colonists and the agents of emigration abroad.

The Official Agency has its office in the centre of the city, that it may more readily attend to, and despatch any business concerning colonization.

On the other hand, the government grants to immigrants the following favours: the payment of the difference of price they ought to pay if they went over to the United-States and that due for their shipment to Brazil ; an advance of the whole passage money to those who embark with the firm purpose of establishing themselves in the colonies of the State, several Brazilian consuls being authorized to defray their respective expenses, particularly those in London, Liverpool, Switzerland, Marseilles, and Hamburg; importation of the objects they bring with them, free of duty, viz: their household furniture in any quantity or quality indispensable to their daily use, the

clothes of their own private use, their bedding of every description, in relation to the condition and means of the immigrants, their crockery ware, agricultural implements or tools,
suited to the trades they intend to follow, and a fowling
piece for each grown up man ; the right of being lodged in the boarding-house supported by government, in the
metropolis of the Empire, where on their landing they find
lodgings and victuals at the cost of about 2 shillings a day
for an adult, and 1 shilling for a minor from 9 to 12
years of age; and finally the right of receiving gratuitously from the colonial agency the informations they may
require and a passage to the colonies of the State, if the
colonists are volunteers, lately arrived, heads of family,
and husbandmen.

The Official Agency also takes under its charge to obtain by its efforts or by advertisements in the papers,
employment for those that wish to remain in Rio de
Janeiro.

State colonies.

The colonies of the State are superintended by directors
appointed by the government, in conformity to what is
determined by the Decree of 1867.

The new settlers are temporarily lodged in a house
suited for the purpose, until they are put in possession
of their respective lots of land.

Whenever they ask for it, they are fed by the Agency
during the first ten days, under the condition of paying
their expenses when they make the reimbursement of the
other advances.

Once in possession of his lot of land, the colonist receives a gift of £ 2, which is equally distributed to every
member of his family more than ten and less than fifty
years of age : as also seeds for the first sowings, the ne-

cessary rural implements, a temporary house, 48,4 ares of felled land or its equivalent in money. These last items granted to the colonists to help them to their task, are to be debited to them along with the land.

The colonists that wish to be employed in the public works of the settlement will find immediate work, receiving a reasonable salary, for the space of 90 days within the first six months after his arrival.

In those colonies where the population is superior to 500 souls, a sum not exceeding 5 °/₀ is deducted from the wages of the workmen and deposited for the benefit of the colony, being applied to its improvements by a board of Commissioners, chosen amongst those colonists that have reimbursed the State of their debts: that sum is also destined to help the Director in the management of the colony.

The lots of colonial lands are divided into urban and rural. The areas of the latter comprehend either 60,5, or 30,25, or 15,13 hectares, and the prices are from 2 to 8 reis: the former are 22 to 44 meters in front by 44 to 110 meters long, varying in price from 1 to 8 réis for every 4,84 square meters.

If the concession be on credit, 20 °/₀ must be added to the price, and the payment made in four yearly-installments, the first to be paid two years after the purchaser is come into possession of the land.

If a colonist anticipates the payment of his installments, he is entitled to 6 °/₀ discount.

There are in all the colonies, primary schools for children of both sexes, and catholic and protestant clergymen, who minister to the colonists the spiritual food.

SANTA LEOPOLDINA COLONY.

It is situated 52,8 kil. distant from the capital of the province of Espirito Santo, there being a free access to it by the river Santa Maria.

It has a population superior to 300 inhabitants, mostly Germans, besides some Dutch and Swiss.

According to the colonial census of 1871, there were in the preceding year, 101 births and 41 deaths.

The production consists of coffee, sugar cane, cereals, and several kinds of potatoes, its exports being estimated at £ 10,400.

RIO-NOVO.

It is also established in the province of Espirito Santo, and contains 1,000 inhabitants.

In 1871 there were 84 births and 13 deaths.

The principal culture is coffee and cereals, and, in the above mentioned year, the production was estimated at £ 8,000; the imports at £ 2,200; and the exports at £ 5,200.

MUCURY.

The territory of this colony is belonging to the province of Minas-Geraes, and it is 389,4 kil. distant from the nearest maritime port, viz: 191,4 kil. through commonroads, and 198 kil. of river steam-navigation.

It is inhabited by 700 persons, almost all Germans.

The surface of the tilled lands comprehends 700 hectares, and of those which are to be marked out for lots, more than 300 hectares.

The culture consists of grain, potatoes, coffee, sugar

cane, and tobacco, besides the raising of several kinds of cattle and domestic fowls.

CANANEA.

Situated in the province of S. Paulo, 23,1 kil. distant from the sea-coast, and not far from the village of the same name, it is inhabited by 478 colonists, mostly English.

Special circumstances, which the public powers have carefully tried to remove, have impeded the progress of this colony.

The place is salubrious, and the lands are extremely fertile.

At present a highway is in construction between this settlement and the nearest port, and other remarkable improvements are about to be effected.

ASSUNGUY.

Settled at the distance of 99 kil, from the capital of the province of Paraná, it numbers about 440 inhabitants, and will rise to a promising condition as soon as the roads, that are now in construction and which will give a free access to it, shall be finished.

ITAJAHY.

It is 46,2 kil. distant from the port of the same name, in the province of Santa Catharina. Its population amounts to 2,300 inhabitants, mostly Germans.

In 1872 there were 73 births and 18 deaths.

The surface which is cultivated comprises 400 hectares and yields sugar, rum, cotton, tobacco, grain, and {potatoes.

The pastures, which comprehend 300 hectares, support several kinds of cattle.

It possesses 18 saw-mills, which are always at work, and prove of great advantage to the colonists.

Its produces are valued at above £ 10,000 a year, and the exportation, which is almost confined to timber, at the same sum.

BLUMENAU.

It is situated in the province of Santa Catharina, in the navigable part of the river Itajahy, having cart roads, and being peopled by 6,329 persons, almost all Germans.

In 1871 the number of births attained 335, and the mortality was below 50.

In the same year, the colony's products which consisted of cereals, potatoes, cotton, coffee, sugar, rum, tobacco, butter, and cheese, the following figures prevail: 6,544,800 liters of maize; 6,544,800 liters of potatoes; 151.483,28 kilogr. of sugar; 16.452,8 kilgr. of butter; 15.424,5 kilgr., of cheese; and 200.630,41 liters of rum.

It also possesses many herds of several kinds of cattle, chiefly swine, which raising amounted, in the last dates, to 5,500 heads.

The exports of the settlement were estimated, in 1871, at £ 13,200, and the imports at £ 16,500.

It was created, in the colony, an agricultural society which has rendered good services, by spreading useful informations among the colonists, promoting agricultural exhibitions, and establishing libraries.

SANTA MARIA DA SOLEDADE.

It was founded by a private association on a spot that offers all convenient requisites, near the municipality of

S. Leopoldo, in the province of S. Pedro do Rio Grande do Sul.

Not being able to defray their charges, they had recourse to the public powers, and, by virtue of a legislative act, issued out in 1866, they surrogated their right to the government in return for the capitals disbursed.

In the beginning of this year, it was inhabited by 1,588 persons of different nationalities.

The population has increased, and is likely to increase still more by the admittance of other immigrants which will soon be sent thither.

The whole population of the State colonies amounts to 16,412 inhabitants ; not including S. Leopoldo, already out of the colonial regime and raised up to a town, in the province of S. Pedro do Rio Grande do Sul, with a population of about 20,000 souls, as well as those in the same condition as the latter, such as: Santa Izabel, in the province of Espirito-Santo with 301 souls; Therezopolis, with 1,631 inhabitants, and Santa Izabel, with 1,213, in the province of Santa Catharina.

The number of colonists, therefore, is greater than it was in 1867, when they amounted to 10,964.

Amongst the colonies emancipated, are worthy of mention the two ones of Nova Friburgo and Petropolis, both lying in elevated localities of the mountain range of Orgãos in the province of Rio de Janeiro.

The former, founded in 1820, at the government's expense, with Swiss and German colonists, is, long since, a flourishing village, sought for by sick persons, on account of its salubrity.

The latter, established with German colonists on land-properties of the Emperor, and subsidized by the provincial government for some years past, is actually, the seat of a beautiful town, with 8,200 inhabitants, of which about 3,000 are either Germans or their offspring.

PROVINCIAL AND PRIVATE COLONIES.

In the province of Rio Grande do Sul there are the following colonies :

Santa Cruz, with a population of 5,550 colonists; its exports amounting to about £ 40,000, and its imports at £ 30,000: — S. Angelo, with 1,316 inhabitants, its exports amounting to above £ 5,000, and its imports to about £ 4,000 : — Nova Petropolis, peopled by 1,221 persons, its exports being calculated at £ 4,200, and its imports at £ 5,000.

In the same province, besides the colony Mont'Alverne, founded in 1859 on the river Taquary, with a population of 348 inhabitants, there are also those of S. Feliciano, of Count d'Eu, and of Princess D. Izabel, lately established, and under the charge of the provincial government.

There is yet, in the same province, the colony of S. Loorenço, on the skirts of Serra dos Taipes with 3,280 inhabitants, several manufactories and 14 schools.

In Sta. Catharina, the D. Francisca colony, that has nearly a population of 7,000 inhabitants, continues to thrive, its exportation, in 1871, being estimated at £23,000, and its importation at £ 22,000 : it is subsidized by the government.

Amongst the provincial colonies, Angelina, in the province of Sta. Catharina distinguishes itself, as being composed of 1,316 native inhabitants.

It is situated at a distance of 59,4 kilometers from the town of S. José, and it is in a flourishing state.

In the province of Minas Geraes, in the municipality of Parahybuna, lies the D. Pedro II colony, containing 1,318 inhabitants and having a cultivated area of 1,622 hectares. It has three schools with 131 children of both sexes.

In the province of Bahia was, last year, established the colony Moniz, which promises to be a prosperous one and has already more than 1,000 inhabitants.

The whole population of the last mentioned colonies is estimated at 23,917 inhabitants, that is, 5,108 more than in 1867. If we sum up this population with that of the State colonies they will make a total of 40,329 inhabitants, not comprising the population of S. Leopoldo, and the emancipated colonies already mentioned.

CONTRACTS FOR THE IMPORTATION OF IMMIGRANTS.

The government has signed several contracts for the introduction of immigrants into differents provinces of the Empire.

The general basis on which they are founded, with some indifferent alterations, according to the nature of the contracts, are the following :

The observance of the statutes concerning the transport of colonists into the Empire ;

On the part of the government, a grant of lands situated in the proximity (13,2 kil., at the most) of railroads, of sea ports, and great markets, or in other places pointed out as the most adapted for culture, at the price fixed by law, and paid up in the term of six years, in installments ; the expenses of measurement being put to the charge of the contractors;

Free passage to immigrants and their baggage in the packets of companies subsidized or befriended by the government, and on the rail-roads ;

The landing free of duties of their baggage, utensils, agricultural implements and machinery ;

An allowance of £ 6 to every adult that be employed as a day-labourer ; of £ 7 to every joint-partner colonist ; of £ 15 to every one who purchases lands to settle in the country, and the half of the said sums to those under 14 to 2 years of age ;

On the part of the contractors, the obligation of not receiving any interests from the immigrants for the first two years, nor to stipulate more than 6 °/₀ interest a year, for the five following ones, when the debt becomes due, and to do every thing in their power to promote the welfare of the colonists till they are finally settled ;

The responsibility of the contractors for the abuses they may be guilty of, not only conveying colonists that are not in the terms of their contracts, which the consular agents or other Brazilian functionaries in Europe, appointed by the government, are to pay a strict attention to ; but also by deceiving the immigrants with false promises or by any way concealing the real facts, the circumstances of the country, the conditions of labour and any others that may assure them a thriving future.

The immigrants above all ought to have a perfect knowledge of the duties and advantages they have agreed upon, and to sign, before going on board, a declaration that they are not going to Brazil at the expense and for the account of the Imperial Government, and that they shall not, in any future period, under any pretence whatever, require from the same government any thing else than that protection which the laws grant, in general, to foreigners.

The non observance of these and other clauses makes the contractors liable to fines and to rescission of their respective contracts.

There are, at present, in vigour thirteen contracts of this nature.

In accordance with them, within the period of ten years, in the maximum, 149,600 immigrants are to be imported into the provinces of Paraná, Santa Catharina, Rio de Janeiro, Espirito-Santo, Bahia, Alagôas, Pernambuco, Maranhão, and others of the north of the Empire.

On that purpose, the government has marked out an extent of land measuring 2,431,324 hectares.

We must mention here the pecuniary aid granted by the government to the province of S. Pedro do Rio Grande do Sul, which signed a contract with a private association for the introduction of 40,000 colonists; and likewise the contracts that the president of Espirito-Santo was empowered to make with two farmers of the said province, under the same clauses that were mentioned above.

Independent of those contracts for the introduction of immigrants into the Empire, the government, acknowledging the necessity they were under of promoting by every means in their power the transition from the system of slave to free labour, did not hesitate, following the example of other civilized nations, to accept proposals for the importation of Asiatic labourers.

With these views the government signed a contract for their introduction, taking every precaution to avoid the abuses which in other countries have been committed, and obliging therefore the contractors to insert in the contracts they sign the formal declaration of the time of service, the salary to be paid, the term when due, and the right of rescission.

It is, moreover, positively enjoined that in making enrollments, and upon their agreements with the labourers, in Asia, they shall abide by the laws and regulations in vigour in the different localities, not permitting them to land any expeditions in any part of the Empire, without the captain of the vessel that imports them being provided with a certificate, that he has fulfilled the said laws and regulations.

We are told that the Asiatic Emigration Company is formed, and that the necessary orders have been already issued for the first shipments of Asiatic labourers. On the other hand, with the firm intention to simplifying to immigrants the purchase of unoccupied lands, the government continues to order the measurement and marking out of lots of land, suited for colonization, affording to them at once the free access to sea ports or to navigable rivers.

Until the year 1867, an extent of 339,405 hectares had been measured and marked out in the provinces of S. Pedro· do Rio Grande do Sul, Sᵗᵃ Catharina, Paraná, S. Paulo, Espirito-Santo, Alagôas and Pará.

Since that time that area was reduced to 295,845 hectares, because 17,424 were reserved for the district of the new colony Prince D. Pedro, in the province of Sᵗᵃ Catharina; 17,424 hectares to extend the limits of the colonial district of Assunguy, in the province of Paraná; and finally, because about 8,712 were occupied by Brazilians, on the south of the province of Espirito-Santo, near the colony of Rio Novo. With the late measurements in the provinces of Sᵗᵃ Catharina, Paraná, and S. Paulo, the area of those lands was again raised to nearly 503,965 hectares, according to the statement of the competent office.

Measurements were also made in the provinces of

Espirito-Santo, Bahia, Pernambuco and Pará, in different allotments, equally intended for immigration, which are not included in that sum, as they still depend upon being better verified and regularly enrolled.

Whilst government is occupied with these studies, and in collecting statistical, topographical, and descriptive data as to the existence of the colonies, their situation, measurement and means of communication and other circumstances, that may better recommend the land-property of the State, the competent office is organizing maps similar to those that were sent to the Exhibition, in Vienna.

One of these maps comprehends different tracts of unoccupied lands, and territories measured and marked out, in the municipalities of Cananéa and Iguape, and in the parish of Itapecerica, in the south of S. Paulo, making up an extent of 230,868 hectares, including the territory of Cananéa, in the district of the colony of the same name.

In the same map is found a descriptive notice of the lands measured and marked out, and their relative position to different points of the sea-shore of the district of Iguape, as also of the distances, and of the present system of roads and those that for the future will best suit the intercourse of its inhabitants. This map also affords sufficient information as to the quality of the lands, to what culture they are most fit for, the excellence of the climate, and other favourable conditions.

The other, a lithographed map of the province of Santa Catharina, also shows the public lands already measured and marked out, the existing colonies, as well as the rivers, roads, villages, and different localities where there is to be found a great extent of unoccupied lands of excellent quality, lying westwards, four leagues from the sea-shore and making up an extent of 3,049,200 hectares.

Two more topographic and descriptive maps of the provinces of S. Pedro do Rio Grande do Sul and Paraná, are to be soon published, which are organized according to the same system, and containing such information as will most intimately interest immigrants in their choice of the lands they intend to purchase from the State.

They will thus be able to find out public lands already surveyed, measured, and marked out, and they can take possession of them in lots of 121 hectares, or in half or in quarter lots, as they please.

Those lots may be sold in public auction or otherwise; its lowest price being one *real* every 4,84 square meters, including the cost of measurement and demarcation.

As a general rule, the price is for ready cash : but if the immigrants wish to make their settlements in colonial and agricultural districts, they shall be allowed the term of five years to pay in installments, with the annual interest of 6 °/₀, to count from the end of the second year of their settlement in the country.

The Cathechising and Civilization of the Indians.

It is estimated at 500,000 the number of Indians, who live in a wandering state, through the wilds and native forests of the Empire, they being quite lost for society, which, nevertheless, is subject to their incursions and ravages.

The government has always endeavoured to cathechise and civilize them, being assisted in this undertaking by the evangelical zeal of the Capuchine and Franciscan Observant friars, who worthily fulfil their noble mission.

In spite, however, of reiterated efforts, it has not yet been possible to obtain a number of missionaries sufficient for the necessities of the service.

For so numerous a quantity of Indians, spread out through a vast territory, there are but 61 Capuchine missionaries, many of which are already weakened by labours and their advanced age; besides those there are 6 Franciscan Observants more.

The system of cathechising generally adopted, consists in assembling into settlements those Indians, who by the apostolical devotion of the missionaries leave off their wandering life and acquire the knowledge of property and a love for labour, settling on a fixed dwelling.

Superintended, at first, by the missionaries, those settlements are afterwards managed by secular directors, either upon the death of their primitive settlers or on account of their being removed to other places of the Empire, where they are more necessary.

The Franciscan Observants, 6 in number, were specially established on the Upper Amazonas, where upon their arrival in 1870, have been founded the settlements of S. Francisco, between the rivers Preto and Madeira, for the natives of the Araras and Iorás tribes; and on the river Solimões that of Caldeirão, which possesses a church and other buildings, and contains 250 souls.

They are about to make a third settlement, near the fifth fall of the river Madeira, in order to establish there the Indians of the Caripuna tribe.

The Capuchine missionaries are distributed in the following manner:

Mato-Grosso	2
Goyaz	5
Pará	6
Maranhão	4
Pernambuco	11
Sergipe	2
Bahia	14
Espirito-Santo	2
Minas-Geraes	8
Capital of the Empire	4
Paraná	2
S. Pedro do Rio Grande do Sul	1

Although the aboriginals, with the exception of but a few not numerous tribes, are endowed of a mild temper, and easily submit themselves to sedentary labours, their natural inclination, however, and their rooted wild habits, make them unpersevering in their new mode of life.

Experience has shown out that, with regard to adults, it is difficult, or rather impossible, to obtain from them satisfactory results; and, therefore, without abandoning them to their wretched fate, the government is determined to operate principally on the new generations, by creating educational institutes for young Indians.

In accordance with this plan, the boarding school of Santa Izabel, was founded in 1870, on the valley of the Araguaya, and it is attended by about 52 children of either sex, belonging to the wild Canoeiros and Tapirapés, and to the mild Guajajaras, of the Tupy tribes; to the mild Chavantes, Cherentes, and Carajás, and the wild Jaraés, Cayapós, Gradahús and Apinagés, of the Tapuya tribes.

The same valley is inhabited by the Indians of the tribes Chambioás, a branch of the Carajás, Apinagés, Canoeiros, Coroados, and others whose names are not known.

The Indians are proverbially sober, very expert in the bodily exercises used by them, and endowed of a great strength.

The children existing at the Santa Izabel boarding-school, easily learn reading and writing, and are already learning the trades of blacksmith and carpenter, at the workshops of the Araguaya Steam .Navigation Company, whilst those of the school are being constructed. The girls are also employed in household services.

Those children, who were at first obtained by presenting their parents with each iron tools as would prove more useful to them, are now often willingly offered by their very parents.

The government hopes that, having thus been educated in the precepts of religion and the habits of a civilized life they will be, in after times, powerful auxiliaries, who will draw their parents and brothers into the social state.

A similar sentiment prevailed on the granting of a subsidy paid by the State for the support of the Young Artisans' College, established at Manáos, upon condition of affording education to a certain number of young Indians.

The government intends to establish another college, either at Mucury or on the valley of the river Doce, for the children of those tribes who lead there a wandering life.

To the old settlements, with somewhat civilized inhabitants may be considered as mixed together with the general population, we must add the following ones, which are governed by missionaries.

In the province of Amazonas — S. Francisco, on the river Madeira; Caldeirão, on the river Solimões; and another settlement, which will be established, in a short time, near the falls of the Madeira.

In the province of Pará.—Capim and Tapajoz on the margins of the so called rivers.

In the province of Goyaz. —S. José de Jamimbú, composed of the Indians Carajás and Chavantes ; Gorgulho on the river Araguaya, consisting of Chambioás, 237,6 kilom. distant from Leopoldina on the river Somno ; and Ibiapama.

In the province of Maranhão. — S. Pedro de Pindaré, founded in 1840, and composed of Indians Guajajaras ; Leopoldina, created in 1854 for Indians of the same tribe; Januaria, established in the same year, for the tribes Creusés and Potegés : and Palmeira Torta, in 1870, for the Guajajaras. The population of those settlements amounts to 4,172 souls.

In the latter province there are still 19 settlements governed by *directores parciaes*; their population amounting to 12,000 souls.

They are composed of Indians of the following tribes :

1st Guajajaras.

2d Caractagés.

3d Canellas.

4th Gaviões.

5th Tymbiras.

6th Jaulegés.
7th Caragés.
8th Caraetés.
9th Caracahys.
10th Tembês.
11th Amanazés.
12th Mutuns.

In the province of Bahia there exists the settlement of Cachoeira dos Ilhéos, in a flourishing condition.

In the province of Espirito-Santo, the Mutum and Pancas tribes are settled on the valley of the river Doce, under the direction of two Capuchine missionaries.

In Minas-Geraes there are four settlements : Mutum, on the valley of the river Doce; Jequitinhonha, on the margin of the river so called ; Nossa Senhora da Conceição, and Mucury, in the neighbourhood of the State Colonies, established in that province.

Another settlement is to be established, on the valley of the Manhuassú, immediately upon the arrival of the missionaries that were sent to the above mentioned province.

In the province of S. Paulo there are the settlements of Itapeva da Faxina and of S. João Baptista.

Finally, in the provinces of Paraná, and S. Pedro do Rio Grande do Sul, there exist 5 settlements, namely : S. Jeronymo, on the banks of the Tibagy, 184,8 kil., distant from the town of Castro, and composed of 142 Indians Canôas, also called Coroados ; S. Pedro de Alcantara, with 768 Indians of the tribes Cayguás and Coroados ; they produce coffee, sugar and grain ; Pirapó, and Paranapanema. Those settlements belong to the first mentioned province. In the second there is the settlement of Nonohay, with a population of 332 Indians of the tribe of the Coroados,

c. 4   17

Foreigners.

Foreigners are very kindly treated in Brazil; their rights are respected, and in their civil intercourse they are protected by the laws.

The primary schools are gratuitously open to them and to their children, in the same manner as to natives; and in the like manner, they are admitted both to the public colleges and to the superior schools.

They can travel throughout the Empire as freely as the Brazilian citizens, and can avail themselves of the guarantee of the *habeas corpus* act.

Observing the prescriptions of the laws, they are permitted to establish and exercise freely all kinds of trade, provided that they be not contrary to good morals and to public health and security; they can possess land property, using it in the same plenitude as Brazilian citizens.

They enjoy the greatest liberty of conscience never being persecuted by religious motives, provided that they respect the religion of the State.

The rights of their children, born in the Empire, deserved a special attention of the powers of the State, it being decided that the legislation that regulates the civil condition of foreigners, residing in Brazil, and not employed in the service of their own country, must also be applicable to the civil condition of their children, but only during their minority.

On attaining their majority, they enter into the exercise of the rights of Brazilian citizens.

A Brazilian woman who marries a foreigner partakes

of the condition of the latter; in the same manner that a foreign woman who marries a Brazilian follows the condition of her husband.

The law acknowledges as valid, for all civil effects, the marriages between protestants, celebrated either within or without the Empire, provided that be performed all formalities required by the laws, and that they be duly registered.

The inheritances or legacies of foreigners dying in Brazil, are regulated by the same laws, proceedings, and authorities, as prescribed for those of the natives, unless there exists a consular convention, in which case they are regulated by the latter.

Consular conventions have been made with France, Switzerland, Italy, Spain, and Portugal.

The authority of consuls is also admitted in the cases and in the manner determined by the decree of the 8th November 1851, in virtue of a simple agreement establishing reciprocity by means of an interchange of notes.

In virtue of a declaration on the side of the Brazilian government, the consular conventions will become of no effect since the 20 February of next year.

The imperial government is inclined to enter into negociations for new agreements, the necessary studies having already commenced.

In order to regulate the extradiction of criminals, Brazil has already celebrated treaties with the following nations : the Argentine Confederation, the Republics of Uruguay, Peru, Equador, Bolivia, Spain, and with the kingdoms of Portugal, Italy, and Great-Britain.

Naturalization.

Naturalization is, at present, very easily obtained in Brazil.

The matter is regulated by the law 1950 of the 12th July 1871, which modified the preceding ones in a more liberal scale.

The government was authorized by it to grant titles of naturalization to every foreigner above 21 years of age who, having resided in Brazil, or been abroad in the service of the State, for more than two years, demands it, declaring his intention to stay in the country or to continue in its service, after his being naturalized.

The government can dispense with the time of residence required:

1. Those foreigners who are married to Brazilian women.

2. Those who possess land property in the Empire or have a partnership in any industrial establishment.

3. Those who have invented or introduced any new trade.

4. Those remarkable for their talents, learning or professional abilities in any industrial branch.

5. The children of foreigners already naturalized, when born out of the Empire before their fathers' naturalization.

For the legal effects it is but sufficient to present certificates extracted from the book of notes and the state offices, as well as written declarations from public authorities and respectable persons.

Titles of naturalization are exempt from taxes and pay but £ 2—10 sh of stamp duties, but they are to no effect if the persons naturalized, l y themselves or by proxies provided with special powers, do not, at the same time, take the oath of fidelity and obedience to the Constitution, and the laws of the country, swearing or promising to acknowledge Brazil as their mother country from thenceforward.

The oath may be given either before the central government or the presidents of the provinces.

Upon that occasion the naturalized foreigner ought to make a declaration of his religions principles and of his former country; whether he his single or married, in the latter case whether to a Brazilian or a foreign woman; if he has got children and how many, with the declaration of their name, sex, age, religion, stato and nativity.

These declarations being sent to the Home Department are inserted in the register of all the naturalized foreigners.

To those who purchase lands on which to settle, or belonging to any colony established in the Empire, as well as to they who come at their own expense to exercise any trade, the title of naturalization is still more easily granted.

For that purpose it is but sufficient that after two years residence, they write down a declaration of their intention before the municipal board or a justice of the peace.

Upon receiving an affidavit of this declaration, the minister of the Empire, in the capital, or the presidents, in the provinces, order the issuing out of the respective tittle free from any fees or expenses.

The foreigners thus naturalized, are exempt from the military service, being only subject to that of the national guard, within the municipality.

The government may dispense with the term of two years residence those colonists thought worthy of the concession.

The parents, guardians, or trustees of minor colonists, born out of the Empire, before the naturalization of their parents, may make the declarations required and obtain, for their children or wards, the respective tittle of naturalization, the minors being free to change their nationality, when they come to maturity.

On the other hand, the legislative power of late years has frequently dispensed with the clauses required by the laws respecting naturalization, by means of a simple petition; and has authorized the government to grant it, independent of the above mentioned conditions.

Not including the colonists, the number of naturalized foreigners was as follows:

In 1867.	. . . .	113
» 1868.	. . . .	106
» 1869.	. . . .	316
» 1870.	. . . .	316
» 1871.	. . . . . .	117
» 1872.	. . , ...	224
	Total . . .	1,192

The naturalized foreigner is at once considered a Brazilian citizen, and enters into the fruition of all the civil and political rights appertaining to those born in the country, with the only exceptions established by the Constitution, concerning the offices of Regent of the Empire, Minister of State and of Deputy to the General Assembly.

Intellectual Culture.

Primary and secondary instruction.

The primary and secondary instruction of the capital of the Empire is under the charge of the General Assembly and of the Government.

The inspection of these matters is exercised by the Minister of the Empire, by a general inspector, a council of direction, and by the delegates of the district.

The exercise of a professorship depends on the authorization of the government : the candidate must prove his legal majority (21 years in order to teach, and 25 in order to be the head of a school), his morality, and ability.

Married women must, moreover, exhibit their marriage contract, or the certificate of their husband's death if they are widows ; and in case of their being judicially separated from their husbands, the sentence which decreed the separation.

These conditions are required not only for the public professorships but also for the private or free ones.

Assistant professors ; those who have passed examinations at the academies of the Empire in the higher courses; those who have been public professors; bachelors of arts of the D. Pedro II college; those who exhibit diplomas of foreign academies, duly legalised ; — finally natives and foreigners recognized as able teachers, may be relieved from these proofs of professional capacity by the government.

The public schools of primary instruction are of the first and second order.

In those of the first order, the teaching is limited to moral and religious instruction, reading, writing, the elements of grammar, the elementary principles of arithmetic, and the comparative system of weights and measures.

Those of the second order, besides the above mentioned studies, comprise: the whole of arithmetic with its practical application, the study of the Gospel and the knowledge of sacred history, the elements of history and geography specially of Brazil, the principles of the physical sciences and of natural history with application to practical purposes, linear perspective, music and singing, the complet system of weights and measures compared with the metrical french system.

There is a class of professors, who under the denomination of assistants, aid the public professors in their scholastic labours and prepare themselves for the profession of teachers.

The professors of primary instruction and the assistants are always appointed after competitive examinations.

The directors of every private establishment of primary, secondary, or mixed instruction must show testimonials of their morality and professional ability.

The directors and directresses of schools of primary instruction, although they do not exercise themselves the professorship, must give proofs of their ability by undergoing an examination in the Christian religion, sacred history, reading, writing, portuguese grammar, arithmetic, and the system of weights and measures in use in the Empire. For the directresses of schools of secondary instruction the examination comprises: reading, writing, arithmetic, geography, french or english; — and for the directors : arithmetic, geography, french or english, latin and philosophy.

The government can exempt from examination all persons who are in the same circumstances as those who for professorship are exempt from it ; — and the general inspector can dispense from testimonials of morality those who enjoy a good reputation and are generally known.

They must further, before opening their establishments, present the programme of the studies and the project of the internal regulations, the indication of the locality, the arrangements, the situation of the edifice and the names and professional titles of the professors.

The heads of schools who do not profess the Roman Catholic religion are obliged to maintain a priest for their Roman Catholic pupils.

They may adopt for the instruction of their pupils the books and methods which they think best, provided that they be not such as are expressly prohibited.

Pupils of both sexes cannot be admitted into the same educational establishment ; — and in those of the female sex no person of the other sex, over 10 years of age, can reside, except the husband of the directress.

Learning, in general, but especially primary instruction, has called forth the persevering sollicitude of the government, as well as the accurate attention of the provincial legislatures, which are competent, by virtue of the constitutional precept, to make laws concerning primary and secondary instructions in the provinces, as also to establish the requisite institutions in order to develop them.

Private efforts, in the most active, encouraging, and effectual manner, are happily coming to the assistance of public power in order to spread out, in a larger scale, throughout the different social classes, the elementary learning, which is as much interesting to society as indispensable to man, however may be his rank and course of life

This general tendency of minds is every day more and more developing itself, and is displayed in an assemblage of facts among which the following ones are the most remarkable:

The creation of evening-schools for adults, both in the capital and in several provinces.

The foundation of establishments for professional learning and the education of paupers.

The institution of normal colleges, in several provincial capitals, for the training of teachers of either sex, with classes of practical teaching.

The creation of popular libraries, both public and private.

The adoption of measures to facilitate the exercise of private professorship, and to render instruction obligatory.

The subscriptions and donatives made to the State, and the spontaneous manner by which many public professors and several persons offer themselves to teach gratuitously, in primary schools, and especially in the evening-classes.

The increase that of late years has been remarked in the expenditure of the general and of all the provincial budgets, for the greater development of popular instruction and education, there being some provinces where the annual expenses, with this only object, amount to above the fifth of the total revenue.

Finally, the issue of papers relating to the subject, and the creation of societies in order to spread instruction, or to assist the general and provincial powers in this capital branch of the public service.

Every thing, therefore, contributes to the hopeful success of one of the noblest and most elevated *desideratums* of civilized nations.

In the municipality of the capital, during the financial year 1872 — 1873, the State spent about £ 28.000 with schools of primary instruction, that is, £ 16,000 more than in 1867.

There are, in the said municipality, 172 schools for both sexes, besides 2 lately created; of this number 67 are public, and 99 private. There are also 8 evening schools.

The primary schools were, last year, attended by 12,498 scholars, including those of the war and navy arsenals, and of other public establishments. The former were attended by 7,175, and the latter by 5,323 students.

There were, then, 4,064 students more than in 1867, and also a greater number than in 1871.

The evening-schools of primary instruction are the following :

That of the municipal school S. Sebastião.

That which was founded and is supported by the society « Aid to National Industry. »

Those established at the parish of Lagôa, and supported by a society called « Propagator of instruction through the working classes »; the course of studies comprehending besides primary instruction, practical geometry, french, and drawing. They receive a monthly allowance from the government.

That of the island of Paquetá, established by the master of the public school in that place.

Those of the parishes of S. José, and of Guaratiba, established and directed by two public teachers, with the special object of spreading the knowledge of the metrical system; and finally, the one lately established by the government at the parish of S. Christovão.

Some private schools of the suburban parishes are subsidized by the government, upon condition of gratuitously teaching the children of the poor.

The last municipal-board founded a public school, under the name of S. Sebastião, in a fine building, erected at Onze de Junho Square, at the expense of the municipality. It is spacious enough to contain classes of primary instruction, with the respective separation, for both sexes; and the last annual attendance amounted to 535 scholars, 333 being of the male, and 232 of the female sex.

All the poor children, who attend that school, are conveniently dressed, at the expense of the « Protecting Helpless Infancy Association. »

In a very short time there will be another fine edifice, of still larger proportions, that the said municipality caused to be constructed for the same purpose, at the parish of S. José, by means of private subscriptions which, at the end of last year, amounted already to above £ 15,400.

Some months ago another vast edifice, with sufficient capacity for 200 students and the respective teachers, was built up, in the parish of S. Christovão, at the expense of the commercial corporation of the capital, and offered to the government, for the purpose of establishing there the public school of the said parish.

Two other fine buildings will soon be ready, which the government ordered to be erected in the parishes of Santa Rita, and of Gloria for the public schools of those parishes; one of them being entirely built at the expense of the national treasure; and the other with the sums offered to the government in behalf of public instruction.

The construction of other edifices, for an identical purpose, is about to be carried on in those parishes where they are still wanting.

Those already finished, as well as others still in construction, have been built up according to plans drawn in conformity with such conditions as experience points out as the best on such matters.

The secondary public instruction is given, in the capital of the Empire, at the D. Pedro II Imperial College, which is divided into two establishments—one for day, and half-boarding scholars (*externato*), situated in the interior of the city; and the other for boarders (*internato*), in one of the healthiest suburbs.

The greater part of the pupils pay a quarterly sum, but so trifling that the government expends for the maintenance of the two establishments the annual sum of about £ 26,281.

In the boarding establishment there are educated at the cost of the government 25 boarders, and in the establishment for day-scholars 15 half-boarding, and an unlimited number of day scholars and of these latter the number in some years has been over 120.

Each of the establishments has a provost charged with the direction and inspection of the classes as well as with the discipline of the college; also a vice-provost, a chaplain and other functionaries.

The professors are appointed by the government after a competitive examination.

The course of studies is divided into seven years at

the end of which the title of Bachelor of Arts is bestowed on those pupils who have attended it.

It consists of the following subjects : religions teaching, portuguese, latin, french, english, german, greek, general geography and cosmography, general history, chorography and history of Brazil, rhetoric, poetry, ancient and modern literature especially the brazilian and portuguese, philosophical grammar, philosophy, elementary mathematics, physics and chemistry, elements of natural history, drawing, music, and gymnastics.

Besides 22 professors there are tutors to assist the pupils to study and prepare their lessons.

The two establishments were last year attended by 370 pupils, of which 8 have since received the degree of Bachelor of Arts; 19 obtained prizes, and 12 honourable mentions.

The number of pupils attending the 54 private establishments of secondary instruction, in the capital, during last year, is estimated at 2,027, including 645 of the female sex.

The latter establishments are 27 for boys, and 27 for girls.

Besides the examinations to which the pupils of D. Pedro II college are submitted, there are general examinations both at the b ginning and the end of the year for those belonging to other establishments of secondary instruction, which are together with those of the above college admitted for the inscription in the superior schools.

In November last, 1873 students were approved in french, english, and other languages; and in February this year, 1,986 in sciences.

In order to spread primary instruction, in the municipality of the Capital, the respective statute has determined that the public teachers should meet once a year, in fixed days, under the lead of the general inspector, to discuss all matters relating to the internal management of the schools, as well as to the methods of teaching.

In those conferences they are to expound their observations, as well as the knowledge they have acquired either in the pratice of teaching or in the special works they have consulted. The results have answered the expectation.

At the first meeting this year, the teachers, in general, gave testimonies of their diligence and learning, delivering valuable lectures, proposing and discussing the alterations to be made, and the measures to be taken, for the development of learning. Some of the latter deserved to be honourably and publicly mentioned by the council of direction and the general inspector of primary and secondary instruction.

One of the above said conferences was honoured by the august attendance of H. M. the Emperor.

Public primary instruction is given gratuitously throughout the Empire, and in conformity with the regulations of public instruction, in the municipality of the Capital, it must become obligatory, when the government judges it convenient.

In many provinces it has already been declared obligatory by the respective laws.

According to what occurs in other civilised nations, the necessity of such a measure is calling the attention both of the general and the provincial governments, and therefore, they are providing for its execution by trying to lessen the difficulties proceeding from great distances, the variety of cultures in the rural districts, where children of a certain age assist their parents in their country labours, and from the scattering of population.

The simultaneous system generally adopted in the private establishments of instruction, the want of a general census, which, however, is being carried on by the Census Office, the dissemination of population, and other causes which are to be removed in time, render the organization of complete statistics on education very difficult.

Notwithstanding this, by the existing official returns we may arrive to the following results, with regard to the provinces.

AMAZONAS.

Its annual expenditure with public instruction amounts to £ 6,132 or rather more than the eighth part of its revenue, which is estimated at £ 51,171.

The number of schools is: 43 primary ones, 38 being public and 5 private, besides a nocturnal course included in the former.

They were attended by 1,217 students, 1,146 belonging to the former, and 71 to the latter.

This amount compared to that of the preceding year, in which the attendance to provincial primary schools did not go above 740 students, the increase is 954, which is striking in the actual circumstances of the province.

It possesses 4 private schools of secondary instruction, and a lyceum where are taught the following subjects : philosophical grammar, portuguese, french, english, pedagogy, accounts and book-keeping, elementary mathematics, history, geography, rhetoric, philosophy and drawing.

Among private schools, the Asylum of Nossa Senhora da Conceição is assisted by the province under the condition of giving board and teaching to ten poor girls, 5 of which Indians.

With respect to the preceding year the increase of attendance in those schools was 360 pupils.

PARÁ.

The province possesses 167 public, and 13 private primary schools, not including the evening-classes ; 15 of the former, however, were not yet working. The attendance of those schools amounted to 6,029 pupils, distributed as follows : public schools 4,581 ; private ones 1,109 ; evening classes 339.

There was the annual increase of 2,134 pupils.

Secondary instruction is given in 6 schools, of which 4, comprising the Pará Lyceum, the Normal School, and a Boarding-School for girls, are public ; and 2 private ones subsidized by the provincial treasure : they were attended by 1,513 pupils.

A sum of £ 30,774, more than a fifth of the whole revenue, which amounts to £ 167,180, is spent with the instruction department.

MARANHÃO.

The provincial budget designs for public instruction the amount of £ 11,600, which is corresponding to the sixth of its revenue, calculated at £ 73,841.

Primary instruction comprehends 150 schools, viz : 117 public, 23 private, and 10 evening schools.

In 117 public schools the attendance was of 4,617 pu_pils; in the private ones of 1,006 ; in the evening classes of 472. The increase, therefore, was 472 over that of the preceding year.

Secondary instruction is given in a lyceum, supported by the province ; in 12 private colleges, and in 3 different classes.

In the private colleges pupils are admitted either as boarders or not, with the exception of that established by the Society « Onze de Agosto » for adults, in evening classes. The number of pupils amounted to 1,416, of which 318 attended the public schools and 1,098 the private ones.

In this department of instruction the increase over the preceding year was of 758 pupils.

PIAUHY.

There are in the province 60 public, and 8 private schools of primary instruction.

The attendance to the latter was of 1,634, and to the former of 172 pupils.

Amongst the public schools is included that of the artisan-apprentices, for professional training, containing workshops for tailor, shoemaker, tinman, joiner, cooper and mason, as well as the teaching of music and of printing.

With relation to the preceding year the school attendance augmented.

The province supports a lyceum, of secondary instruction, which was attended by 55 students, and it applies the fifth part of its revenue, that is, £ 35,279 to the instruction department, the expense thus amounting to £ 7,108.

CEARA.

The annual expense is £ 21,710, or the fourth part of its revenue, estimated at £ 85,000.

The number of schools of elementary learning is 221, including 49 private ones.

The public schools were attended by 10,135 pupils of both sexes; and the private ones by 2,706, summing up 12,841.

In the attendance of the former there were 3,390 pupils more than in the preceding year.

The province supports in its capital a lyceum with 10 classes, as also in different localities 6 classes of latin.

There are 3 private colleges of secondary instruction, including the boarding-school for artisans-apprentices, assisted with the annual sum of £ 300, under the condition of feeding and teaching 70 poor orphans; there are besides, the Atheneum and the Ceará college.

Those establishments were attended by 860 scholars, of which 473 frequented the public, and 387 the private ones, thus being 181 over the preceding year.

RIO GRANDE DO NORTE.

The annual expenditure with public instruction amounts to £ 6,462 or more than the fifth of its revenue, calculated at £ 35,767.

It maintains 82 public schools of primary instruction, a college of secondary instruction named « Rio Grandense Atheneum », 4 detached classes, besides a private one of latin grammar; there are more 9 private schools, and 1 nocturnal course attended by 38 students.

The primary schools were attended by 2,928 pupils; the Atheneum and the detached classes by 114, and the latin private school by 5.

PARAHYBA.

Primary instruction is distributed by 109 public, and 8 private schools, that were attended by 3,648 pupils, of which 198 belonging to the latter.

Secondary instruction is given in a lyceum and 3 latin classes, at the charge of the province; they were attended by 109. There are 4 private classes more of geometry, latin, french, and english, attended by 69 students.

The revenue of the province was calculated at £ 60,000 : the sum voted to this department being £ 11,969, the provincial treasury applied a fifth part of its income to public instruction.

PERNAMBUCO.

Primary instruction was given last year in 456 schools, comprising 8 nocturnal courses and 111 private classes.

The number of pupils ascended to 13,520, viz : 11,288 of the public schools, 1,942 of the private, and 290 of the nocturnal courses.

Compared with that of the preceding year the school attendance had an increase of 3,408 pupils. Secondary, instruction was given to 1,153 scholars, of which 395 belonging to public, and 758 to private schools.

This number is distributed by a Gymnase for boarders and day-scholars, a Normal School, and 4 detached classes, 3 of latin and 1 of latin and french, all supported by the province, and by 32 private colleges, one of which subsidized by the provincial treasury.

The total amount of scholars, in 1871, rose to 331 more than that of the preceding year.

The provincial revenue is £ 242,519, and the sums intended for the instruction department amount to £ 45,995, that is, more than the fifth of its income.

ALAGÔAS.

It applies the sum of £ 12,538, that is, more than the fifth of its revenue, calculated at £ 68,741, to public instruction, the State of which is as follows :

Primary instruction : 136 public, 1 nocturnal, and 73 private schools, attended by 6,026 pupils, including 35 of the nocturnal course.

Secondary instruction : 1 Normal School for both sexes, 1 Lyceum, 1 french and 2 latin classes, supported by the province, besides 3 private colleges.

They were attended by 369 scholars, 92 of which belonging to the former, and 277 to the latter.

SERGIPE.

There are, in the province, 148 public, 1 nocturnal, and 30 private schools, the former attended by 4,477 pupils, the nocturnal school by 44, and the latter by 538, there being an increase of 1,045 pupils over those of the preceding year.

It also possesses 5 public and 7 private establishments of secondary instruction, attended by 247 students, 192 belonging to the former, and 55 to the latter.

The subjects taught in the nocturnal course, also exist-ing, and attended by 19 students, are the following : portuguese grammar, french, book keeping, history of Brazil, the Constitution of the Empire, linear drawing, and mathematics.

The provincial revenue is estimated at £ 50,551 and the sum designed for public instruction was of £ 10,688 or almost the fifth of the former.

BAHIA.

It contributes with about £ 33,524 to primary and secondary instruction, that is, more than a fifth part of its revenue, which is calculated at £ 188,530.

Primary instruction is given in 274 public, 11 nocturnal,

and 21 private schools, five of the latter being subsidized by the provincial treasury.

The attendance amounted to 15,540 pupils, of which 14,461 belonging to the public, and 532 to the private schools. The nocturnal courses were frequented by 547. With relation to the preceding year there was an increase of 3,462 pupils, including in the private schools the 547 pupils of the nocturnal courses.

It possesses 9 establishments of secondary instruction, of which 3 are public and 6 private. Amongst the former the most important are a Normal School for both sexes, and a provincial Lyceum.

The attendance amounted to 1,142 students, 171 of which belonging to the public, and 971 to the private ones.

ESPIRITO-SANTO.

Although its annual revenue be but £ 27,593 it, however, destines £ 6,486, or more than a fourth of it, to this important branch of public service. It has 81 public, and 5 private schools.

The former were attended by 1,590, and the latter by 105 pupils.

Secondary instruction is given in 2 public establishments, one named « Holy Ghost College, » for boys, and the other called « Our Lady of Penha College » for girls, both of them being frequented by 72 pupils, either boarders or otherwise.

Besides these, there are 2 private colleges, attended by 13 pupils.

RIO DE JANEIRO.

It contributes to primary and secondary instruction with a sum equivalent to above the seventh part of its revenue, for in a budget of £ 443,700, an amount of £ 62,958 is destined to that service.

The number of public schools, including 6 nocturnal courses, is 435; and that of the private ones 135.

Among the former, however, only 272 were working, being attended by 10,151 pupils. The private ones, of which 21 are assisted by the provincial treasury, were attended by 3,625 pupils.

The total amount was then 13,776, there being an increase of 4,707 pupils over that of the preceding year.

The province possesses a Normal School for both sexes, 3 classes of english, french, and latin, all supported by it, and 14 private colleges, 10 of which for boarders. The attendance amounted to 171 in the former, and 971 in the latter.

There is besides, in the capital, an asylum for girls, under the name of Santa Leopoldina, which is spoken of in an other place.

S. PAULO.

It expends with the instruction department the annual sum of £ 31,561, or more than the sixth of its revenue, calculated at £ 211,078.

The number of public schools amounted to 422, and were attended by 11,520 pupils of both sexes.

There are nocturnal courses in different towns of the province. That, in the capital, was attended by 88 students, and they are all maintained at the expense of the inhabitants.

Secondary instruction is, in general, given in the classes of the course of preparatory studies, annexed to the Faculty of Law, and at the charge of the imperial government.

In the town of Itú there is a class of latin and another of french, which were attended by 42 scholars, as well as an important seminary.

PARANÁ.

This is the state of instruction in the above province :

The 47 public schools were attended by 1,917 pupils ; and the 17 private ones by 333.

There have been created 37 public schools more, but they are not yet working.

For secondary instruction there are 6 establishments : 2 public and 4 private, with the attendance of 188 students.

There was no sensible alteration in the frequency, with regard to the preceding year.

The revenue of the province is £ 62,195 and the sum allotted to public instruction £ 9,258 or nearly a seventh of its whole amount.

SANTA CATHARINA.

It has 93 public primary schools which expend about £ 6,361, a sum nearly corresponding to the fourth of the whole provincial income, which is £ 24,369.

It possesses 40 private schools and the attendance of both the public and the private amounts to 4,150 pupils ; 3,112 belonging to the former, and 1,038 to the latter.

With respect to the preceding year there was an increase of 648 pupils.

S. PEDRO DO RIO GRANDE DO SUL.

There are in this province 246 public, and 116 private primary schools.

The attendance was of 7,573 pupils, in the public, and of 4,738 in the private schools; the total amount being 12,311 pupils.

The province subsidizes 24 private schools. The increase of the school attendance was of 2,850 over the preceding year, and has been always rising since 1867, when the attendance amounted to 3,849 pupils.

There are 23 establishments of secondary instruction: 4 public, and 19 private.

The former were frequented by 72 scholars, and the latter by 351, summing up 423.

The province possesses amongst its public establishments of secondary instruction an Atheneum and a Normal School for both sexes.

The provincial revenue is estimated at £ 185,080, of which £ 25,000 are applied to public instruction, thus being correspondent to more than the seventh of the whole revenue.

MINAS GERAES.

From its revenue calculated at £ 141,294 it expends £ 41,184 or more than a third, with primary schools and other literary establishments.

The number of public primary schools amounts to 554, and that of private ones to 124, thus summing up a total of 678, frequented by 18,770 pupils, of which 17,337 belonging to the former, and 1,433 to the latter: of those 95 attended schools subsidized by the province.

The number of scholars in the primary schools went 5,125 beyond that of the preceding year.

There are in the province: a course of pharmacy, divided into 2 years, at which are taught: chemistry, botanics, materia medica and pharmacy; 49 different classes of secondary instruction, being 1 of latin, 44 of latin and french, 1 of french and english, 1 of english and geography, and 2 of mathematics, all supported by the province ; and 87 private establishments, including 5 colleges subsidized by the same province, 1 of which for the female sex.

The attendance amounted to 988 pupils, 836 in the above mentioned classes, and 152 in the latter establishments. The course of pharmacy was attended by 36 scholars.

The increase was of 617 pupils over the preceding year.

GOYAZ.

The annual expenditure with public instruction is £ 4,525 or a little more than a third of its revenue, which is calculated at £ 14,892.

The number of schools of primary instruction is 73, of which but a single one is private. The attendance was of 2,143 pupils of both sexes, against 1,899 in the preceding year, the difference, therefore, being 244.

It possesses an establishment of secondary instruction under the name of « Provincial Lyceum », wherein 102 scholars were inscribed.

MATO-GROSSO.

The expense with public instruction is, in this province, calculated at £ 2.396, more than the ninth part of its provincial revenue, which amounts to £ 22.600.

Its schools are 32 in number, viz : 27 public and 5 private, attended by 1,236 pupils : 1,176 belonging to the former, and 60 to the latter.

There are besides 9 classes, the teaching of which is :

mathematics, geography, history, latin and french; attended by 26 scholars.

Recapitulating all that has been said concerning primary instruction in the Empire, it is seen that in 4,653 schools, both public and private, of which informations were obtained, the attendance amounted to 155,058 pupils of both sexes.

Attending to the difficulty of collecting this kind of information in so vast a country, and so scattered a population, it will be recognized that the results obtained are much below the truth, not only with regard to the number of schools, but yet as to that of pupils of either sex that really attend on them.

It must also be noticed that in those imperfect and deficient statistics are not comprised such children as learn primary and secondary instruction in their home.

Many Brazilian farmers, residing at a considerable distance from towns, choose to have at their farms or plantations, primary schools and classes of secondary instruction, to which, besides their children, are admitted those ones of the less wealthy neighbours.

In the meantime, the statistical returns compared to those of 1866, it is seen that there was an increase of 218 primary schools and of 47,575 pupils, the annual mean being 7,929 pupils.

The following table shows, by provinces, the number o schools and classes of primary instruction, the pupils that frequented them, and also the different provincial revenues, and the sums allotted to public instruction.

PROVINCES.	PRIMARY SCHOOLS.	ATTENDANCE.	PROVINCIAL REVENUE.	EXPENDITURE WITH PUBLIC INSTRUCTION
			£	£
Amazonas..	43	1,217	51,171	6,132
Pará..............	180	6,029	167,180	30,774
Maranhão........... ..	150	6,095	73,844	11,600
Piauhy...............	68	1,806	36,279	7,108
Ceará................ ..	221	12,841	85,000	21,710
Rio Grande do Norte ...	92	2,028	35,767	6,462
Parahyba	117	3,648	60,000	11,969
Pernambuco...........	456	13,520	242,519	45,993
Alagóas	210	6,026	68,741	12,538
Sergipe	179	5,059	50,554	10,688
Bahia.............. ..	306	15,540	188,530	33,524
Espirito-Santo	86	1,695	27,593	6,486
Rio de Janeiro	570	13,776	443,700	62,958
Municipality of the capital.............. ...	174	12,498	....	28,000
S. Paulo.............	422	11,520	211,078	34,564
Paraná............	101	2,250	62,195	9,258
Santa-Catharina........	133	4,150	24,369	6,361
S. Pedro do Rio Grande do Sul..............	362	12,311	185,080	25,000
Minas-Geraes	678	18,770	141,294	41,184
Goyaz	73	2,143	14,892	452
Mato-Grosso	32	1,286	22,600	239
Summingup.	4,653	155,058	2,192,386	416,233

Religious Instruction.

The teaching of preparatory studies and divinity is given at the seminaries existing in the 12 dioceses.

Their number amounts to 19, and are divided into two classes, under the name of high and petty seminaries, according to the subjects taught.

With the exception of that of S. José, founded in the city of Rio de Janeiro, the only one which possesses a sufficient estate for its support, the rest are subsidized by the State with an annual expense of £ 11.500.

By the last official returns, those seminaries, with the

exception of that of the province of S. Pedro do Rio Grande do Sul, which building was not yet concluded, were attended by 1.428 students, that is, the petty seminaries by 1.090, and the high seminaries by 338, as it is shown by the following table :

DIOCESES.	SEMINARIES.		NUMBER OF STUDENTS ATTENDING.		TOTAL.
	Petty.	High.	The high.	The petty.	
Pará {Belém. . . .	1	. . . .	. . . .	72	72
Pará {Manáos. . .	1	. . . .	. . . .	30	30
Maranhão.	1	1	13	177	190
Ceará	1	1	37	118	155
Olinda.	. . . .	1	48	. . . .	48
S. Salvador. . . .	1	1	39	130	169
Rio-de-Janeiro . .	1	1	54	. . . .	54
S. Paulo.	1	1	12	103	115
Marianna	1	1	48	338	386
Diamantina. . . .	1	1	25	76	101
Goyaz.	1	. . . .	. . . .	46	46
Cuyabá	. . . .	1	62	. . . .	62
	10	9	338	1,090	1,428

Last year 111 students have taken orders at the seminaries mentioned in the following table :

DIOCESES.	ORDERS.			
	Minor.	Of sub-deacon.	Of deacon.	Of presbyter.
Ceará.	. . . . .	6	7	7
Olinda	. . . . .	. . . . .	. . . . .	13
S. Paulo.	. . . . .	. . . . .	7	8
Marianna.	15	14	10	13
Diamantina	3	2	2	2
Cuyabá.	. . . . .	. . . . .	. . . . .	2
	18	22	26	45

To that number must be added 3 more presbyters, who are professors in the petty seminary of Belem, province of Pará, besides 9 students of the seminary of Bahia, who ended the course of divinity, but by an impediment of the respective Archbishop have not taken the orders of presbyter.

It is, moreover, to be noticed that in the Latin-American Seminary, founded in Rome by H. H. Pius IX, are studying 38 Brazilians from the provinces of Ceará, Bahia, Rio de Janeiro, and S. Pedro do Rio Grande do Sul.

The plan of studies in both classes of seminaries is not the same in all the dioceses, but they comprehend:

In petty seminaries: the portuguese, latin, greek, french, hebrew, and italian languages, religious instruction, universal history, history of Brazil, geography, elementary mathematics, natural history, philosophy, rhetoric, music, singing and drawing.

In high seminaries: sacred and ecclesiastical history, exegetics, hermeneutics, moral and dogmatical divinity, natural law, canonical law, lithurgy and ceremonials.

Military Instruction.

The military studies are performed in the following establishments, which are under the care of the War department.

Regimental schools; Preparatory schools; Military school; General school of gunnery in Campo Grande; Central college, and Deposit of artillery-apprentices.

REGIMENTAL SCHOOLS.—The regimental-schools intended to train up non-commissioned officers for the army, comprise the following subjects for the three arms:

reading, writing, christian doctrine, the four first rules
of arithmetic, vulgar and decimal fractions, metrology,
linear drawing, the principal prescriptions of the military penal legislation, the duties of a common soldier,
of a corporal, a quarter-master and sergeant in all circumstances both of peace and war; and further for
each arm the special pratical instruction laid down in
the programme organized by the educational council
of the military school.

PREPARATORY SCHOOLS.—The preparatory schools comprise the study of the subjects required for the inscription
in the superior military courses, and for the elementary
practical instruction in the use of the different arms.
The course of studies, in those provinces where the government shall judge convenient to create them, shall last
for two years, during which are studied portuguese
and french grammar, history and geography, especially
of Brazil, arithmetic, elementary algebra, geometry, trigonometry, linear perspective, practical geometry and the
administration of companies and battalions.

The preparatory school of the Capital of the Empire
is annexed to the military school.

Its course lasts 3 years, and besides other studies it
also comprehends gymnastics, swimming and fencing.

MILITARY SCHOOL.—The military school has a course
of three years;—the subjects taught are: the higher principles of algebra, analytic geometry, experimental physics,
preceded by ideas of mechanics, inorganic chemistry and
its application to military pyrotechnics, topographical
design, topography and examinations of territory, tactics,
strategy, castrametation, military history, temporary
and permanent fortification, elementary principles of

ballistics, principles of the law of nations, elements of the law of nature and of common law in all relating to military affairs, the military code, design of projections, descriptive geometry, comprising the study of numbered plans and their application to defilements; differential and integral calculations, mechanics, theoretical and practical ballistics, military technology, artillery, the principal system of permanent fortification, the attack and defence of strong-holds, military mining, design of fortifications and machinery of war, the manual exercises, gymnastics, swimming, and practical exercises.

The two first years form the course of cavalry and infantry, and three years that of artillery.

For the Staff and for Engineer corps there is besides these three years a supplementary course at the Central college, which, for the Staff, comprises:— the study and practical exercise of geographical design, astronomy, topography, geodesy, botany, zoology and the elements of organic chemistry; and for the Engineer corps, the study and practical exercise of mechanics as applied to constructions, the principles of civil architecture, the property and resistance of materials of construction, ideas on the course of rivers and the movement of bodies of water, in canals and aqueducts, natural and artificial internal navigation, railways and telegraphs, mineralogy and geology, architectural design the arrangements, and decoration of civil and military edifices and the execution of plans.

The Military academy is governed by a commandant — a general officer who must have belonged to one of the three arms and not be employed in teaching; and by a sub-commandant — a superior officer, assisted by one or two adjutants — officers of the army — and by a secretary in charge of the correspondence.

The educational staff is composed of 6 professors, 4 assistant professors, 2 teachers and one or two assistant teachers.

The military school has a library adapted to its special purposes, a cabinet of physics, a chemical-pyrotechnical laboratory, a chapel, and an infirmary.

The professors are appointed by the government after a competitive examination.

The government was lately authorized to reestablish the militar school that once existed in the Province of S. Pedro do Rio Grande do Sul, adding to the other studies a course of hippiatrics.

The superior course of the school was attended, this year, by 112 students, and the preparatory course by 193 students.

GENERAL SCHOOL OF GUNNERY IN CAMPO GRANDE. — It is intended to the training of instructors for the different corps of the army by a theoretical and practical knowledge of gunnery as well as of arms of all descriptions, the respective teaching being pursued according to the method prescribed by Panot in the course of gunnery in St. Omer.

In this school, which has been advantageously attended by a considerable number of pupils, the following matter is taught : — The nomenclature of the various kinds of cannon, their framework, limber, caissons, carriages, tackle, forges and other furniture; the nomenclature, use and manufacture of the various kinds of projectiles; the nomenclature and service of the different instruments of force, employed in mounting and dismounting guns; the practical means of judging distance; the nomenclature and use of the various tools for the extraction or insertion of fuse, and for sighting and pointing the different guns ; the theory and practice of firing guns and congreve rockets, that is, direct, horizontal, plunging, and ricochet firing ; the graduation of fuse to the different distances and corresponding trajectories; estimation of the explosive force of gunpowder by the various methods known.

There is a long range of fire and other dependent departments.

It is near the capital of the Empire to which it is connected by the D. Pedro II rail-way and by a fine cart-road.

It was separated from the military school, and has of late received a new organization.

Central College.— This establishment is chiefly destined for the teaching of mathematics and the physical and natural sciences ; its course lasts six years and comprises the following subjects : — algebra, geometry, plane and spherical trigonometry, linear and topographical perspective; topography, analytical geometry, the general theory of projections, differential and integral calculations, mechanics, experimental physics, the graphic resolution of problems of descriptive geometry and their application to the theory of shading : inorganic chemistry and its analysis ; the sketching of machinery ; astronomy, topography, geodesy, botany and zoology ; principles of organic chemistry, geographical design, mechanics as applied to construction, civil architecture ; the theory of river systems, the movement of bodies of water in canals, navigation, roads, bridges, rail-ways, telegraphs, mineralogy, geology, architectural design, the arrangement and decoration of civil and military edifices and the execution of plans ; hydrodynamics practically applied , motive power of hydraulic machinery, improvement of rivers, as regards navigation and floods, navigable canals, canalisation and supply of water ; artesian wells, the safety and preservation of ports ; the removal of banks and formation of anchorages ; political economy, statistics, the principles of administrative law; sketches for building and for hydraulic machinery and practical exercises during the vacations.

This college has two courses for civil students ; one for the profession of civil engineer, and the other for that of geographical engineer.

The former is composed of the study of all the above mentioned subjects, and of the corresponding practical exercises. The latter comprises the studies of the four first years of the general course, which include : algebra, analytical geometry and the general theory of projections ; the elements of differential and integral calculations ; mechanics, plane and spherical trigonometry ; topographic astronomy ; geodesy, experimental physies, inorganic chemistry, botany, zoology, principles of organic chemistry ; the graphic solution of the problems of descriptive geometry and their application to the theory of shading ; linear and topographical perspective ; sketches of machinery and geographical design ; practice at the Observatory, geodetic operations, and practical exercises.

The college is under the charge of a director, who must be a general officer of one of the scientific arms and not a public professor. He is assisted by two adjutants—one of them a superior officer, of a scientific arm, and by a secretary entrusted with the correspondence.

The educational staff is composed of 11 university professors, 5 assistant professors, 2 drawing-masters, 2 assistant drawing-masters, and several teachers.

It has a library, a cabinet of physics, a laboratory of chemistry, a mineralogical cabinet, and a room for models of the most important constructions and of machinery.

The professors are appointed by the government after a competitive examination,

The government is authorized, by law, to reform the internal regulations both of this college and of the military school, in order that the latter may contain a complete course of military engineering and the necessary studies for the degree of Bachelors of mathematics and physical sciences; the central college being removed to the Home department, since it being rather intended for civil purposes, it will thus assume its real position of a school for geographical, and civil engineers, and those who may wish to superintend industrial, agricultural, and mineralogical works.

The central college is at present attended by 464 students.

Last year, the inscriptions amounted to 483 students, of which 408 passed their examinations with full success.

IMPERIAL ASTRONOMICAL OBSERVATORY. — It is a dependence of the Central College, and is destined to the teaching of practical astronomy to the students of the fourth year attending the said college, and to the publication of astronomical and meteorological observations.

It is there that the chronometers of the war and marine departments are regulated, and it signals daily the *mean* time.

It has published an important work consisting of meteorological tables with the different curves.

It is situated on an eminence, in the city of Rio de Janeiro; its employés have often been sent in commission to various parts of the Empire to study and make observations.

The meteorological facts observed during each day are published in the daily papers on the following morning.

In order to raise it to the same foot with other similar establishments, the government is caring about the means of improving its scientific store. The director is in Europe for the purpose of acquiring and bespeaking such instruments and apparatus as be adapted to the studies at the charge of the observatory.

This establishment is about to be reorganized so that it may fulfill, in a more perfect way, its leading purposes, by increasing the circle of its observations, specially for the list of stars, and training a personnel with the necessary abilities to carry on geographical and geodetic pursuits.

There is also an observatory in the capital of the province of Pernambuco.

Native and foreign scientific commissions have been usefully occupied in the study of these matters in various parts of the Empire.

Naval instruction.

The naval department possesses several establishments of instruction.

In the Naval College, sitting on board a ship of war, are taught all the branches of mathematics as applied to astronomy and navigation, physics and chemistry, meteorology, steam-engines, artillery, hydrography, and naval tactics.

The naval cadets learn english, french, maritime law, history of navigation, and all matters required for the professional learning, both military and scientifically considered.

The practical teaching is given on board either in the coasting or sea going voyages that are annually made.

The preparatory studies for the Naval College are taught at the expenses of the State in a day-scholar establishment, which is intended to be converted into a naval boarding-school.

The studies above mentioned consist of: portuguese, geography, universal history, arithmetic, algebra to the equations of second degree, and a slight knowledge of french, english, and drawing.

The professors and assistants of the naval college are appointed by the government after a competitive examination.

For mariners and marines there is a practical school of artillery.

Those who attend the school of geometry applied to arts and that of engine works are entitled to the post of machinists on board ships of war and are apt to be employed in the workshops of the navy arsenal.

Not only in the national schools, but also in the most renowned European establishments, many Brazilians are giving themselves up to the study of naval construction, steam-eugines, hydraulics, artillery, and pyrotechnics.

Thus, within a short time, Brazil will be possessed of a numerous personnel with the abilities required for all naval technical pursuits.

The directors of the workshops are already Brazilians, some of which advantageously known in Europe where they have pursued their studies.

One of them, who has successfully altered the line

of naval construction, received in England a patent for
his invent; the other built the first iron-clads launched
out from the stocks of Rio de Janeiro.

Still with regard to instruction, there is in the Capital
a naval library, which is spoken of in another place.

The ships of the navy have all their libraries, more
or less copious, according to their respective crew.

The officers of the navy have distinguished themselves
for their learning, and some of them have published important works concerning the subjects of teaching, and
professional questions.

There being already, in the capital of the Empire, an
Observatory which determined its astronomical position,
new charts must be drawn up, rectifying those actually
used in the Imperial Navy, which generally refer to the
meridian either of Greenwich or of Paris.

The three years theoretical studies being over, the
naval cadets are appointed midshipmen and sent out
in a voyage, under the command of a scientific officer,
and the immediate charge of several competent teachers,
in order to obtain the practical knowledge.

Upon their return, the commander and teachers deliver minute reports concerning the voyage, and the midshipmen exhibit the proofs of their diligence and abilities.

Since 1857, with the exception of the five years during the war against Paraguay, several voyages of practical
instruction were made to Europe, some of them calling
at the United States.

The steam-corvette *Nictheroy* is employed at a like commission; she was bound to the United States, and from
thence will call at several ports of Europe, where there
are naval important establishments.

The imperial navy has also performed several exploring voyages, the most remarkable of them being that of the corvette *Bahiana*, in 1867; since, by overcoming serious difficulties, she doubled the cape of Horn, and called at several ports of the Pacific.

This same corvette, which is a specimen of the solidity and excellence of naval constructions, in Brazil, still performed with success a long voyage through the Atlantic ocean, calling at several islands among which those of Tristan da Cunha, Ascension, Cape de Verd, and many other places in the western coast of Africa.

In 1861 the Brazilian steam-corvette *Beberibe* started from the port of Rio Janeiro, in order to sound several points between the Cape de Verd islands and the coast of Brazil, by verifying the existence of the different hidden rocks and shoals, pointed out on the charts.

The statement of this voyage proves the zeal and the skill of the officers of the Brasilian navy, and may be consulted, with advantage, since it contains useful information as applied to the study of submarine phenomena.

The Brasilian steam-corvettes *Vital de Oliveira* and *Paraense* are assisting the soundings and other preliminary pursuits of the english commission at whose charge was the laying down of the submarine cable, that is to connect the brazilian coast with Europe.

All the ships of the navy, belonging to the second naval district, have received orders to perform the above mentioned service, when required.

A small squadron is employed, on the south of the Empire, at hydrographical pursuits, and is to rectify the sea-charts, along the whole extent of the River Plate.

The naval college was attended, last year, by 88 students, of which 24 were promoted to midshipmen as having completed the course of studies.

From 1863 to 1872, by the same reason, 187 naval-cadets were promoted to midshipmen.

In 1872, the naval college gave titles of machinist to 46 persons, viz :

1st class machinists.. 11
2d class   »   5
3d class   »   11
4th class   »   19

                                    Total   46

In the capital of the Empire there are 259 artisans-apprentices, and 144 mariners apprentices; in several provinces there are 93 of the former, and 803 of the latter.

They all receive both the professional and the primary instruction.

When the respective lists be completed, the number of mariners-apprentices will amount to 2,500, both in the capital and the provinces of the Empire.

Faculties of Medicine.

There are two Faculties of Medicine, one in the capital of the Empire, and the other in the province of Bahia, both using the same plan of studies, which comprises 6 years and the following subjects : general physics specially as applicable to medicine, inorganic chemistry, mineralogy, descriptive anatomy, anatomical demonstrations, botany, zoology, organic chemistry, physiology, general and pathological anatomy, general, internal, and external pathology, internal and external clinics, midwifery, diseases of the pregnant women and new-born children, topographical anatomy, medical operations, several surgical apparatus, materia medica, therapeutics, hygiene, history of medicine, medical jurisprudence.

These subjects are taught by 21 professors. There are also 21 assistant-professors, who take the places of the professors, in case of any impediment, and who attend to the practical studies. All of them are appointed by the government after competitive examinations.

The Faculties have a special course of pharmacy and another of obstetrics.

The 1st is for 3 years, and comprises the following studies: physics, chemistry, mineralogy, organic chemistry, botany, materia medica and pharmacy.

The course of obstetrics consists of 2 years, and is formed of the chair of midwifery, in the medical course, and of the corresponding practice at the Misericordia-Hospital.

Each faculty possesses a chemical laboratory, a cabinet of physics, of natural history, of anatomy, of materia medica, a surgical arsenal, a pharmaceutical laboratory, and the necessary amphitheatres for the lectures and demonstrations.

The gardens situated in the neighbourhood of the Faculties supply the want of special botanical gardens.

Each faculty is governed by a Director and a Board composed of the professors of the faculty; it has a secretariate for all its correspondence, and a library.

n the faculty of medicine of the capital, 470 students inscribed their names in the years 1872 for the medical course, 113 for the pharmaceutical course, and 3 female students in the obstetrical one.

In the first course, 52 students received the degree of Doctor of Medicine;—21 completed the second course and obtained their diplomas as apothecaries.

In the facnlty of Bahia, 193 stndents inscribed their names for the medical course; — 69 for the pharmaceutical course.

Twenty three of the former received the degre of Doctor of Medicine, and 27 of the latter obtained their diplomas as apothecaries.

The Doctors or Bachelors of medicine and the Surgeons, as well as midwifes and dentists authorized to practise in virtue of diplomas from foreign Academies or Universities, must pass an examination before one or other of the faculties, if they come to exercise their profession in the Empire.

To be admitted to this examination it is necessary to present their diplomas or original titles, and in the absence of these, some other authentic documents which replace them with authorisation of the government, proof of personal identity, and documents attesting the morality of the pretendant.

These titles, diplomas, or documents must be viseed by the Brazilian consul resident in the country where they are made out.

Acting or retired professors of the Universities, or of Schools of Medicine, recognised by the respective governments, are exempt from this examination as soon as they prove this fact before either of the Brazilian faculties, by means of certificates of the Diplomatic Agents or of the Brazilian Consul residing in the countries where they have been professors.

Candidates who desire to inscribe their names for the medical course, must have passed examinations in latin,

french, eng'ish, history and geography, rational and moral
philosophy, arithmetic, geometry an l algebra up to equations of the first degree.

For the course of pharmacy: in french, arithmetic
and geometry. For the obstetrical course: in reading,
writing, the 4 first rules of arithmetic, and french. The
government spends annually with these 2 faculties the
sum of £ 21,691.

Faculties of Law.

For the teaching of the social and juridical sciences
there are two Faculties of Law; one at S. Paulo, capital
of the Province of that name, the other at Recife, capital
of the Province of Pernambuco.

They are both governed by the same regulations.

A course of preparatory studies, necessary for the
inscription in the superior course, has been annexed to
each Faculty. These preparatory studies are: french, portuguese, english, latin, arithmetic, geometry, history,
rhetoric and philosophy.

The superior course is divided into 5 years and
eleven chairs, comprising: the law of nature, universal
law, analysis of the Constitution of the Empire, law of
nations, diplomacy, the elements of Roman Law, ecclesiastical Law, civil Law, with analysis and comparison
with the Roman Code, Criminal Law, Military Law, Maritime and Commercial Law, juridical hermeneutics, civil,
criminal and military proceedings, forensic exercises, political economy and Administrative Law.

Each Faculty of Law is under the immediate superintendence of a director to whom it pertains to inspect

the studies, and, besides his other attributes, to preside over the assembly of professors, which is charged with all that relates to the economy and discipline of the Faculty.

The faculties have a secretariate for their correspondence, and a library.

In the year 1872, 474 students inscribed their names at the 2 Faculties of Law, of which 102 completed their course and received the degree of Bachelor, which enables them to be admitted as judges or to the bar.

The Faculty of Recife was attended by 300 students, of which 75 received their degree of Bachelors; and that of S. Paulo by 174 students, of which 27 received the degree of Bachelors.

For the preparatory examinations, 1,620 students were inscribed, being 1,073 approved; 1,286 inscriptions pertaining to the Faculty of Recife and 890 students approved, and to that of S. Paulo 334 inscribed and 183 students approved.

This degree enables the recipient to teach in the superior course of the said degree.

Each of them has 11 university professors, and six substitutes; one and the other appointed by the government after a competitive examination.

The annual expenditure of the two law faculties amounts to £ 17.320.

Commercial Institute of Rio de Janeiro.

The subjects taught at the Commercial Institute of the capital form a course of 4 years and are the following: — linear drawing, calligraphy, french, english, german, arithmetic as applied to commercial operations, algebra as far as equations of the second degree, geometry, geography, commercial statistics, commercial law, and the customs and consular legislation compared with those of the countries in the closest commercial intercourse with Brazil, history of commerce, book-keeping, and political economy.

The institute is inspected by the Minister of the Empire, through the intermediary of a government commissioner, and by the director.

The most important questions respecting the establishment generally, or the teaching and discipline, are decided by a board composed of the professors appointed by the government, and the director as president.

The professors are appointed by government after a competitive examination.

During the past year 53 pupils inscribed their names for attendance at the course of the Institute, besides 17 hearers who attended the classes.

The annual expenditure is £ 2.080.

Imperial Institution for Blind Children.

It consists of a boarding-school, where children of both sexes are taught primary and secundary instruction, moral, litterary, and professional education, as suitable to their age and capacity.

It is superintended by a director, appointed by government, and subordinate to the minister of the Empire, who through a commissary has the inspection of the establishment; besides the director it has a chaplain, a physician, and other functionaries.

It is at present established in the interior of the city, but is to be removed to one of the most healthy suburbs, at a convenient distance, as soon as the building which is now in construction, with capacity enough to contain 500 inmates, shall be finished.

The course of studies is generally divided into eight years, comprehending, as to the moral and literary department, the following matters: reading, writing, cathecism, and explanation of the Gospel, portuguese grammar, french, arithmetic, algebra to the equations of second degree, geometry, general notions of mechanics, physics and chemistry, modern and ancient history, geography, the history and geography of Brazil.

Although the English language was not included in the plan of studies, it has lately been taught, with advantage, to some students.

The professional study, actually, comprehends: vocal and instrumental music, harmony, rules of counterpoint and instrumentation, printing, book-binding, and the tuning of pianos for male pupils; music and needlework for girls.

As soon as the number of the boarders shall have encreased and the new building finished, work-shops for turners, wicker-work, shoemakers, tailors and other trades fit for the peculiar condition of the children, will be opened, and an elementary school of gymnastics, adapted to the condition of the blind.

The Institution has a library with nearly 1000 volumes, and a fund, that in October last, was already mounting to £ 7,742, mostly owing to private donations and some receipts of public theatres.

The classes are under the direction of six professors,

appointed by government, who teach more than one matter, and by four tutors, that help them, three of which were once pupils of the institution.

Some of the ancient pupils now gain their livelihood as music masters and piano tuners.

Last year the number of pupils amounted to 29, of which 20 of the male, and 9 of the female sex.

They are almost all educated at the government's expenses; the annual expenditure with the Institution being £ 4,800.

The government is also taking into serious consideration, how to employ the poor blind students, who, upon finishing their studies, will not be able to find occupation in the Institution, on account of the small number of workshops there existing.

With these views, the committees of public instruction, and of the budget of the chamber of Deputies have lately presented the project of a bill, in which the subject is treated in an ample way; these being its most important provisions: 1st, the admission of an unlimited number of pupils in the public establishments; 2d, to give greater expansion to the study of music; 3d, to increase the number of workshops; 4th, to create a fund of £ 200,000, as proposed in the same project; 5th, to establish in the provinces of Maranhão, Pernambuco, Bahia, Minas-Geraes, and S. Pedro do Rio Grande do Sul, institutions dependent of, and similar to the central one in the Metropolis. 6th, to give portions of £ 100 to each helpless blind girl, upon her leaving the institution.

Deaf and dumb Institute.

It was founded in 1856 by a private undertaker, H. M. the Emperor contributing with purses for two pupils, the imperial government with ten, the province of Rio de Janeiro with five, and the religious orders of S. Benedict and of the Carmelites with the necessary sums for letting a house for the Institute.

Having been afterwards yielded up to the government by the said undertaker, in return of a sum of money, it was, in 1868, converted into a public educational establishment, with which the State expends £ 3,400, every year.

It is a boarding school founded with a view to give to the deaf and dumb the instruction they are able to receive, within the limits prescribed by the respective statutes.

It is situated at about three miles distance from the city of Rio, in one of the best suburbs, the house being spacious enough for the actual number of boarders, there also existing a small farm with yards for gymnastical exercises, pleasure grounds, and ponds of abundant and excellent water.

The actual attendance is 21 boys and 5 girls.

The subjects taught are, at present: religious doctrine, portuguese language, by the intuitive method, used in the Paris Institute, practical arithmetic, sacred history, the geography and history of Brazil, drawing, and artificial articulation and reading by the movement of the lips; this last subject is taught by an assistant professor, who is also deaf and dumb.

Those pupils who are above 12 years of age are also taught horticulture and gardening, at which they employ some time every day during the most convenient hours : some of them work at the shoemaker's shop, existing in the Institute, and which makes all the shoes required for the pupils.

The girls are taught sewing, embroidery, and every kind of household service.

The staff is composed of a director, 2 teachers, 1 writing mistress, 2 tutors, one of which was once a pupil in the institute, a drawing master, and a chaplain, who is also charged with the religious teaching.

The classes are furnished with the principal objects for that special teaching, comprising : engravings, icono-logical tables, which have been so advantageous in the German schools, an apparatus made at Rio, by order of the actual director, for the teaching of Arithmetic accor-ding to Dessuseau's method, and several ones for gym-nastical exercises.

There is also a library of which a special mention will be made hereafter.

The institute's property consists of £ 3,000 in bonds of the public debt, which are proceeding from private donations and theatrical rehearsals.

This sum is destined, as well as any other thus acquired, to make up a capital fund for the assistance of those poor pupils, who having terminated their education, may not find easy and ready means of livelihood, on their leaving the Institute.

Academy of the Fine Arts.

It is intended for the teaching of the fine arts, and is superintended by a director, assisted by effective and honorary professors.

The course of studies is divided into five sections :

The 1st section comprises the classes of : — geometrical design ; ornamental design ; and civil architecture.

The 2nd section the classes of : ornamental sculpture ; engraving of medals and of precious stones ; and statuary.

The 3rd section the classes of: sketching of figures; landscapes ; flowers and animals; historical painting; and living models.

The 4th section the chairs of : application of mathematical principles : anatomy and physiology of the passions ; history of the arts; æsthetics ; and archœology.

The 5th section is formed by the conservatory of music.

The instruction is divided into two courses: one diurnal, and the other nocturnal.

In the latter are taught : industrial, ornamental, and figural design ; ornamental and figural sculpture ; elementary mathematics, including practical arithmetics and geometry ; the elements of mechanics, and living models.

The nocturnal course was established as an industrial school for the advantage of the working-men, who have gladly availed of it.

The effective professors are appointed by the government after competitive examination ; the honorary professors are appointed by the absolute majority of votes of the Academic body, on the proposal of the director or of

three members of any of the sections, and their appoint-
ment afterwards receives the approval of the government.

The honorary professors are obliged, when named by
the director, to fill the place of the effective ones in case
of any impediment. They cannot take possession of their
offices without presenting to the academy body one of
their works, which remains the property of the establishment. There is also a class of corresponding members
composed of distinguished artists residing out of the capital.

The classes of the Academy were last year attended by
164 pupils, including those of the nocturnal course. Of
those who passed their examinations, 16 were approved.
Every year there is opened for the space of three days in
the saloon of the Pinacotheca a public exhibition of the
works of the different classes, and after this ceremony is
over, the distribution of prizes takes place. Every two
years there is a general public exhibition of all the works
of art executed in the capital and in the provinces: this lasts
for 15 days.

All native or foreign artists have the right to exhibit
their works, when these are accepted by the Academical
jury.

Twenty nine pupils obtained prizes for the works they
exhibited at the last public exhibition.

There is an extraordinary prize for the most distinguished Brazilian pupil; — this consists in a yearly pension for him to study in Europe, during six years, if he is
a historical painter, sculptor or architect; and during
four years if he is an engraver or landscape-painter.

The Academy has lately received some works that show
the application and progress of one of its pupils, who
as a pensioner of the state is residing at Rome whither

sometime ago, was sent another pupil who obtained that prize.

The academy possesses a library, a Pinacotheca, and a secretariate for its correspondence.

The annual expenses of the Academy are £ 3,756.

Conservatory of Music.

Although this establishment is a section of the Academy of the fine arts, it is nevertheless governed by a special director, with a special code of regulations, is in a separate edifice and has its own revenue.

The instruction, which is completely gratuitous for both sexes, is composed of:—the elements of music and solfeggio, and the general principles of singing for the male sex ;—the same subjects for the female sex ;—singing for both sexes; — the rules of accompaniment and of organ; of string and wind instruments.

Classes for composition and others will be established, as soon as the resources of the conservatory permit of this, and the progress of instruction demands it.

The administration of the conservatory is composed of a director, a treasurer and secretary entrusted with the correspondence.

Several excellent pupils have come out of this establishment; some of them, who were once without any fortune, have earned the means of subsistence of which they now dispose.

The classes were last year attended by 152 students inscribed, of which 60 male and 92 female-students, excluding 27, who were not inscribed.

Of those who passed their examinations, 64 were approved and among them 38 obtained prizes.

Natural History Museums.

NATIONAL MUSEUM.—It was created in 1817, in the city of Rio de Janeiro, and is intended for sciences having connexion with Natural History. It is considered as the most important one of South-America.

It is formed of four sections: 1st of comparative anatomy physiology and zoology; 2nd of botany, agriculture and the mechanical arts; 3d of mineralogy, geology and the physical sciences; 4th of numismatics, the liberal arts, archeology, the usages and customs of modern nations.

Each section has a director, who may be helped by one or more assistants, one supernumerary clerk, and the necessary apprentices. Its Director-in-chief is appointed by the Government from amongst the four directors.

The Directors and their assistants compose the administrative board, at the charge of which is the management of the establishment.

The Museum has, besides, several corresponding members in the national and foreign scientific societies, and there are actually two naturalists travelling through the Empire, for the purpose of making collections.

The principal object of the National Museum is: to collect and study all the natural products of the country, and to deliver public lectures on the sciences of its province, spreading among the people theoretical and practical knowledge, in a simple style, adapted to their comprehension.

Every sunday the museum is open to the public, but

it may be visited on any other day (except thursdays) on asking for a permission, which is easily granted. The average member of visitors, each sunday, is one thousand.

The most remarkable collections of this establishment are those of geology and mineralogy, distributed into three large rooms, and mostly composed of those once belonging to the celebrated Werner, and of a great many minerals collected by Sellow, who was for sometime at the service of the museum.

The zoological collections are likewise remarkable, the richest amongst them being the ornithological and ethnographical ones relating to the Brazilian Aborigenals.

The edifice is vast, and contains several large rooms; but it has no longer the sufficient capacity on account of the constant increasing of its collections and the improvements it has had these last years.

The museum now keeps correspondence with the European establishments of the same description, and willingly exchanges the duplicates of its collections for those of foreign museums.

The government intends to create in the provinces several museums dependent of that one in the capital of the Empire, that they may exchange among one another the respective products of each one, receiving at the same time from the central one, not only the necessary instructions for the classification and study of the collections, but even its superabundant duplicates.

PARÁ MUSEUM. — It consists of a cabinet of Natural History and was created three years ago, in the town of Belém, and organized nearly as the national museum.

It is maintained by the province and possesses several very remarkable collections.

Among them the most important is the archœological one, mostly proceeding from the island of Marajó and the western mountains of the province.

An ornithological collection there existing comprehends a great many remarkable birds of the Amasonas.

In the town of Santarem, in the same province, there is a newly created museum belonging to the « Santarem Ethnographic Society. »

MINAS-GERAES MUSEUM. — This new museum has been created about two years ago, in the city of Ouro-Preto.

It is a cabinet of Natural History possessing already a valuable collection of geological and mineralogical specimens.

CEARÀ MUSEUM. — It was created and maintained at the cost of a private Brazilian gentleman, who after having spent a few years labour in getting the collections, gene-rously offered it to the province about two years ago.

It contains several collections of products of the province, amongst which there are to be noticed some hundreds of mineralogical specimens, a great many animals stuffed or preserved in alcohol, a small collection of compared anatomy, zoological monsters, fruits, fibres of plants and many other curious objects.

Besides these cabinets, which are all lately created but which promise to thrive, there are several others annexed to establishments of public instruction in the Empire.

Such are the cabinets of Natural History of the Central College, in Rio de Janeiro; the small cabinets of the Faculties of Medicine of Rio de Janeiro and Bahia; those of the Lyceum of the latter province and of the Gymnase of Pernambuco; and finally a small museum of natural and archœological products, lately founded at the province

of Alagôas, under the protection of the Archœological Institute of Alagôas, and subsidized by the provincial assembly.

Libraries.

The National Public Library is the most important
establishment of the kind, in the capital of the Empire,
attending to its numerous, excellent, and precious collection of books.

Besides some important paleotypes and several editions
of the most famous printers of the xv, xvi, and xvii
centuries, it possesses more than 100,000 printed volumes, methodically arranged in twelve large rooms.

The theological section contains about 15,000 volumes,
amongst which are to be found the famous and rare
polyglotic bibles of Ximenes, Arias Montanus, and others,
as well as many valuable treatises on different branches
of ecclesiastical science.

The section, which comprehends history, biography and
voyages, contains 24,000 volumes, including very remarkable ancient works and the best productions of modern
writers.

The scientifical section contains 39,000 volumes on
moral, political and physical sciences.

In the first class, which comprehends 24,000 volumes,
are to be noticed many ancient works of a recognized
merit, especially concerning juridical matters.

The second class contains 15,000 volumes of most precious
works and is about to be enriched with the acquisition
of some modern works respecting sciences, which are
constantly progressing.

The section of greek and latin classics forms a precious and varied collection of 4,000 volumes, with beautiful bibliographical curiosities, comprehending editions of the most renowned printers of former ages, and many paleotypes.

The section of belles lettres contains 16,000 volumes on linguistics, rhetoric, poetry, novels, and philology.

This section possesses an interesting and varied collection of lexicons, the works of the principal national and foreign literary men, as well as those of the most distinguished modern philologers, besides a great many polygraphs.

Among the latter a special mention should be made of Ortiz (various treatises, 1493) on account of its rarity, and Frederic the 2ᵃ (œuvres, 1846, Berlin) for its elegant and rich edition.

The section of national and foreign newspapers and reviews is also a very important one. Its number amounts to about 3,000 volumes, comprising collections of the papers published in Rio de Janeiro, before and since the Independence of the Empire, as well as many of the best scientific, literary or periodical publications of Europe, especially of France.

The section of maps, topographic charts and plans forms a collection of 620 volumes, in the most part concerning different provinces of the Empire.

The section of manuscripts and drawings, although not amounting to more than 1,200 volumes, still contains many valuable and ancient rarities, besides an interesting collection of original sketches of some of the most renowed painters.

The National Library also possesses the whole collection

of Martius *Flora Brasiliensis*, the publication of which was assisted by the government, and that of Velloso's *Flora Fluminensis*, which has become very rare.

The books on arts and trades, that must form a distinct section as soon as the necessary accommodations be obtained, amount to about 3,500 volumes, comprehending many important works on ancient and modern painting and architecture.

All persons decently dressed are admitted into the National Library, every working day, from 9 to 2 o'clock in the morning, and from 6 to 9 o'clock in the evening.

The establishment has a reading room large enough to admit 60 persons, at ease, and at night it is lighted with gas.

The monthly public attendance may be estimated at 1,000 to 1,300 readers.

To the present time the government expended every year £ 2,500 with the National Library; but that sum was raised up to £ 6,785 by the last budget law.

The government intends either to construct or to purchase a larger building, with a view to increase some parlours and reading-rooms more, and for a better accommodation of the books already existing, and those which are to be acquired in time.

In the capital of the Empire there exist several other libraries, either special and belonging to public establishments or possessed by religious communities, and private societies.

Amongst the former we must mention :

1st That of the Faculty of Medicine, comprehending 5,200 volumes bound, besides a great number of printed pamphlets, relating to the different sciences that constitute the medical course of studies, there being amongst them many modern works of the most renowned french, english, and german authors.

Its annual attendance may be estimated at 3,000 readers, the greatest number of them, students and professors of the faculty ; every one, however, can be admitted to it, asking permission to the respective librarian.

It is probable that the attendance to this establishment will increase henceforward, since measures have been taken for it being opened during some hours in the evening.

2ᵈ That of the Central College, with 6,000 volumes distributed into three sections, namely : of mathematics, physical sciences and books on subjects not relating to those of the college course. It is opened every day in the morning during the school-time, and at the disposal of the professors and students.

3ᵈ That of the Naval College, with 13,000 volumes, 5,200 maps and different plans, besides 22 models of vessels and several instruments adapted to cosmographical pursuits.

Being, for the most part, formed of important works on nautical subjects, it possesses, nothwithstanding this, a considerable number of others on the various branches of human learning.

4ᵗʰ That of the Military School , composed of books and manuscripts about the different branches of the military profession, the arts and trades as applied to the service of the army, mathematical and physical sciences, as also of maps and collections of military laws, regulations, and ordinances.

5ᵗʰ That of the National Museum which, though scarcely

containing 6,000 volumes, is perhaps the richest of all the special libraries, owing to the value and selection of its works, amongst which there are many of the best that have been published on natural history. Although these works are specially destined to be of assistance to the directors of the different sections of the museum, they are, however, often perused by such persons as desire it.

6th The Library of the General Board of Statistics comprehending 1,103 volumes.

7th That of the Academy of Fine Arts, containing about 1,000 volumes.

8th That of the Imperial Institute for blind children possessing above 1,000 volumes, concerning its special province.

9th That of the Deaf and Dumb Institute, which contains geographical maps and globes, complete collections of models of the weights and measures of the metrical system, school-books in portuguese, and special works about the education of the deaf and dumb.

10th Those of the State Offices.

Amongst the libraries belonging to religious communities and private societies, we shall mention :

1st That of S. Benedict's Monastery, containing an excellent collection of 8,000 volumes, almost all of them being ancient works on ecclesiastical matters.

2[d] Those of the convents of Santo Antonio and of the Carmelites, comprehending each of them 2,000 volumes on religious subjects.

3[d] The Library Fluminense founded 26 years ago by a private association ; it possesses 40,000 printed volumes, comprehending a rich collection of official documents concerning the history of Brazil, and more than 100 manuscripts of an historical value, besides a great number of papers and pamphlets published in the Empire.

Although it was established for the benefit of its shareholders to whom, according to the respective statutes, it pertains the exclusive right of reading or retaining for some time in their power whatever books they please, the entrance to it is permitted to every body who may desire it.

4th The Portuguese reading-room Library, which was founded in the year 1837 with 3,000 volumes, and possesses at present 52,000 on all branches of human knowledge.

It contains many and valuable works in latin, italian, spanish, german, and some ones in russian and greek ; its greatest riches however, consist of french and specially of portugnese books, which are numerous. It also possesses 100 maps, 240 engravings, and 92 pictures.

This establishment belongs to a portuguese association, but subscribers and readers of every nationality are admitted to it. It is open in the morning from 8 to 2 o'clock, and in the evening from 4 to 9 o'clock.

During the last year the shareholders and subscribers removed from the library about 40,000 books, and the attendance was superior to 3,000 readers, and 150 visitors. The capital stock of the establishment amounts to about £ 20,000.

The association intends to erect a building with the convenient accommodations for such an establishment, having already spent £ 8,000 on the acquisition of grounds and several improvements.

5th The British Subscription Library, maintained by

the society which succeeded to the ancient english literary club. It possesses 6,219 volumes, amongst which are specially remarkable some english works and newspapers. This establishment is very much frequented.

6th The Germania Association Library, founded in the year 1832, possessing at present 5,500 volumes mostly of german authors, and is regularly frequented by its associates.

Each of the societies — Literary Essays — Imperial Typographical Association of Rio Janeiro — Portuguese Literary Retiro — possesses a library the 1.st of which containing 2,600, the 2.d 560, and the 3.d 1820 volumes.

Such is the case with other scientifical and literary associations of the Capital, deserving a special mention the following ones :

1st The Library of the — Historical Geographical and Ethnographical Brazilian Institute — the most important of such societies. It possesses 5,000 printed volumes, almost all of a great value concerning the history of Brazil, and offered by the associates ; it also possesses an abundant collection of manuscripts acquired with much pain and perseverance.

Amongst the printed volumes deserves a special mention the american library that belonged to the celebrated Dr. Martius, which was offered to the Library by His Majesty the Emperor.

The manuscripts are, in great part, copies of very important registers existing in the archives of Portugal, Spain, and Holland, taken by order of the government.

2d That of the society — « Aid to National Industry » — in which there are important works on industry and agriculture.

Next to these can be mentioned those of the — Imperial Academy of Medicine — of the Brazilian Polytechnic Institute — of the Society « Lover of Instruction » — of the Brazilian Advocates'Institute — of the Bachelor of Arts'Institute — and some others.

It was founded some time ago by the efforts of the late Town Council president a municipal library, which has already acquired a great number of books, mostly by gifts.

The foundation of libraries in the Capital and in all the provinces of the Empire is now the object, not only of the government's sollicitude, but also of individual efforts.

In the several provinces of the Empire there are the following libraries :

In that of the — Amazonas — one was established in the — Lyceum — containing 800 volumes and is maintained by the provincial treasury.

In the province of Pará there are two libraries, a public one and another belonging to the «Gremio Litterario Portuguez», both of them in the capital.

The first, containing about 3,700 volumes in several languages including greek and hebrew, is attended by more than 500 readers, in a year; the second contains 2,755 volumes and has nearly the same attendance of readers.

A library has been of late created at Santarem, a town in he said province ; it contains already above 1,000 volumes.

In the province of Maranhão, the Popular Library, possessing 3,700 volumes, and visited by above 500 readers ; that of the — Portuguese Reading-Room with 5,500 volumes, visited by 400 persons.

In that of Ceará a public library with 4,000 volumes.

In that of Rio Grande do Norte, a reading-room which the provincial government endeavours to increase.

In that of Pernambuco, besides the library of the Faculty of Làw possessing 2,700 volumes, there exist the — Provincial Library with 3,600 volumes, and that of the — Portuguese reading-room — containing 9,500 volumes.

The annual attendance to the second being superior to 500 persons, and to the third of 800 readers monthly.

In the province of — Alagoas — there is a public library in the capital, comprehending 4,700 volumes, and was attended during the last year by 826 persons; besides another one under the denomination of — Popular Library — in the city of Penedo, containing 357 volumes and frequented by 62 persons.

In that of — Sergipe — there exists a reading-room founded a few years ago.

The province of — Bahia — possesses the following libraries: that of the — Faculty of Medicine — with 9,700 volumes, visited last year by 3,700 persons; that of the — Portuguese reading-room — with 3,000 volumes and frequented by 500 persons; the — Provincial Library — with 20,000 volumes and visited annually by 5,000 persons; that of the — Lyceum — established a few years ago, with 573 volumes, and that of the society « Gremio Litterario » with 5,700 volumes, and daily average attendance of 40 persons.

The same province possesses in the municipality of Valença a private library containing 363 volumes, its access being free to the public, besides another one recently founded by the — Imperial Agricultural Institute of Bahia.

In that of Rio de Janeiro has been ordered by the

presidence the foundation of — Popular libraries — in th cities of Paraty, Parahyba do Sul, Barra Mansa, Valença, Vassouras and Campos, besides the Reading-Rooms actually existing in Vassouras and Nova Friburgo.

In the capital of S. Paulo there are the libraries of the — Faculty of Law — with 9,700 volumes of interesting ancient works in its greatest part on juridical matters; the — Popular Library — with 2,413 volumes, frequented last year by 3,650 persons; and that of the society — Germania. In the city of Campinas there is a Reading-Room containing above 1,000 volumes, besides others in the cities of Santos, Sorocaba, Pindamonhangaba and Itú.

In the provincial Lyceum of Paraná was recently established a library.

In the province of Rio Grande do Sul it will soon be established a — Popular Library — by virtue of a provincial law passed in the year 1871. In the capital there exists already the library of the — Rio Grandense Atheneum — and the city of Rio Grande has a Reading-Room containing above 5,000 volumes.

In the capital of Santa Catharina there exists a — Provincial Library — with 1,800 volumes, which was frequented last year by 650 readers.

In the province of Minas Geraes there are two public libraries, one in the capital containing 1,500 volumes, and the other in the municipality of S. João d'El-Rei with 2,100 volumes, besides the Reading-Rooms established in some other cities.

In that of Goyaz there is the library of the — Goyano literary cabinet — which possesses 4,350 volumes and is visited by 100 readers.

According to the calculations made at the general

department of statistics concerning the last year, the number of books of every description put in all the Empire at the disposal of the people can be rated at 339,892; and at 28,272 that of persons who frequented public-rooms both in the capital and in the provinces.

To obtain this computation, the said department collected the result of partial tables, received from some of the above mentioned establishments, having also in attention the informations that could be obtained about those that did not send the said tables.

The Press.

In the capital of the Empire the following daily papers are published :

Diario Official do Imperio do Brazil. — (Official Journal of the Empire of Brazil) — It is in its 11th year, and has a daily circulation of 1,300 copies, printed in very good paper, 1,2 meter long, and 0,8 meter wide; the sheets are 0,52 meter long, and 0,34 meter wide.

It publishes all the official acts of the government and is printed at the National Printing Office where there are 4 steam engines, 13 manual presses, and 140 operatives.

The government intends to endow the National Printing Office with all necessary means in order to raise it up to the degree of perfection that is to be desired.

Jornal do Commercio. — (Commercial Journal) — It was published for the first time in 1821, and there are now 15,000 copies daily distributed, printed in three hours time, and almost always of 6 pages each, very often of 8 pages, having each page 8 columns, and being, 0,71 meter long and 0,63 meter wide.

It consumes annually 9,100 reams of the largest sized

paper, weighing 520,000 kilgr., and 900 kilgr. of ink. If we add that which is consumed in printing the annals of the Chamber of Deputies, the catalogues so frequently published, and the *bulletins* distributed a short time after the arrival of steamers from Europe, the consumption amounts annually to 10,100 reams of paper.

Printed in *mignon* generally the subject of a sheet can make a volume in-octavo of 300 pages.

It works with three large Marinoni's machines of 4 cylinders each, and three smaller ones of 2 cylinders for secondary printing : they are all moved by steam.

. Its personnel is : 8 internal or external directors ; 80 correspondants including those who are in Europe, in the United-States and in the Empire, and 242 operatives, employés, and clerks, for the composition, revision and printing, distribution, business of the office and other purposes.

In order to be of assistance to the typographic class, the *Jornal* founded an association under the title of — Beneficent Association of the Compositors of the *Jornal do Commercio*, the funds of which are formed by means of a small contribution deduced from each workman weekly wages, which now are amounting to £ 1,000 notwithstanding the great expenses which it incurred on since its foundation. The association protects or helps them as well as their families, in case of disease, by granting loans and pensions when its associates are unable to work.

The *Jornal* has annexed to it a printing-office for the works of every description, in which 12 persons are constantly occupied.

Diario do Rio. — It was founded in 1817 and is the most ancient paper of the capital.

Its circulation is of 4,700 copies, of 4 pages each, having 0,75 meter long, and 0,5 meter wide, mostly printed in types *gaillard* n. 8.

It consumes every year 2,000 reams of double-sized paper ; and possess two reactive steam-engines and a numerous body of workmen.

Reforma. — Founded in 1870, it is a daily paper of 4 pages, each being 0.48 meter long, and 0,33 meter wide.

Next to the above mentioned come the following ones :

Nação. — (1st year). It is published every evening ; 0,32 meter wide, and 0,49 meter long.

Jornal da Côrte. — (1st year). Published every evening, just like the preceding one.

Republica. — (4th year). 4 pages, being 0.48 meter long, and 0,33 meter wide.

PERIODICAL PUBLICATIONS.

The Apostolo. — (7th year). It is a religious paper, 0,32 meter wide, and 0,48 meter long. It publishes the official acts of the bishopric, and discutes all religious questions of the State.

Instrucção Publica. — (1st year). Weekly paper of 8 pages each. It publishes the official-acts concerning its special department and discusses all questions relative to primary, secondary and superior instruction, in the Empire.

Gazeta Juridica. — (1st year). Of the same size as the above paper ; ill treats of all subjects of its special province.

Monitor do Povo. — (2nd year).

Archivo do Retiro Litterario do Rio de Janeiro.

Arte Dentaria.

Bibliotheca Romantica.

Boletim do Grande Oriente do Brazil.

Bons Exemplos.

Brazil.

Brazil Musical.

Brazil e Portugal. — (3ᵈ year).

Centro Academico.

Conselheiro das Damas.

Constitucional.

Crença. — Religious paper.

Echos do Povo.

Gazeta Medica. — Medical paper.

Imprensa Medica.

Jornal das Familias.

Leitura de Carapuça.

Locomotora.

Lyra de Apollo.

Lyra Eolica.

Minerva.

Monarchia.

Novo Album de Modinhas Brazileiras.

Palestra.

Periodico dos Pobres.

Revista Juridica.

Revista de Legislação e Jurisprudencia.

Revista Litteraria.

Revista Mensal do Instituto dos Cirurgiões.

Revista da Sociedade Ensaios Litterarios.

Tupy.

Verdadeira Instrucção Publica.

Voigt's Shipping Intelligence.

Pantheon. — Distributed gratis. A paper for advertisements.

Anjo Familiar. — Id.

Gazeta do Povo. — (1st year.)

Familia. — (1st year.)

Entre-acto. — (1st year.)

Imprensa Evangelica. — (9th year.) The organ of the evangelical religion.

Luz. — (1st year.) Historical and Literary Paper.

D. Pedro II. — (5th year).

Brazil Historico. — A pamphlet. (5th year). It publishes official documents relating to our national history.

Gazetilha. — (1st year.) A daily evening paper.

Rio Commercial Journal.

Anglo-Brazilian-Times. — It is written in English and treats different subjects particularly concerning Brazil.

Futuro. — (1 st year.)

Cosmos. — (1st year.)

Pelicano. — (1st year.)

Brado do Povo.

Amongst the Reviews of the Scientific, Literary and Industrial Associations we must mention :

Revista do Instituto Historico, Geographico e Ethnographico Brazileiro. — It is a quarterly review forming every year two large quarto-volumes of 350 or 400 pages each. It is intended for the study of the Brazilian history, and was created in 1839 and has now 35 volumes.

Auxiliador — A review of the « *Sociedade Auxiliadora da Industria Nacional* (Aid to National Industry), forming every year an octavo volume of 550 or 600 pages. It was founded in 1833 and is in its 40th volume.

Annaes Brazilienses de Medicina — A review of the « *Academia Imperial de Medicina.* It forms every year an octavo volume of 480 pages, and is in its 25th year.

Revista do Instituto da Ordem dos Advogados Brasileiros. — A quarterly review concerning legislation and

jurisprudence. It forms every year two small quarto volumes of 350 or 400 pages each.

Revista do Instituto Polytechnico Brasileiro.

*Revista do Imperial Instituto Fluminense de Agricul-
tura*, with engravings. It is in its 17 th volume.

Revista Academica.

Illustrated papers:

Archivo Contemporaneo. — (1st year).

Semana Illustrada.— It is in its 13th year and has a
weekly circulation of 5000 copies of 8 pages each, printed
in very good paper at the «*Imperial Instituto Artistico;* »
and uses 10 lithographic and 3 typographic presses.

Vida Fluminense.

Mosquito.

And many other papers of less important litterary and
scientific associations.

In the provinces the following papers are issued:

AMAZONAS.

In the capital:

Amazonas.— (7th year.)

Reforma Liberal.— (4th year.)

Catechista.

Argos.

Commercio.— (3d year.) Large sized paper.

Rio Negro.— Weekly paper.

PARÀ

Diario do Grão-Pará.— (20th year) Issued out in the
capital.

Jornal do Pará.—(10th year), id

Liberal do Pará. — (4th year), id.

Diario de Belem.— (5th year), id.

Jornal do Commercio.

Tribuna.— Id.

Pelicano.— 1st year), Id.

Bôa Nova.— (2n¹ year), A religious paper ; id.

Luz da Verdade.— A weekly paper ; id.

Santo-Officio.— Id.

Regeneração. — Id.

Pyrilampo.— Id.

Patria. — Id.

Tacape. — Id.

Futuro.— Id.

Tocantins.— Id.

Conservador.— Id.

Regeneração.— Id.

Reforma Liberal.

Diario do Commercio.

Liberal.

MARANHÃO.)

Publicador Maranhense.— In the capital.

Paiz.— (10th year), id.

Telegrapho.— (2nd year), id.

Constituição.— Id.

Apreciavel.— (7th year), id.

Liberal. — (5th year), id.

Diario do Maranhão.— Id.

Jornal Caxiense. — In the town of Caxias.

PIAUHY.)

Piauhyense. — In the capital.

Patria. — (3d year), id.

Amigo do Povo.— (5th year), id.

Piauhy.— Id.

Imprensa. — Id.
Oitenta e Nove. — Id.

CEARÁ

Pedro II. — (33^d year.) In the capital.
Cearense. — (25th year), Id.
Constituição. — (10th year), id.
Futuro. — (1st year), id.
Voz da America, — (1st year.) At the city of Aracaty.
Aracaty. — Id.

RIO GRANDE DO NORTE.

Constitucional. — In the capital.
Conservador. — Id.
Assuense. — (4th year.) In the town of Assú.
Liberal.
Mossoroense. — In the village of Mossoró.

PARAHYBA.

Publicador. — (9th year,) Of the capital.
Jornal da Parahyba. — (11th year), id.
Despertador. — (14th year), id.

PERNAMBUCO.

Diario de Pernambuco. — (48th year.) Of the capital. It is a large-sized paper and has a circulation of 6,000 daily copies.
Jornal do Recife. — (14th year), id.
Diario da Constituição. — id.
Diario Liberal. — (1st year), id.
União. — id.
Verdade. — (1st year), id.
Provincia. — (1st year), id.

Cigarra.— (1st year), id.
Jornal do Commercio.— (1st year), id.
America Illustrada.— (1st year), id.
Reformista.— In the town of Victoria.
Liberal Victoriense,— (3d year), id.
Correio de Santo Antão.— (3d year), id.

SERGIPE. ✓

Jornal do Aracajú.— (3d year.) In the capital.
Jornal de Sergipe.— (7sh year), Id.
Conservador.— Id.
Liberdade.— Id.

ALAGÔAS. ✓

Diario das Alagôas.—(15th year.) Of the Capital.
Jornal das Alagôas.—(3d year), id.
Liberal.—(4th year), id.
Constitucional.
Partido Liberal.
Tribuna.
Pyrilampo.
Penedense.— In the town of Penedo.
Revista do Instituto Archeologico Geologico Alagoano.

BAHIA. ✓

Diario da Bahia.—(27th year.) Of the Capital. It has a
large circulation.
Jornal da Bahia.—(20th year), id, id.
Correio da Bahia.—(2nd year), id, id.
Horizonte.—(1st year), id.
Sentinella da Liberdade.—(1st year), id.
Revista Commercial.—(1st year.)
Apostolo.

Revista Medica.

Academico. —(1st year.)

Constitucional.—Id.

Alabama.—A satirical paper which is in its 10th year ; id.

Revista da Instrucção Publica.—(3^d year.) A monthly paper ; id.

Abolicionista.—(2nd serie.) A fortnight paper ; id.

Renegenerador.—In the town of Nazareth.

Crise.—(4th serie.) In the town of Santo Amaro.

Popular.—Id.

Americano.—(4th year.) In the town of Cachoeira.

Ordem.—Id.

Progresso.—Id.

Perola.—(1st year.) A literary paper.

Jornal de Valença.—(3^d year.) In the town of Valença ; a weekly paper.

ESPIRITO-SANTO.

Correio da Victoria.—(24th year.) Of the Capital.

Jornal da Victoria.—Id.

Espirito-Santense.—(2nd year), id.

Conservador.—(1st year), id.

Estandarte.—In the town of Cachoeiras de Itapemerim.

União.—Id.

RIO DE JANEIRO.

Patria.—(17th year.) Of the Capital.

Rio de Janeiro.—(1st year), id.

Nacional.—Id.

Monitor Campista.—(35th year.) In the town of Campos.

Gazeta de Campos.—(1st year), id.

Independente.—(5th year), id.

Mercantil.—(16th year.) In the town of Petropolis.

Germania. —(10th year), id. It is written in the German language.

Tribuna do Povo.—(4th year), in the town of Macahé.

Telegrapho.—(6th year), id.

Cantagalense.—In the town of Cantagallo.

Correio de Cantagallo.—Id.

Parahybano.—(9th year.) In the town of Parahyba do Sul.

Agricultor.—(1st year), id.

Regenerador.—In the town of Valença.

Astro Rezendense.—In the town of Rezende.

Artista.— In the town of Angra.

Época.—(1st year.) In the town of S. João da Barra.

Primeiro de Março.— Id.

Regeneração.— In the town of Cabo Frio.

S. PAULO.

Correio Paulistano.—(19th year.) Of the Capital.

Diario de S. Paulo.—(17th year), id.

Opinião Conservadora.—(4th year), id.

Vinte e dous de Maio.—(1st year), id.

Revista Commercial. —(23d year.) In the town of Santos

Imprensa.—(3d year,) id.

Americano.—(2nd year.) In the town of Sorocaba.

Sorocaba.—(1st year), id.

Ipanema.—(1st year), id.

Gazeta de Campinas.—(3d year.) In the town of Campinas.

Correio de Taubaté.—(1st year.) In the town of Taubaté.

Echo Bananalense.—(2nd year.) In the town of Bananal.

Esperança.—In the town of Itú.

Mosquito.—In the town of Arêas.

Areense.

Americano.—In the town of Pindamonhangaba.

Diario de Santos.

Lorenense.—In the town of Lorena.

Municipio.

Meteoro.

Omnibus.

Constitucional.

Diario de Santos.

Pindamonhangabense.

Parahyba.

Jornal do Povo.

Paulista.

Estrella do Oeste.

Tribuna.

Progresso.

Independente.

PARANÀ.

Dezenove de Dezembro.—(19th year.) Of the Capital.

Antonina.—(1st year.) In the town of the same name.

Commercio do Parand.—(10th year.) In the town of Paranaguá.

SANTA CATHARINA.

Despertador.—(1st year.) Of the Capital.

Regeneração.—(4th year), id.

Conciliador.—(1st year), id.

Colonie-Zeitung.

S. PEDRO DO RIO GRANDE DO SUL.

Jornal do Commercio.—(9th year.) Of the Capital.

Rio Grandense.—(7th year), id.

Reforma. —(4th year), id.

Democracia. —(1st year), id.

Constitucional. —(2nd year,) id.

Deutsche Zeitung. —A paper written in German, id.

Diario do Rio Grande. —(25th year). In the town of Rio Grande.

Commercial. —(15th year), id.

Echo do Sul. —(18th year), id.

Investigador. —(1st year), id.

Artista. — (10th year), id.

Tempo. —An evening paper, id.

Jornal do Commercio. —(3d year.) In the town of Pelotas.

Diario de Pelotas. —(5th year), id.

Cruzeiro do Sul. —Id.

Razão. —In the town of Bagé.

Prelo. —(1st year), id.

Voz do Povo. —(4th year.) In the town of Jaguarão.

Onze de Junho, —(4th year), id.

Revista Gabrielense. —(1st year.) In the town of S. Gabriel.

Echo de Camaquam. —In the village of Camaquam.

Emigrante Allemão.

Jornal do Pantheon Litterario.

Album Semanal.

MINAS-GERAES.

Pharol. — (4th year.) Of the Capital.

Noticiador de Minas. —Id.

Monitor Sul Mineiro. —(1st year.) In the town of Campanha.

Monarchista, —(2nd year), id.

Jequitinhonha. —In the town of Diamantina.

Pharol. —In the town of Parahybuna.

GOYAZ.

Provincia de Goyaz.—(4th year.) Of the Capital.
Alto Araguaya.
Correio Official.

MATO-GROSSO.

Situação.—(5th year.) Of the Capital.
Primeiro de Março.—(3d year), id.
Liberal.—(1st year), id.

There are in Rio 39 printing offices, besides the above mentioned ones, where printing is done very nicely, just as nice as that in many towns of Europe.

In the provinces there are also 200 printing offices where are printed the above said papers and a great many literary works.

Scientific, literary and industrial associations.

I. There are many scientific, and literary associations, in the capital of the Empire, and in the provinces.

Amongst them the first rank is undoubtedly occupied by the *Brazilian Historical, Geographical and Ethnographical Institute,* founded in 1838, and intended for the study of our national history, by collecting, commenting, and publishing all documents concerning it.

Its review is called — *Historical Institute Quarterly Review,* it is in its 35th volume and is being regularly continued : the pamphlets annually published make up a volume of 800 pages, and sometimes more.

The Institute celebrates fortnight meetings in the

Imperial town-palace ; His Majesty the Emperór being always present to them.

The *Imperial Medical Academy* inaugurated in 1829, is divided into 3 sections : the medical, the surgical and the pharmaceutical sections, studying all subjects concerning to each of those branches of the medical profession. Since 1831 a monthly review is published under the name of *Brazilian Medical Annals.*

Weekly meetings are held at the town-hall and every year, on the day of its foundation, a solemn session takes place at the Imperial town-palace, and on this occasion some medical questions are proposed for prize. Either natives or foreigners may concur to those prizes, but all are obliged to present their memoirs, in two years time.

The *Polytechnical Institute* is intended for the study of mathematics and their applications, of engineering, and military sciences ; and occasionally publishes a review.

The *Institute of the Order of Brazilian Advocates* is intended for the discussion of the theoretical and practical questions of jurisprudence.

It was founded in 1843 ; its meetings are weekly, and since 1853 a review is published, which is in its 9th volume.

The Vellosiana Society, founded in 1850, and reorganized in 1869, is devoted to the study of natural sciences, particularly the native productions of the country, the history and habits of the aborigenals ; the first volume of its review was already published.

The *Pharmaceutical Institute of Rio de Janeiro*, the *Vellosiana Society* and the *Pharmaceutical Academical Atheneum*, study all the matters composing the official course of the apothecaries' art.

The second one publishes a monthly paper called *Abelha* (The Bee).

The *Bachelor of Arts Institute*, founded in 1863, the *Literary Institute*, the *Historical Atheneum*, and the *Cicero's School*, cultivate literature, except the first, the province of which is vaster since it also comprehends the study of natural sciences. Scarcely a volume of their review has been published.

The *Literary Essays Society* inaugurated in 1860, the *Portuguese Literary Lyceum*, and the *Portuguese Literary Retiro* are intended for the same purposes of the preceding ones, and maintain classes of the portuguese, french, and english languages, geography, elementary mathematics and rhetoric. The first issues a review since 1862.

The *Directors' and Professors' Institute* is devoted to pedagogical matters.

The *Association of Instruction for Workmen* is consecrated, as its name shows, to a special purpose, also comprehending the study of literature.

It maintains evening-classes, which are very much frequented, in one of the city suburbs.

The *Book-keepers' Society*, founded in 1869, is devoted to the study of every thing concerning that branch, and to the promoting of the prosperity of trade and particularly that of Brazil. It possesses a library, and intends to issue a monthly review and maintain classes adapted to its speciality.

The Industrial Associations are still few in number, but they begin to have such a development that promises successful results.

There are in the capital of the Empire the following ones :

The *Society for the Aid of National Industry*, intended for the discussion of subjects relative to national husbandry and industry, and to effect the improvements and reforms, which are indispensable to the progress of those two branches of the public wealth. Since long it maintains a review called *Auxiliador da Industria Nacional* and since 1871, two evening classes for adults, which are very much attended, and promise to be of great service to the instruction of workmen.

The *Fine Arts Promoter Society*, founded in 1856, does all in its power to encourage the progressive development of arts in the Empire, by means of practical and theorical teaching, in a lyceum instituted for that purpose, and maintained by it; and also by means of a review; of exhibitions; and of public concourses. This Lyceum has now 15 evening classes very advantageously attended by great many artists of all ages.

The government assists it with a pecuniary aid, and shows itself disposed to grant many other favours.

Last year, 1,233 pupils attended those classes; and lately there was inaugurated a class of physics applied to arts and industries, which possesses already a very good cabinet for experiments: it is about to be created a class of industrial chemistry, with its respective laboratory.

The government intends to build an edifice for the Lyceum, large enough to have the indispensable rooms in order to train up the pupils in the practical exercises of arts and trades.

The *Imperial and Agricultural Institute of Rio de Janeiro*, recently created, maintains a normal farm, an agricultural asylum, and a manufactory of Chili straw-hats, all of which are in a flourishing condition.

Its funds are increasing, and its review continues to be published regularly, as it was already said.

There are still other societies worthy of mention, such as the *Imperial Rio Typographical Association*, destinated to the development and progress of printing; the society *Aid to Mechanical and Liberal Arts*, and many others.

In the Provinces there are, amongst many others, the following ones worthy of mention.

At Maranhão — The *Literary Institute*, the *Maranhense Atheneum*, and the *Onze de Agosto*, which maintain an evening school, comprehending several classes for adults, and attended by more than 400 students; besides the *«Festa Popular»* founded on the purpose of promoting Provincial Exhibitions, either agricultural or industrial.

At Pernambuco.— The *Archeological and Geographical Institute of Pernambuco*, and the *Mechanical and Liberal Artists' Association*, which maintain several classes attended by 167 pupils.

The *Promoter of Public Instruction Society*, composed of great many associates of either sex, lately founded a normal-school for women devoting themselves to professorship. which is already attended by 80 female scholars.

At Alagôas.— The *Archeological Geographical Institute of Alagôas*, besides issuing a review, maintains a museum for natural products and a numismatic cabinet; in the same province there are other Commercial, Typographical, and Agricultural Associations.

At Bahia.—The *«Historical Institute of Bahia»*, presided

by the metropolitan Archbishop, the *Gremio Litterario*, and the *Portuguese Library*.

At S. Paulo. —The *Literary Atheneum*, *the Juridical Nucleus*, and the *Germania*, in the capital of the Province; the *Scientific Culture* (a German association), the *Literary Society*, the *Artistical Beneficient and Promoter of Instruction Society*, at Campinas; the *Amparense Society* intended to promote and develop intellectual culture, in the town of Amparo; the *Literary Talk Club*, at Sorocaba; the *Literary Society*, and the *Bragantine Club*, at Bragança.

Theatres.

In the capital of the Empire there are 10 theatres, 3 large ones, 2 small ones, 3 suburban and private theatres, 2 playing-rooms.

The *Opera Fluminense* situated at *Campo da Acclamação*; *D. Pedro II*, recently built at *Guarda-Velho* Street and *S. Pedro de Alcantara* theatre, at the *Praça da Constituição*, afford splendid accommodations to the public, the two first ones being destinated to musical performances, and the latter specially to dramatic plays.

There take place sumptuous masked-balls, the inauguration of which, in the carnival of 1845, put an end to the old *Entrudo* of colonial times, carrying on a remarkable change in the habits of the people.

In the small theatres, *Gymnasio* and *S. Luiz*, some dramatic troops give performances, in the national language; and those who are fond of the *vaudeville* will find in the popular theatres *Alcazar*, *Phenix*, and *Casino* such plays performed by a french troop in the 1st, a national one in the 2ⁿᵈ, and both by french and national troops in the 3¹ one.

In the private theatres of *S. Christovão* and *Botafogo* only amateurs play.

A great many french and italian singers ; french, spanish, and italian actors, amongst them the most renowned european celebrities, very often arrive at Rio de Janeiro, on account of the facility and rapidity of transantlantic communications, and perform on our stages.

There are theatres in the capitals of all the provinces, as well as in many towns and villages.

The government intends to organize the Brazilian Theatre, and raise it up to a degree convenient to the civilisation of the Empire.

Thus it was created a new dramatic conservatory, in order to obtain the great aims pertaining to it ; to avoid by the examination of the dramatic compositions, appointed to be played, and by the internal inspection of the theatres, any offense to moral, religion and decency ; and to exercise, in those subsidized by the State, a literary censure, so as to improve the taste with the adoption of good models, and by good examples and encouragement, to contribute for restoring and promoting dramatic literature and art, in the Empire.

Those useful measures for the foundation of a normal theatre and of a course of dramatic art, depend of the consent of the legislative power.

A concourse was opened for the construction of an Opera-house and several plans were presented.

To the best one was granted the promised reward, the others being rewarded too.

The southern side of the *Campo da Acclamação* was

disapropriated by government, for the construction of the new building. Very shortly the works will begin.

Charitable Institutions.

The principal charitable Institution in the Empire is « the Santa Casa da Misericordia, » founded upwards of 1545.

It may, with full confidence, be asserted, that the print cipal cities of the world cannot boast of possessing, nor have any thing that can compete with either the General Hospital or the Lunatic Asylum of Rio de Janeiro.

In the compromissorial year of 1872 to 1873, 14,539 sick were treated, in its general hospital; 10,526 of these left the hospital cured, 2,946 died, and 1,067 continued their treatment there.

If we take out 317 that died in the first 24 hours of their admittance into the hospital, the mortality list was 18, 5%, independent of the ponderous circumstance tha-many of the patients that were sent to the hospital arrived there in a dying condition, and during many months of that year the city of Rio de Janeiro had to struggle against two epidemic diseases.

The hospital is constantly kept in the state of the great-est cleanliness and order; and the patients are treated with every attention and sentiment of human benevolence. The same mode of treatment is carried on in the D. Pedro II Lunatic Asylum, exclusively adapted to those that suffer from mental derangement, the number of which in the same year amounted to 393 lunatics.

In both these hospitals the sick, who are admitted as

of a poor condition, receive their treatment gratis, without any distinction to class, nation or religion. But there are also private apartments for boarders.

The revenue of its patrimonial fund is nearly £ 30,000.

The management of the sick, and the internal and economical management of the Hospital is entrusted to the sisters of Charity, of the Congregation of S. Vincent de Paula.

The Hospital « Santa Casa de Misericordia » independent of the above mentioned hospitals, and of other infirmaries that it supports in different localities, and of those that it immediately establishes, whenever any epidemies begin to show their denseness and ravages, has founded four permanent consulting medical offices, one being annexed to the Hospital, and 3 in different parts of the city and its suburbs, where medical advice is given gratis as also the medicines, and where the poor find physicians to visit them in their homes when they cannot go out. In one of these consulting offices called « Sala do Banco » in the Hospital, 7,050 poor sick received medical advice during the last year.

The following are dependencies of the « Hospital da Santa Casa da Misericordia :

The Foundling Hospital, that possesses patrimonial property to the value of £ 20,800.

The Orphan Asylum for girls, that contains 135 inmates, of which, during last year, 2 of them died, 18 left the asylum, and of these 8 to be married. Its fund consists of 119 Brazilian bonds in the value of £ 12,400.

In this asylum there is a reserved dowry account kept, which possesses in Brazilian bonds a sum of £ 21,540, that in 1872 gave a revenue of £ 2,200.

The Asylum of Sta Thereza, with a fund of £ 3,000, occupies a magnificent building, where girls destitute of support receive an asylum, are fed, clothed, and educated. They were twenty in number, last year.

The income of the General Hospital and of all those Institutions annexed to it, in the compromissorial year of 1871 to 1872 was £ 177,262, and the expense £ 160,578, which leaves a balance, in favour, of £ 16,683.

The « Santa Casa Hospital » supports 2 cemeteries in the suburbs of the city, called S. John Baptist of Lagôa, and S. Francisco Xavier.

During the last year, the Board of direction executed many important works in order to render some of the establishments under their charge, more spacious, particularly the general hospital, the D. Pedro II lunatic asylum, and the two cemeteries. Within the precincts of the cemetery of S. Francisco Xavier, a new one was opened, solely for Protestants; it is held with the same care and respect as the Catholic ones.

The Santa Casa da Misericordia, including its dependencies, has a patrimonial fund valued nearly in £ 1,700,000, namely: in buildings £ 1,380,000 ; in Brazilian bonds £ 167,600; in furniture, clothes and linen, utensils and other objects £ 100,000, and on leased lands £ 50,000.

Its board of commissioners aided by the State and by public charity, devote all their energy to promote as much as possible, the pious intentions of the founders of the Santa Casa and of its annexed charitable institutions; and to give a more perfect idea of their ardent zeal, in the last compromissorial year, it was clearly proved that independent of the great expenses which they had to occur to, there was not one of their general estimates of expenses that did not leave a balance in favour of each of them.

LAZARS' HOSPITAL. — It is specially intended for those suffering from elephantiasis of the greek ; the number of them amounted to 79, viz: 47 adults and 9 minors of the male sex; 18 adults and 5 minors of the female sex. Of them 7 men and 4 women died ; 4 men and 2 women left the hospital.

The receipts amounted to £ 10,356, the expense to £ 8,518, thus leaving a balance, in favour, of £ 1,837.

The edifice, that is being constructed, is much advanced, the sum of £ 6,011 having already been expended.

The property of the lazars' hospital consists of £ 36,660 on bonds and leased grounds, as also legacies on houses, bonds and Bank of Brazil's shares.

The State grants a yearly allowance of £ 200.

As to the provinces of Rio de Janeiro, Bahia, Pernambuco, S. Paulo, Maranhão, Ceará, Minas Geraes, S. Pedro do Rio Grande do Sul and others, they each have their « Santa Casa de Misericordia » with hospitals, in general, well organized, where the poor patients are treated gratuitously with the greatest care and humanity.

All the cities and even towns and villages of the interior of the province have their « Misericordias » or Institutions of Charity, which will be long to enumerate.

The province of Bahia has, besides asylums and institutions for the protection of poor girls, the S. Lazarus hospital for morphetics, and the asylum of S. John de Deos for lunatics, for which they have already laid down the foundation stone.

There are also asylums for morphetics in Pará, Maranhão and Mato-Grosso.

The capital of S. Paulo has an asylum for lunatics and another for morphetics; the cities of Itú, Constituição, and Campinas have also one each, and Guaratinguetá has its college for educating poor girls, under the name of Asylum of the « Bom Pastor. »

The province of S. Pedro do Rio Grande do Sul, has also asylums for the education of children of both sexes destitute of means; and also in the cities of Rio Grande and Pelotas; in the capital of S. Catharina there is an asylum for girls.

The province of Rio de Janeiro has the Asylum of Sta. Leopoldina, already mentioned in another place; a fine hospital, in the city of Nictheroy, supported by the treasury of the province; and in all the cities charity asylums, some of them very well organized. In the last year the expenses for the supporting of those institutions amounted to above £ 6,200.

Beneficient and philanthropical associations.

The beneficient associations are very numerous and undeniably testify the philanthropical sentiments of the Brazilian people.

Some of them possess considerable patrimonies and according to their forces succour the helpless poor, even at the cost of enormous expenses.

Others possess modest capitals, but though the aid be little, they yet help, whenever they can, those that stand in need of it, without distinction either of nationality, class or religion.

RELIGIOUS ORDER OF S. FRANCISCO DA PENITENCIA. — Its institution dates from 1619, and besides the divine worship, it is intended for the assistance of its poor brethren. Its patrimony consists of 169 town buildings, the revenue of which amounted to £ 21,647, rented grounds

and government policies to the nominal value of
£ 2,740.

Its hospital is vast and completely furnished with what
is required for the treatment and comfort of the sick,
that in number of 1,106, were treated here, having gone
out 965, died 48, and 93 continuing in treatment. The
average mortality is little more than 4 %. With the hospital the Order spent £ 4,515 ; with monthly and extraordinary alms £ 63,26 ; the rest being employed in
divine worship, burials, and in the cemetery works,
which require yet a sum of £ 35,000, for their conclusion.

ORDER OF NOSSA SENHORA DO MONTE DO CARMO. — Instituted for the same purpose, in the year 1638, the patrimony of this order consists of 63 houses, bonds of
the public debt, to the nominal value of £ 17,340 ;
policies of the province of Rio de Janeiro, amounting to
£ 3,200, and shares of the Bank of Brazil, representing
a value of £ 480.

The rent of the houses to the total sum of £ 8,600, and
the other articles of receipt amounted last year to
£ 21,500, the expense being £ 21,200.

In its vast hospital, at which it spent about £ 50,000,
1,552 sick brethren were received, 1,413 of which went
out, 60 died and 79 continued in treatment. The mortality was below 4 %.

The expense was distributed by the following articles :
for the hospital £ 3,968 ; for monthly alms and other
assistances £ 4,649, for religious acts, burials, management of the cemetery and others £ 12,592.

ORDER OF THE MINIMI OF S. FRANCISCO DE PAULA. — Its
institution dates from 1756.

Its patrimony consists of 26 edifices, which rent amounted last year to nearly £ 2,100 policies of the public debt to the amount of £ 59,850 and policies of the province of Rio de Janeiro to that of £ 10,000.

The Order spends nothing with the management of its excellent hospital at which, in the same period, 622 sick brethren were received and treated; of these 30 died, and 19 continued in treatment; the charity both of the brethren and of the board of administration, that is annually renewed, provides for all the expenses, which very often go to above £ 100 a month.

Its expenses, however, amounted to £ 14,200 and its revenue to £ 14,900, thus realizing a balance of £ 700, including the sum of £ 1,799 spent in support of sick brethren, on their burial, the management of the cemetery, and the amortization of the debt contracted for the rebuilding and improvement of their magestic church.

ORDER OF SENHOR BOM JESUS DO CALVARIO DA VIA SACRA. —Created in 1724 as a simple congregation for divine worship and charitable purposes, it was only formed into a Third Order, in the year 1830.

Notwithstanding its having constructed an excellent edifice to serve as hospital for its sick brethren, the want of income prevented the inauguration of the respective service, and limited them to help and assist the poor brethren, the expense, during last year, amounting to £ 1,246. The patrimony consists of 14 houses, which give a yearly income of about £ 2,600; of government policies to the value of £ 35,720, and policies of the province of Rio de Janeiro to that of £ 500.

The receipts amounted to £ 7,100, and the expenses to £ 6,100, leaving a balance of £ 1,000.

ORDER OF THE IMMACULADA CONCEIÇÃO. — The old society nnder this name was raised to the rank of a Third Order

Destined to the same purposes as those of other Religious Orders, it supports an Asylum of Charity in which, without any distinction whatever, hospitality is given to helpless women of good hehaviour, but under equal circumstances the preference is given to the sisters of the Order.

The Order possesses 9 houses and £ 4,000 in policies. The income of these properties and other sources of revenue amount to £ 1,734, making a total of £ 5,267, if the balance and eventualities of the last year are added.

The expenses, including those of the church, the repairing of which amounted to above £ 10,000, were £ 4,259, and the balance £ 1,000.

Within the asylum 13 women are maintained, but besides these the Order gives support to its sisters to the amonnt of £ 122, during the last year.

BROTHERHOOD OF SANTISSIMO SACRAMENTO DE NOSSA SENHORA DA CANDELARIA.—Founded in the year 1669 to maintain the splendour of religion and to practise pious works, it has under its charge the administration of the Hospital of the Lazars.

It has 100 houses which rent amounts to £ 13,038, and £ 29,880 in policies. The income was £ 17,123 and the expenditure £ 13,321, leaving a balance of £ 3,801.

It assisted 575 persons, of which 59 are brethren or the widows of brethren, distributing amoug them the sum of £ 3,520.

With its temple, which was commenced in 1775, it has already expended about £ 200,000.

THE IMPERIAL BROTHERHOOD DE SANTA CRUZ DOS MILITARES.
— This brotherhood was created in 1628, for the purpose
of celebrating religious acts, and to assist the widows and
children of deceased brethren. It belongs exclusively to the
military of the first line of the army, pertaining to the garrison of the Capital, and of the province of Rio de Janeiro, to which or to their widows and children it allows
pensions of the amount of their half pay, in case of losing
it, or if they have fallen in want.

It has 23 buildings let at an annual rent of £ 7,460,
and 905 policies with a yearly revenue of £ 5,063. It
spends in pensions the sum of £ 7,269.

Its receipts were £ 17,556; its expenditure £ 14,976;
leaving a balance of £ 2,582.

BROTHERHOOD OF NOSSA SENHORA DO ROZARIO AND S. BE-
NEDICTO. — This is considered one of the oldest religious
societies of the capital of the Empire, and was founded
by negroes.

It admits even slaves as members, and promotes their
becoming free, according to the means at its disposal, out
of a special fund for charitable purposes.

The selection of such members as are slaves and are
to be set at liberty, is made by drawing lots. It supports brethren in want and their widows.

Its patrimony consists of 16 houses and 44 policies
of the nominal value of £ 100 each. The receipts amount
to about £ 1,500; the expenditure to £ 1,350.

Besides these religious orders and many societies,
which give aid to members in want, or infirm, the Capital has many philantropic associations, both national
and foreign.

Amongst the national ones there are the following :

União Beneficente, commercio e artes. — Founded in 1863 it has at present a patrimony of more than 150 policies of the public debt, and supports needy members, in accordance with its statutes.

União beneficencia. — Founded in 1852, it supports, out of monthly contributions, the helpless families of its deceased members.

Rio grandense. — Established in 1857 for the same purpose as the preceding one, it has a capital upwards £ 3,000.

Paulistana. — Created on the occasion of the inauguration of the statue of José Bonifacio de Andrada e Silva, on the 7th September 1872, its object is to assist those born in the province of S. Paulo, who have fallen in distress.

Mineira. — Recently established for the purpose of assisting those out of the province of Minas Geraes, residing in the capital of the Empire.

Typ ographica fluminense. — Founded in 1853. It has a patrimony of 46 policies of the public debt ; its purpose is to assist helpless members and their respective families ; it founded an asylum for those unable to work and for the development and progress of the typographic art.

Caixa municipal de beneficencia e congregação de santa thereza de jesus. — Inaugurated in 1860, its purpose is to aid poor people in their homes, to give portions to poor young women of exemplary morality, and to erect an asylum for helpless old people.

Efficiently aided by the congregation of the sisters of Santa Thereza de Jesus established in 1861, with the aim of improving the fate of beggars, of founding an asylum for them, the foundation stone of the respective building has been laid in 1871 in one of the suburbs of the capital of the Empire by Her Imperial Highness Dona Isabella.

Its patrimony, which is formed of donations obtained by the director, members, and brethren of the congregation, already amounts to £ 13,000.

AMANTE DA INSTRUCÇÃO. — This association commenced very modestly in the year 1831, and now maintains a day and a boarding school, where instruction to poor children is ministered.

Its patrimony consists of £ 8,340, in policies of the public debt.

UNIÃO BENEFICENTE DAS FAMILIAS HONESTAS. — It commenced in 1862 with a capital of 120 policies of the public debt, and distributes annually about £ 3,000, in allowances to different families.

ASYLO DA VELHICE DESVALIDA. — Founded in 1872 for the purpose of establishing asylums for old people of both sexes.

Besides these, there are the following associations: «Brazileira de Beneficencia», « Beneficencia e Humanitaria », « Beneficente Perfeita Amizade », « Seculares Empregados da Igreja», and others of the same kind, too numerous to be mentioned.

Amongst the foreign benevolent societies the following ones rank as the most distinguished, for the purport indicated in their respective titles.

FRANÇAISE DE SECOURS MUTUELS. — Founded in 1856, it has a patrimony of £ 4,487.

BRITISH BENEVOLENT SOCIETY. — Inaugurated in 1837. Without any patrimony. It derives its income from annual contributions, and donations; and spends the same in monthly or dayly alms.

DER DEUTSCHE HUELFSVEREIN. — It was founded in 1844. Its patrimony is limited to 5 policies of the public debt; but from the income of said policies, from an annual subscription amongst the Germans residing in the capital, and a subsidy from some governments of Germany and Austria-Hungaria, it distributes assistances to Germans and Austrians in need of them.

SOCIÉTÉ BELGE DE BIENFAISANCE. — It commenced in 1853. Its income consists of the produce of subscriptions both here and in Belgium, monthly contributions of its members, and the income of its patrimony of 17 policies of the public debt.

SOCIEDAD ESPAÑOLA DE BENEFICENZA. — Instituted in 1859, it has 37 policies of the public debt.

SOCIETÀ BENEFICENTE ITALIANA. — It was formed in 1854. Its capital consists of 25 policies of the public debt, besides the money which they have always at band, for the object of its creation.

SOCIEDADE PORTUGUEZA DE BENEFICENCIA — It has 23 years of existence ; and has erected in one of the suburbs of the capital of the Empire a magnificent hospital, called S. João de Deus, which was opened in 1859. For the erection of the building, furniture and embellishment of the same, the association spent £ 30,000. Its patrimony is above £ 40,000 in public funds.

CAIXA DE SOCCORROS DE D. PEDRO V. — It is a Portuguese association, formed in 1863, with a patrimony of more than £ 40,000, and by means of monthly contributions and extraordinary assistance, it does not only pay the expenses for the treatment of many sick people, of consultations, medical visits and the necessary medicines, but it promotes also the education, the employment, and accommodations of children of helpless Portuguesemen.

PHILANTROPICA SUISSA. — Founded in 1821, with a patrimony of about £ 4,000, in public funds.

BENEFICENCIA UNIÃO ISRAELITA DO BRAZIL. — It is of recent formation.

Besides the above mentioned, there are the association « Americana de Beneficencia » ; the « Portugueza Amante da Monarchia e Beneficente » ; the « Madrepora » and others of a similar nature.

In nearly all the capitals of the provinces and populous towns similar associations are to be met with, both national and foreign, which distribute assistances to their respective members and to helpless persons.

Mounts of Piety. (*)

In Rio de Janeiro there are three mounts of piety, viz : « General Mount of piety for State functionnaries », « the General Mount of piety » and « the Navy Mount of piety. »

---

* Mounts of Piety.

Mounts of Piety, in Brazil, are associations different from the *Monts de piété*, in France, and the *Lombard-houses*, in England, and in the United States. The Brazilian — Mounts of Piety— are public associations, either under the inspection of the government, or of a board of subscribers, their purpose being for the insurers or pensioners to leave after their death an yearly allowance to their families. It is a sort of public life-insurance association. Under the name of Monte do Soccorro (Mount of Assistance) there is a public office for a purpose like that of the *mont de piété*, or the *lombard-house*.

The first was established in 1835, and all persons of either sex, who exercise any public charge liable to the payment of duties, may belong to it, provided they don't exercise them *ad interim*, or as simple commissions.

The stock of this mount of piety is £ 321,000, in policies, besides an annual subsidy granted by the State. The inscriptions and contributions are regulated according to the plan approved in the year 1870.

The « General Mount of piety » dates from 1841, and its stock is £ 573,000, in policies. This establishment admits of persons of both sexes and of every condition, and its pensionaries do not lose, as in the above mentioned, their pensions, even when they have attained their majority.

The pensions are instituted only in benefit of the person assigned by the pensioner ; every one, however, may establish a pension for himself.

Each annual pension cannot, but in special cases prescribed by the respective statutes, amount to above £ 160.

Every one may establish pensions to the sum of £ 400, in behalf of any person ; and up to £ 600, for the benefit of his wife, children, and grandchildren.

The « Navy Mount of piety » was established in favour of navy officers' families, which receive after the death of their heads the correspondent half pay.

All naval officers contribute every month with a day's pay for the maintenance of this mount of piety, which is ruled according to the plan approved in the year 1795, when it was established, as well as by other subsequent legislative regulations.

In the army, instead of pensions paid by a mount

of piety, the widows, unmarried daughters, and minor children of officers, are entitled to the half pay which their husbands or fathers should receive if they had retired from active service, according to law.

In case of the dead officers being unmarried, their mothers, when widows, are entitled to the half pay.

The government, besides this, allows pensions, dependent on legislative approval, to the widows, unmarried daughters, sons under age, mothers, and sisters unmarried of officers dead in campaign, or in any other public commission considered as highly important.

Houses of Correction.

In the capital of the Empire, and in many of the provinces, there are houses of correction for the confinement of prisoners or of convicts.

That of the capital of the Empire, which is still unfinished, has quite ready one radius for prisons, and two for working-houses, besides other buildings dependent on the establishment. The system adopted in it is that of Auburn.

The radius for prisons, already finished, comprehends 200 cells. To complete the edifice, according to the original plan, three radii more for prisons and two others for work-shops are to be constructed, as well as a central tower and the necessary accommodations for its employés.

The establishment possesses a primary school, and a library for the convicts' use, a washing-place, a bakery, and a quarry, under the charge of the administrator, and has also a photographic laboratory for the necessities both of the establishment and of the police department.

The expenses during the year 1871 — 72 amounted to £ 18,528, and the receipt was £ 9,600.

Different objects made in the establishment, and sent to the Vienna Universal Exhibition, prove the excellence of their workmanship and the advantages derived from the system adopted in.

Next to the House of Correction of the capital of the Empire, the one that is the most adapted to its designs is that in the city of S. Paulo, not only on account of its being situated in one of the most picturesque suburbs and in a vast edifice with several important working-houses, orchard and gardens, but also by the order, cleanliness, and morality that presides over its several departments.

Next to this establishment we must mention the houses of correction of Pernambuco, and those of the capitals of the provinces of Bahia, Rio de Janeiro, and other cities of the Empire, wherein the so called penitentiary prisons have not yet been constructed.

Lighting.

The Capital of the Empire is lighted with gas.

The service is performed by an English Company, to which were transferred the rights and obligations set forth in the contract made, in 1851, with the Baron of Mauá.

The number of burners is 5,205, and the expense amounts to more than £ 60,000 per annum.

The cities of Recife, Nictheroy, Campos, S. Salvador, Fortaleza, Belém, S. Paulo, Santos and S. Luiz, are also lighted with gas, and the necessary operations for applying the same mode of lighting to other cities of the Empire are in course of execution.

The legislative assembly of Mato-Grosso has of late authorized this system of lighting, in the city of Cuyabá.

Municipality of the Capital of the Empire.

The municipality of the Capital of the Empire, called also the neutral municipality or municipality of the Court, has a special administrative organization.

The affairs which in the provinces are at the charge of the provincial assemblies and of the presidents, in the municipality of the Court are submitted to the General Assembly and the Government, to which the Town-Council is immediately subordinated, being of its competence to approve temporarily the municipal regulations, to fix annually the income and expenses of the municipality, on proposal of the Town-Council, and to decide the recourses interposed of its deliberations.

In the capital of the Empire, the municipal income proceeds from the following articles: municipal taxes, leases of grounds belonging to the municipality, the produce of fines of police and infractions of regulations, rents of the marine grounds, licences conceded for opening shops, commercial houses and other branches of industry, comprehending theatres and other public amusements, and finally an increase voted on the house tax, which is specially destined for the pavement of streets with parallelopipeds.

The patrimony of the municipality, which is large enough, consists, besides the edifice, that is used as townhall, and other houses, of tracts of lands, granted in different dates, market-places, public slaughterhouses and the buildings of the two schools constructed by means of its intervention.

The last year's income amounted to £ 89,995, and the expense to £ 87,332.

The municipal receipt has always progressively increased since 1830, in which year it scarcely amounted to £ 3,122.

In 1866 it was of £ 67,043, the balance, therefore, in favour of last year being £ 22,952 over the latter year, and £ 86,873 over that of 1830.

Certain taxes, that belong, in the provinces, to the provincial receipt, are in the Capital of the Empire, considered as general ones, their produce being in the last financial year £ 706,200.

In compensation the government defrays the expenses with different services, that in the provinces are paid by their respective treasuries or by the municipal ones, as for instance, public lighting, water-supply, fire services, house of correction, police force, properly said, and others.

The city of S. Sebastião of Rio de Janeiro, the capital of the Empire, is situated on the west side of the bay of Nictheroy. Its astronomical position is 22°, 53' 51", S, lat. and 0° 0' 56" E. long. from the Meridian of the Imperial Observatory of Rio de Janeiro, situated on the Castello Hill. in the same city, or 43° 8' 30" O. Greenwich.

The Bay of Nictheroy is, in circuit, more than 19,8 kil.; and its bar offers free entrance to the largest vessels; its profundity generally varying from 22 to 23 meters, and in some places attaining 110 meters.

In the circumscription of the city are comprehended 7 islands and in that of the Municipality 33, besides some small islands.

The area of the municipality, excluding the islands, comprises a space of 1,394 square kil.

The city, strictly speaking, does not occupy more than a surface of 21,780,000 square meters.

The city has 11 parishes with the respective parish churches and 69 filial churches and chapels, where divine service is regularly celebrated.

Of late there were created two parishes in the suburbs of the city, which are not yet canonically provided.

The construction and the ornament of some of the parish and filial churches distinguish themselves for their magnificence.

There are 7 convents, 6 religious Third Orders, more than 100 brotherhoods and fraternities, a great number of devotions and 2 houses of prayer, founded and maintained by protestant communions, one for the British Episcopal Worship, the other for the German Evangelic community.

The municipality contains besides the former, 8 parishes more with their parish churches, almost all containing other filial churches and chapels, 3 police delegacies, that exercise accumulative attributions in the whole municipality, 22 subdelegacies and 25 justice of the peace districts.

The perimeter of the city contains 23.523 houses, subject to house-tax, representing the local value of £ 1.971.381, 82 public buildings and 622 exempt from the above said tax.

Of those edifices 6,208 are 2 stories high, 1,456 of one story and 15,859 on the ground floor.

The following public buildings deserve mention :

The Mint, one of the best constructions of the Empire, situated on the west side of the Campo da Acclamação, comprising an area of 4.698.8 square meters, including the second pavement on the front. Here the 2^d National Industrial Exhibition was held.

The War Office and Head Quarters with military barracks, occupying the whole northern face of the same camp, with an extension of 281,6 meters long, by 320,1 meters wide.

The National Museum, on the east side of the same camp, with spacious halls, adapted to its purpose.

The house in which the Supreme Court of Justice and the Court of Appeals of the district of Rio de Janeiro hold their sessions.

The Academy of Fine Arts, an elegant structure, with halls adapted to the respective classes and to the annual exposition of painting and sculpture, together with the Pinacotheca, a deposit of valuable pictures and gypsum models.

The Central School, at which courses of mathematics, engineering, and physical sciences are given, and the General and Industrial Exhibitions of 1861 and 1873 were held.

The National Treasury, actually in reconstruction, remarkable for its vast proportions.

The Conservatory of Music, constructed a short time ago for its special purpose, and distinguished for its beautiful form.

The Military Hospitals and that of the Navy, with accommodation corresponding to its purpose.

The new public schools of primary instruction of S. Sebastião, S. Christovão, S. José and Gloria.

The Boarding and Day-schools of secondary instruction of the Imperial College of D. Pedro II, the former in one of the suburbs, the latter in the interior of the city.

The House of Correction occupying a great space at one of the extremes of the capital.

The Custom-house, comprehending large edifices and very important works, among which excel vast docks, in construction, and not far from these the Imperial dike, built at the Island of Cobras, as well as another one, which is being constructed beside it.

The Episcopal Palace, the residence of the Bishop of Rio de Janeiro, on the top of Conceição Hill.

The Episcopal Seminary of S. José, destined for the instruction of the clergy.

The Bank of Brazil, a true palace, solidly constructed for the seat of the most important establishment of credit of the Empire.

The D. Pedro II Central Rail-Way Station built on the western end of the Campo da Acclamação, of a pleasant appearance and a few years since augmented with large and spacious ware-houses, work-rooms and a garden in front.

Worthy of attention are also :

The vast Gas Manufactory with an area of 23,435 square meters.

The Hospital of the Santa Casa da Misericordia, with two parallel wings, after its completion is to be 181,5 meters in breadth, and 54 meters in width, and having an area of 9,782,85 square meters, being in size and perfection of work one of the most notable edifices of the world and containing magnificent infirmaries for 1,100 sick.

The Lunatic Asylum of D. Pedro II belongs also to the « Misericordia » and is dedicated to the treatment of the lunatics. As monumental as the precedent edifice, it comprises an area of 7.560,1 square meters, its front being 290 square meters.

The Hospital of Lazars, in the suburbs of S. Christovão.

That of S. João de Deus, belonging to the Portuguese Beneficient Society.

That of the Religious Order of Nossa Senhora do Monte do Carmo.

That of the Religious Order of S. Francisco da Penitencia.

That of the Religious Order of the Minimi of S. Francisco de Paula.

That of the Order of Senhor Bom Jesus do Calvario.

That which is being built at the expense of the French Society of mutual succour, situated on a hill, in one of the most delightful suburbs.

The theatres *D. Pedro II*, the largest, *Lyrico Fluminense* and *S. Pedro de Alcantara*, besides *Gymnasio*, *Phenix Dramatica* , *Casino Franco-Brésilien* and the *Théatre Lyrique Français*.

The edifices of the State Offices of the Home Department, and those of Justice, Navy and Foreign affairs and the one in construction on the D. Pedro II square for the Agricultural Office.

Those of the Navy and War arsenals, of the Public Library and the *Casino Fluminense*.

The Imperial Quinta of Boa Vista.

The Asylum for the Military Invalids at the Island of Bom Jesus.

The Beggars'Asylum, calculated at £ 30,000, which the society of municipal beneficence is constructing.

The factory of arms in the fort of Conceição and the pyrotechnical laboratory of Campinho.

There are 302 streets, besides 76 larger and 45 smaller lanes, 53 squares, and 18 ascents. The Campo da

Acclamação, situated nearly in the centre of the city, is 594 meters in breadth, and 308 meters in width.

When the gardening of that Campo, which is already being made, be accomplished and the monument, which is projected, to commemorate the victories obtained by the armies of Brazil in Paraguay, shall be erected, it will become one of the finest squares in the world.

There are in the city 8,943 houses of business, 1,680 belonging to natives and 7,263 to foreigners, comprehending in this number 11 custom-house stores, different workshops and manufactories.

Commercially considered, the Capital of the Empire is the principal commercial place of South America, and in North America only the city of New-York ranks over it.

The average import of the annual movement of external commerce of the city of Rio de Janeiro, comprehending the exportation and importation, was in the last liquidated financial years, of £ 18,182,900.

To this movement, effected in 2,245 ships that entered with 954,956,691 kilgr. tonnage and 2,062 ships which left with 1,007,710,523.4 kilgr. tonnage, we should add the traffic by land between the municipality of the capital, and the provinces of Minas Geraes, S. Paulo, Goyaz and Mato-Grosso, and which we cannot estimate at less than £ 2,000,000, in value.

The Custom House is one of the most profitable of the world.

The average income it produced within the last three financial years of Import and Export duties amounts to £ 3,284,900.

If to these figures the average sum of £ 660,000 is

added, which has been collected by the Receipts Departement of the municipality within the above said years, we have a total of £ 3,944,900, with which these two fiscal stations contributed towards the general receipts of the Empire.

The position of the port of Rio de Janeiro, being almost in the centre of South America, makes it a natural emporium for the sea traffic of the United States of North America, and of Europe for the ports of Asia and those of the Pacific Ocean.

The city of Rio de Janeiro has a faculty of medicine, a central college, a military, a navy day and boarding school, a general surveying office for public works. a general directorship for Telegraphs. where the telegraph wires of the government lines meet, a fire-brigade, two police-corps, barracks for the garrisons both of the army and the navy, general directorship of the Post, Exchange, General inspectorship for public instruction, commercial institute, institutions for blind, and deaf and dumb children, conservatory of music, Academy of Fine Arts, Lyceum of Arts and Trades, museum, public archives, military museum, dramatic conservatory and many libraries.

Rio de Janeiro likewise has a central board of public health, which watches, in general, over the sanitary service of the city, an institute for vaccination with branches in all the provinces, an excellent hospital on the seashore far from the town, which is opened when the sanitary state requires it, board of health for the port, for the army and navy, hospitals and houses of beneficence and one for foundlings, besides two for orphans, a fine public garden within the boundaries of the city, on the sea shore, lighted with gas, and where many foreign and native plants are to be met with.

In one of the suburbs, about 2 kil, from the centre of the city, the Botanical garden is situated, with numerous varieties of exoctic plants, extensive gardens and grassplots, and close by it a model school for agriculture, an agricultural asylum, a manufacture of Chili hats, and the breeding of silk-worms, under the immediate inspection of the Imperial Institute of Rio. There is a necrosterium, lately finished, for the reception of human bodies found on the streets, and on the beach; 5 cemeteries outside of the city, viz: 3 private and 2 public ones, the former belonging to the religious orders of S. Francisco de Paula, of Carmo, and of Penitencia; and the latter, called S. Francisco Xavier, and S. João Baptista, under the charge of the Santa Casa de Misericordia, besides 1 cemetery for Protestants.

The establishments of credit, those of anonymous companies and societies both commercial and industrial, amount to a high figure : literary, scientific, and recreative societies are mentioned elsewhere.

It is notable that since some years, especially since the year 1867, there has been a great tendency on the part of the proprietors to give to the houses which they build in the city as well as in the suburbs more elegance, in conformity with the principal rules of architecture.

Some of these buildings are magestic, and ornamented with much taste and magnificence.

Nearly all the streets are paved with parallelopipeds, and most of the squares are planted with trees.

There are the following principal squares, viz :

of the directive-board of the primary and secondary instruction of the municipality of the capital, ex-president
of several provinces, and ex-deputy to the General Assembly.

Assistant-Commissary.

FRANCISCO ANTONIO GONÇALVES. — Officer of the Order of
the Rose.

_____

Brazilian Committee at the Vienna International Exhibition.

President.

H. R. H. D. Lewis Augustus Maria Eudes of Coburg and Gotha, Duke of Saxe. — Admiral and President of the Naval Council of Brazil, Grand-Cross of all Brazilian Orders and decorated with the Uruguayana Medal.

Vice-president.

Baron of Porto Seguro. — Member of H. M. the Emperor's Council, Chevalier of the Order of Christ, and Commander of that of the Rose, Grand-Cross of the Russian Imperial Order of S. Stanislas of the 1st Class, Grand-Cross of the Austrian Imperial Order of the Iron-Crown, Commander of number of the American Royal Spanish Order of Isabel the Catholic, and Extraordinary Commander of the Royal and Distinguished Order of Charles the 3^{d}, Envoy Extraordinary and Minister Plenipotentiary at Austria-Hungary.

Secretary.

Manuel de Araujo Porto-Alegre. — Grand-Dignitary of the Order of the Rose, Chevalier of the Order of Christ, ex-professor of the Central College and of the Academy of Fine Arts, Member of the Historical, Geographical and Ethnographical Brazilian Institute, and of many other scientific societies, either national or foreign, Consul General of the Empire, at Lisbon.

Members.

BARON OF CARAPEBUS.—Grandee of the Empire, Chamberlain to H. M. the Empress, Officer of the Order o the Rose, Commander of the Order of Christ, and Commander of the Order of Nossa Senhora da Conceição de Villa-Viçosa of Portugal.

BARON OF NIOAC.—Chamberlain to H. M. the Empress, Chevalier of the Orders of Christ and of the Rose.

Assistants.

JOSÉ DE SALDANHA DA GAMA.—Officer of the Order of the Rose, Chevalier of the Order of Nossa Senhora da Conceição de Villa-Viçosa of Portugal, Chevalier of the Italian Royal Order of the Crown, Assistant-professor at the Central College, Member of the Fiscal-board of the Imperial Agricultural Institute of Rio de Janeiro, and many other scientific societies, Gentleman of the Palace.

JOAQUIM JOSÉ DA FONSECA JUNIOR.

OSCAR ADOLPHO DE BULHÕES RIBEIRO.—M. D., Bachelor of Arts, Chevalier of the Order of the Rose.

JOAQUIM JOSE DA FRANÇA JUNIOR, Bachelor of Law.

GUILHERME SCHUCH DE CAPANEMA. — Commander of the Order of the Rose and Chevalier of that of Christ, Professor at the Central College, General Director of the Telegraphs, Fellow of the section of mineralogy, geology and physical sciences at the national museum, Corresponding-member of the Acclimating-Society of Paris, and of many other scientific associations, either national or foreign.

BENJAMIM FRANKLIN RAMIZ GALVÃO.—M. D., Bachelor of Arts, Bibliothecary of the National and Public Library,

Assistant-Professor at the Faculty of Medicine of Rio de Janeiro.

João Joaquim Pizarro. — M. D., Assistant-Professor at the Faculty of Medicine of Rio de Janeiro.

Joaquim Monteiro Caminhoá.—M. D., Professor at the Faculty of Medicine of Rio de Janeiro, Officer of the Order of the Rose, Chevalier of Christ, decorated with several war-medals.

Luiz Alvares dos Santos.—M. D., Professor at the Medical School of Bahia, Officer of the Order of the Rose, Chevalier of Christ, decorated with several war-medals.

Rufino Augusto de Almeida. —Bachelor of Law, Commander of the Order of the Rose.

Luiz da Costa Chaves Faria.—M. D., Bachelor of Arts.

Miguel Antonio da Silva.—Officer of the Order of the Rose and Chevalier of the Orders of Christ and Aviz, professor at the Central School, member of the Imperial Agricultural Institute of Rio de Janeiro.

Carlos de Almeida.

Henrique Hermeto Carneiro Leão.—M. D., Bachelor of Arts, Officer of the Order of the Rose.

Luiz Philippe Saldanha da Gama.—Post-captain on the Navy, Chevalier of the Orders of the Rose and Christ.

Antonio Januario de Faria. —M. D., Professor at the Faculty of Medicine of Bahia, Commander of the Order of Christ.

Alfredo Antonio Simões dos Santos Lisboa.

Antonio Luiz da Cunha Bahiana.—Bachelor of Law.

Joaquim Antonio Alves Ribeiro.—M. D., Chevalier of the Orders of Christ and of the Rose.

Antonio Gabriel de Paula Fonseca.—M. D., Chevalier of the Order of Christ.

CONTENTS

———

Rio de Janeiro. Typographia Universal de Laemmert
Rua dos Invallidos, 61 B.

9 783337 271374